The
LONG SEASON

by JIM BROSNAN

With a New Preface by the Author

IVAN R. DEE

CHICAGO

THE LONG SEASON. Copyright © 1960, 1975, 2002 by James P. Brosnan. This book was first published in 1960 by Harper & Row, and is here reprinted by arrangement with HarperCollins Publishers. First Ivan R. Dee paperback edition published 2002. All rights reserved, including the right to reproduce this book or portions thereof in any form. For information, address: Ivan R. Dee, Publisher, 1332 North Halsted Street, Chicago 60622. Manufactured in the United States of America and printed on acid-free paper.

Library of Congress Cataloging-in-Publication Data:
Brosnan, Jim.
  The long season / Jim Brosnan ; with a new preface by the author.-- 1st Ivan R. Dee pbk. ed.
    p. cm.
  ISBN 1-56663-418-0 (alk. paper)
  1. Brosnan, Jim. 2. Baseball players--United States--Biography. I. Title.

GV865.B75 A3 2002
796.357'092--dc21
[B]
                                                    2001047606

The
LONG SEASON

Jim Brosnan was born in Cincinnati, Ohio, and grew up there. After graduating high school he was signed to a minor-league contract by the Chicago Cubs, and later played major league baseball for the Cubs, the St. Louis Cardinals, the Cincinnati Reds, and the Chicago White Sox. In eight and a half major league seasons as a pitcher, he won 55 games, lost 47, and had an earned run average of 3.54. He is retired and lives in Morton Grove, Illinois.

Preface to the 2002 Edition

"Why did you write the book?"

That is the question I've been asked countless times by baseball fans ever since *The Long Season* was first published in 1960. The new millennium seems a good time for an answer.

At the age of eleven I had an epiphany. Rare for a subteen, but manifestly possible. It happened at the Westwood Public Library in the Western Hills suburb of Cincinnati. All those books on all those shelves! What joy I got from digging into that small literary treasure!

WHAT A KICK YOU'D GET IF YOUR NAME WAS ON ONE OF THOSE BOOKS! It was the voice of that cunning imp, Ambition, sowing a seed that would grow for twenty years.

My mother wanted me to be a concert pianist. My two maiden aunts wanted me to be a priest. I had neither talent for the former nor a vocation for the latter.

At Cincinnati Elder, the local parochial high school, I learned to read Latin, play the trombone, and write essays, one of which pleased the history teacher no end but failed to impress my father, who wanted to know what I was going to do for a living.

The only useful thing I could do, apparently, was throw a baseball faster than the average sixteen-year-old. Pitching for Bentley Post, a perennial powerhouse among American Legion teams, gave me a chance to be seen during the summer by major league scouts in four states.

The only one interested was Tony Lucadello of the Chicago Cubs. He had seen me pitch shutouts in the regional and sectional tournaments. When he learned that I had already graduated from high school, he offered me a bonus of $2,500 if I'd sign a minor league contract.

My diary for 10/24/46 read: "Eureka! Manna from Heaven! Merry Xmas to me! Merry Xmas to me!"

I should have checked the contract first. It would pay me $125 per month for the four-month season. Even if I won all my games, I'd surely lose weight on such paltry pay.

During the next four minor league seasons I won as often as I lost—which, in the Cubs organization at that time, meant promotion to a higher classification. I was ticketed for Triple-A ball in 1951 when the Selective Service System called my number. I'd be in the army for the next two years.

A grizzled, baseball-loving sergeant told me how to play the old army game. "Get to know the first sergeant, the supply sergeant, and the mess sergeant. Treat them right and they'll take care of you."

As company mail clerk I made sure to hand deliver their mail twice a day. In return I got the occasional weekend pass, a brand-new winter coat, and all the food I could stuff in my mouth. In two years I put on forty-five pounds.

I had promised myself that I'd write a book about my army experiences. Hemingway did it, didn't he? Mailer. James Jones. Irwin Shaw.

The trouble was this: my only army experience worth writing about was my honeymoon. PITCHER MARRIES PITCHER should have been the headline when, on June 23, 1952, Anne Stewart Pitcher married Jim Brosnan, pitcher, in the chapel at Fort Meade, Maryland. She was a freckle-faced Virginia belle, a civilian employee of the army, and she would dance all night at the Civilian Club on the post. She taught me how to dance. Then she taught me how to drive her Chevy convertible. So I had to marry her and promise never to write about that long summer night.

Out of the army and back in the International League, I had a pretty poor season (4 wins, 17 losses) for a pretty poor team in Springfield, Massachusetts. The subsequent invitation to spring training with the Cubs was a pleasant surprise, actually making the team was a shock, and working with pitching coach Howie Pollet proved to be the turning point in my career.

"You have a live arm and you change speeds well," he said. "You need a breaking ball you can control. I'm going to teach you how to throw a slider."

It proved to be the perfect pitch for me. I won eight out of nine decisions in the Texas League, was 17 and 10 in the Pacific Coast League, and was in the Big Show for good in 1956.

Two undistinguished years later I met Bob Boyle of *Sports Illustrated*. He had heard that my ambition was to write a book about big league baseball. "Why don't you write an article for us?" he asked. "If something significant happens—a no-hitter or something like that."

How about if I were traded from the Cubs to the St. Louis Cardinals (for shortstop Alvin Dark)? "A mutt for a pedigreed pooch," wrote one reporter. "A real steal for the Cubs."

Bah, humbug, I scrooged, and wrote all about it for *SI*.

"Loved it," said Boyle. "Why don't you write a book about a whole season?"

For the rest of the story, turn to page one.

JIM BROSNAN

Morton Grove, Illinois
November 2001

Introduction

The following journal is my personal account of the 1959 baseball season . . . the way I saw it. Certain names, places, and events will be recognized by many readers. Some readers will remember the players, scenes, and action just as I did. In some cases I may have seen things differently. But then no two people can truly say that they see the same thing exactly the same way. Occasionally my viewpoint will prove to be unique; no one else could have seen things just that way. But that's the way I saw it.

Professional baseball in America is not a game, nor can it be called an ordinary business or occupation. Baseball is a pastime—a habit—with millions of people . . . baseball fans. Anyone fanatically attached to baseball considers himself privileged to enter and enjoy the private world of the baseball players. Identification of the fan with the ballplayer goes beyond the playing field, where it traditionally belongs. Many ballplayers (some of whom are not baseball fans) resent an intrusion into their personal lives. The means by which most fans learn what they want to know about the players leaves much to the imagination. The feeble defense with which the players try to prevent the fans from getting to know them too well does little but create confusion. Perhaps that is the way it should be.

The 1959 National League season was my twelfth year as a professional baseball player. It was my fourth season in the major leagues, and, in most respects, a typical year in the average ballplayer's career. (With no false modesty I call myself an average professional baseball player.) One season doesn't make a career, of course, but the fan who follows me as I re-create the 1959 season will probably get a little different viewpoint of baseball.

The daily life of the professional baseball player is not really so exciting that it should attract as many adolescent ambitions as it does. Yet, the ballplayer's life does have its rewards. In my twelve years in organized baseball I've played professionally in forty-one of the fifty States, several Caribbean islands, and some Far Eastern countries, including Japan. Had I joined the Navy in 1947 instead of the Chicago Cubs organization I doubt if I would have seen much more of the world. And the pay has been better.

Each and every baseball season has its share of satisfactions and disillusionment, its thrills and despair. Perhaps my account of the 1959 season is less emotional than it actually seemed to others, but then I was born a cynic. The professional life, moreover, grinds and polishes the emotions to a fine, hard core —the professional spirit. Amateur baseball fans may resent, at times, the apparent lack of constant, noisy enthusiasm that is one part—but only a part—of athletic spirit. The professional player has more skill and needs no false hustle to do his job. A player who loves his craft and has the patient determination to do the best job he can creates a personal efficiency that is as much a pleasure to watch as it is a help in winning ball games. Running full speed with his mouth open does not always contribute to a player's success. The professional stores up, treasures that winning spirit, for there are many long days in the baseball year.

This journal—*The Long Season*—tells the story of one professional ballplayer's life during a championship season. This is the way I saw it.

The
LONG SEASON

Morton Grove, Illinois

THE official National League schedule says the 1959 season opened on April 10—San Francisco at St. Louis. For me the season started three months earlier, on January 10, in Chicago. I was still working at the Meyerhoff advertising agency, and I had called home to see if there were enough olives for the martini hour.

My wife, Anne Stewart, said, "The contract came. Guess how much?"

I never would have.

We had been looking for the contract in the mail each day. We had talked about it for six months.

Even before one season ends, a ballplayer estimates next year's contract. In late September of the 1958 season I reviewed my record with pleasure and concluded that I didn't have much more time to improve it. With each game I pitched I felt better and better about my prospects in 1959.

"Good old Bing," I had said one night as the season came to an end. "I think I'm going to enjoy talking contract with him."

"You should. This will be the first time you ever had anything to say to a general manager," my wife said.

I'd won twice as many games as I'd ever won before in one year in the majors, and in addition, I had saved seven more games in relief as the Cardinals staggered through the last month. The only question in my mind was how much of a raise I'd get. Here I had proved that I could do two jobs well —start and relieve. What price versatility?

Did Bing Devine, the Cardinal general manager, look upon me with the rose-tinted, dreamy-eyed gaze of a pennant-waver? Or would we two battle for the bare bones of a typical baseball business contract? I cut out from the agency in time to get the first commuter train home. My wife greeted me with her fighting smile, and handed me the registered letter from St. Louis.

One quick glance confirmed my most pessimistic fears. All winter we'd waited, hoping for a reward, a pat-on-the-back that would pay all the old bills. Hanging my coat and hat in the closet, I took the martini my wife held out to me, and gulped down the olive that had risen in my craw.

"Good God, I'm no better off after a good year than I was the year I got out of the Army. This doesn't mean a thing! A thousand-dollar raise! He'll spend that much on phone calls before the season starts!"

"You aren't thinking of signing that, are you?" Anne Stewart asked, shaking her finger at the folded paper that read:

UNIFORM PLAYER'S CONTRACT

NATIONAL LEAGUE OF PROFESSIONAL BASEBALL CLUBS

. . . .

2. For performance of the player's services and promises hereunder the Club will pay the Player the sum of ———.

"What are you gonna do?" I asked, an almost plaintive cry hardly calculated to answer her question. "Maybe he's trying to test my sense of humor. Turn the thermostat up; it looks like it's going to be a long, cold winter."

Devine had written, "Please find enclosed your St. Louis contract calling for salary of $16,000. If this is satisfactory, return to me as soon as possible."

My typewriter keys quickly clicked out an answer. I boiled over for one full page, spilling anguished indignation. Hell, I had been tempted to ask for $25,000!

How insulting can you get? You give a bushel of money to any healthy kid who comes along, hoping he'll be the one in

2

ten who ever wears a major-league uniform. Here I proved I could do the job for you and you throw me a bone, you offer a token raise! Well, I sure as hell am not satisfied, and you can take this contract and stuff it in your files!

Sincerely,

Then, yanking these unmailable comments from the typewriter, I paused to regroup forces. I wasn't even going to get $20,000, which was the original compromise I had in mind. How much would he pay? A ball club's first offer is generally hopeful, not necessarily sincere, and hardly final. Now, how do I start negotiating without seeming stubbornly antagonistic?

Anne Stewart said, "You tell him you're gonna get $20,000 or you won't sign. You finally had a good year. Now make 'em pay for it."

I sat in my half-paid-for lounge chair in our heavily mortgaged home, with Chicago winter weather running the fuel bill into five figures. Spring training would start February 20. The annual reverie would soon invade my cocktail hour . . . sea gulls, palm trees, fishing boats lazing on the blue Gulf. . . . I needed a plan.

"The first principle of contract negotiation," said Stan Musial one day, "is: don't remind 'em of what you did in the past; tell them what you're going to do for them in the future. They know what you're selling; they've bought it before. Now promise greater things to come."

Once, during the 1958 season, Devine had said to me, "We must get together to talk about your potential. We bought you from the Cubs because you look better than your record. We still think so." He had said this after my string of incomplete starts had reached six straight games and Hutchinson had decided to try me in the bullpen. Devine added, "I think we'll enjoy talking to you. After reading that article you wrote for *Sports Illustrated* I'm going to bring along a dictionary." (A portion of my 1958 diary had been published during the season, causing some predictably surprised reactions. I swore a hundred oaths that I had really and truly written every word myself. Ballplayers are supposed to have their opinions written for them by sportswriters. It is a tradition.)

Devine is no slouch with words himself. His speeches during our postseason tour of Japan indicated a not unusual facility for a baseball general manager. He features lengthy, high-speed oratory, pausing for breath every twenty-two seconds during which time he floods the mind with two facts and thirty-one extraneous comments. His machine-like chatter would talk the ears off a donkey, and I wasn't about to let him make a horse's ass out of me.

I would duel him with air-mail letters. Three hundred miles is too far for vocal mesmerism. His first move was obviously a feint. A thousand-dollar raise was ridiculous. My counteroffer would be equally unrealistic, accompanied by a flourish of last year's statistics, since I was on fairly solid ground there.

My pleasant, so-glad-to-hear-from-you reply contained the barest hint of a possible compromise. "Perhaps you could reconsider, on the basis of an assurance on my part to do as well in 1959 as I did in 1958. If my record (see above) is as good as it looks, any improvement would obviously be worth twice your offer."

The die was cast but I'd be damned if I was going to cross the Missouri till I was satisfied with my own conscience. The postman slogged through a snowstorm to carry off my letter, and the wild winds of Morton Grove piled four and a half feet of snow in front of my garage door. Jamie stared sadly at the blizzard, her four-year-old wistfulness almost hiding the conniving echo of her mother's suggestion. "Daddy, when we go to Flo-wa-da, can I go fish with Mommy?" Every baseball family eagerly awaits the new season.

Devine played it cool. I fidgeted nervously each time I was asked, "Have you signed your contract for next year?" The

4

publicity releases from Busch Stadium in St. Louis quoted Solly Hemus: "Brosnan will be the long man in the bullpen!" Demoted before I even threw a pitch! "Long Man . . . that's the lowest form of pitcher, isn't it?" asked my best friends, unkindly.

"Yeah, well, it's damn good money," I assured them, hopefully, anxiously. The fever was getting to me. Snow was colder every day; sand never seemed so heart-warming. Three weeks went by, and not a word from St. Louis.

January 26—Morton Grove, Illinois

"LET's pack up and go to Staunton," I suggested, as January gradually froze my ambitious hopes for a big contract. "We'll visit with your father, maybe drive to South Carolina and visit your brother Scholey and Uncle Vernon. Then, if Devine and I ever do get together, I'll have a running start to St. Pete." The itch to start the season was irritating me more than Devine's silence. What the hell was he mad about, anyway?

Thirty days had exhausted my patience, so I called to let him know where I'd be for the next two weeks. He apologized most graciously for not getting in touch, engulfing me in a burst of warm-windy wishes that "we should really get together for a long talk." My ear grew numb and I wished I'd called collect. I had warned myself—"Duel by air-mail"—and here I was, enfiladed through my own careless impatience.

Devine wheeled up his big guns for the usual general manager's barrage. "There are three elements that affect a ball club's basic salary budget for players: (1) the statistics of the player's performance in the preceding year; (2) the player's future—how long can he be expected to last; (3) the ball club's position in the standings. If you finish out of the money, in the second division, you can't be expected to pay bonuses."

5

This carefully calculated harangue, in expert hands, would obviously reduce all the Cardinals to beggary. Who, by those standards, could get a raise after the 1958 season?

"Bing," I interrupted, "we're not arguing about last year. Let's stick with next season, okay? If you even suspected that I was going to win twenty in '59 you'd be happy just to have me satisfied. Right?

"Now, twenty thousand dollars is a symbol of success to me. When I first started playing pro ball I made $125 a month. My goal in my career became symbolized by that twenty thousand dollars per year. Without straining credulity too much, you might say I'm close to realizing that goal. I don't feel that I should compromise at this time."

"Life is a series of compromises," he opined. "I'd like to be making as much as I think I deserve, too."

He finally mentioned a figure, halving the difference between his original offer and my planned-for compromise. His almost offhand figure-dropping suggested that he still wasn't being serious. I smiled my way off the phone and backtracked into the typewritten argument that "I enjoyed talking with you again" and "Since you've been quite busy, you may have forgotten my position. I'm getting older. My career-expectations are less great, and more practical. I can't promise you twenty wins, but I can do a better-than-average job. What do you call a better-than-average salary for a pitcher?

"I'll be in Staunton, Virginia, for ten days. You can reach me at Col. S. S. Pitcher's home."

If Devine had me on the run, I'd let him chase me a little, anyway.

February 2—Staunton, Va.

THE Shenandoah Valley glowed hospitably under a prespring zephyr. Soft showers stirred the apple-blossom buds, and I savored some of the best free-loading in baseball. My in-laws serve only Virginia Gentlemen! That is good bourbon, suh!

I was sipping the same when the Last Offer came. "This is the best I can do," said Devine. "We've talked Security, Pennant, High Cost of Living, Financial Goals in Life, Prospective Parenthood." (One of the common, last-ditch, desperation arguments is the Pregnancy Problem. "How can I afford another baby?") "Now," said Devine, "let's get serious." He spoke slowly and distinctly and finally.

"Give me five hundred more, and I'll settle," I said.

"Why argue about five hundred dollars?" he said.

February 4—Staunton, Va.

HAVING agreed to terms I celebrated. An extra shakerful of martinis was shaken, savored, and swallowed. The Colonel said, "There's a bottle of champagne out back in the 'Cool Place.'" But, as I chewed my fourth olive, I waved aside his suggestion. What greater grapes grow than are pressed into Vermouth! "Save it till I have a really good year," I said.

"I was saving it for the day I retire," he said.

"Bet I'll beat you to it," I countered. My mind was fuzzing up properly. The present was happy, the future rosy. "Is there an extra bit more gin for this memorable moment of triumph?" I asked.

"Don't you think you've had enough, honey?" my wife asked. "We've got a long drive ahead of us tomorrow."

"Don't worry, babe," I said. "Old Broz can do it."

An extra head appeared in the morning-sunlit mirror. We were supposed to hit the road at six A.M., and we set a new family record by leaving only one hour and forty minutes late. Packing a car with two kids, a dozen toys, and enough clothes for a two months' trip takes special training. Although we must do it half a dozen times a year it is an exhausting, sometimes frustrating job.

A dozen suitcases, grips, bags, and boxes can be quickly

and neatly stacked between the driver's seat and the kids. But, invariably, I end up with this huge hatbox outside the car on the ground, looking like a lost carburetor. "Why in hell do you need a boxful of hats?" I'd ask. "For six years I've wrestled with this thing!"

"You never know when you may need them," my wife would reply.

"There's one hat in here you haven't worn since we've been married."

"Put it in the car, Meat."

At least we have a station wagon in which to travel. The cargo area behind the back seat carries four dolls, a bat and ball, two blankets and four pillows (for the dolls, of course), two large balloons, two baskets of small toys, writing pads and crayons, books to color in, and two children who barely fit. With a six-foot-wide no man's land of suitcases between them, parents and children are free to play and scream on an adult or infantile level. The last stage of our trip to Florida blasted off.

"It's going to rain all the way to Charleston," Anne Stewart said, in gloomy, heavy-headed pessimism. "That's what the man said last night on the news."

Weather forecasters make quite an impression on our family. The last thing we see at night is the weather map on TV saying that "rain from the Gulf" will spoil our off-day, or that the "winds from the southwest" (home plate as we see it) will be practically cyclonic and all God-fearing pitchers should stay in the dugout, or better yet at home.

Two meals, five rest-room stops, a torn fan belt and ten hours later we drove into Charleston, S.C., a solidly segregated city trapped against the sea by Negro communities extending in an arc from Florence to Savannah. "Haven't seen a white man since we left Florence," I said to a Carolina cousin. "Won't see any till you get to Savannah," said he. "How about a little bourbon and water?" I stripped off my raincoat (it finally started to rain just as we reached Charleston,

8

ruining our day as predicted) and we toasted, silently, Jefferson Davis and John Waring, mayor of Charleston, for preserving our heritage, or whatever they have been doing over the last century. When in the South, do as the white men, so we did our duty by a bottle, discussing secession . . . seriously.

I was told that a reporter for the local paper wanted to know if he could interview me sometime during the weekend. "We didn't know if you wanted the publicity or not," said the cousins. (Only smallpox would prevent me from promoting a chance to see my name in the papers.)

Over the phone the reporter said that Charleston had a new baseball team, Frank Scalzi was the manager, the White Sox had a working agreement with the local owners, and the principal stockholder of the ball club had plenty of money. He also has a charitable mind or a wise accountant with a tax-angle, if he chose to operate a ball team in Charleston, S.C. The mosquitoes alone would discourage patrons, not counting the heat, the gnats, and the segregation issue. (A Chicago ball club would have to have Negroes in the outfield, at least, and what sort of example would that be for young children to see?) But there is no accounting for the mind of a baseball fan, and a minor league owner has to be fanatic, if not about segregation then why not baseball?

Mention of Frank Scalzi's name piqued my memory, though, and I asked the reporter to arrange for us all to get together if he could. Skeeter Scalzi had managed me in the summer of 1948, when I played for Fayetteville, N.C. Once, after I had disgusted him by throwing a gopher ball with the bases loaded he had gathered the infielders around the mound and asked, "Who wants to pitch?"—a rather unqualified dismissal, I thought. My feelings were hurt so badly that I took them, my glove and spikes, and bought a bottle of port wine into which I poured my complaints. As the bottle emptied, my despair increased. My search for the bathroom became ridiculously erratic and my roommate could not stop laughing long enough to dissuade me from leaving on the next plane for

Cincinnati. Scalzi was left short-handed for pitching just as he took his team on the road for a series with the other pennant contenders. He gave me an "F" for deportment in his weekly report to the front office, but he had no choice but to welcome me back when I finally recovered my senses five days later. By then every pitcher on the team was bushed and I had to work, gopher balls or not. Within a week I pitched a no-hit game and started to win. At the end of the season, Frank was manager of a championship club and I was full of an equal measure of bright hopes for the future.

Like all minor league managers working with young kids Scalzi had to act the father confessor and student counselor to some of his players. In the midst of my hopelessness I had asked Frank if he thought I should quit baseball to dig ditches. And he dispelled my brooding with a bit of practical optimism. He said, "I want to make you a proposition. Sign a contract with me, giving me ten per cent of all of the money you make from baseball in the next five years, and I'll give you a thousand dollars right now . . . today. How about it?"

Had I been wiser and not so young I'd have taken the deal. The money would have been useful when I went into the Army two years later. But by the time I finished preening myself after this not so subtle pat on the back, Scalzi put me in another game and I was bombed again. Those first few years learning the game were often rough on my pride. Today, Scalzi could say "I told you so" and I'd enjoy every word of it.

The *News and Courier* sportswriter arrived a minute late, accepted a bourbon and water (I was getting used to the customs), and disappointed me thoroughly with his first two statements.

"Scalzi left yesterday for his home in Portsmouth," he said. "Let's shoot a picture of you playing the piano."

Here, I had hoped for a baseball bull session, to which a reporter would be an invited observer. The ultimate sports interview! Scalzi is frank, I am brassily opinionated. What a chance for a reporter with sharp questions and attentive ears!

Our session had none of these. Dutifully I posed, plunking the piano. . . . "Brosnan Plays Beethoven, Bartok and Baseball." Delightedly I paraded parental pride in my children. . . . "Brosnan Loves Baseball, Children, the South." Diplomatically I praised Mantle, panned Mays. . . . "Brosnan Finds White Center Fielders Superior." Effusively I lied about how much I enjoyed the interview. . . . ("Brosnan a Prevaricating Bastard," my mind's eye read.)

Unfortunately for both sportswriters and ballplayers the Interview has become stereotyped, and the limits and confines of communication have been drawn. Player suspects Writer. ("He misquotes me, makes me say things I wouldn't think of saying—*just to get a story!*") Writer sneers at Player. ("He hasn't said anything new since he first cried 'Goo' at the age of two. What can I do with a character like this?")

February 14—Charleston, S. C.

DURING our stay in Charleston my wife's uncle, Vernon Whitaker, and his wife, Eula Mae, dispensed Southern charm with a practiced glad hand. "What I like about your relatives," I commented, as we packed again to continue our trip, "is that they're obviously not baseball fans. Nobody has bugged me about baseball for three days, and it has been a true vacation."

"In their own way they do like baseball," Anne Stewart said, "but you know Vernon is my mother's brother. And remember what Mother said when I told her you played baseball? 'Why that's nice. What does he do for a living?' I thought Daddy would die!"

"You know," I said, "that must have been the reason I felt so comfortable with your mother. She didn't know whether or not I ever got Duke Snider out, and she cared less. And she still liked to have me around for free-loading. All of the people I've met here in Charleston are pretty much the same way, I guess. I do believe they think the segregation issue is more important than the opening of the baseball season. Do you think Vernon would be shocked if he knew we invited Ernie Banks to our housewarming?"

She blanched at the suggestion, but said, "I think Vernon and Eula Mae know your sentiments. You've deliberately agitated everybody who ever brought up the question. And Eula Mae still asked me if we wanted the beach house for a vacation after the season. Oh, Meat, it's so beautiful on Sullivan's Island in October!"

"Their generosity is limitless. I hope this weekend is a good omen for the season. Let's go bid them *au revoir*. If we get into the World Series we'll come back in October."

February 19—St. Petersburg, Fla.

THE day we arrived in St. Petersburg, the sportswriters were gleefully describing the number of "holdouts" on the Cardinal club. Each major league baseball team has its share of stubbornly discontented ballplayers in the spring. (Most of them sign, but some of them stubbornly insist on a measure of content.) The practice of printing the salary of each signed player causes a great deal of depression among the less fortunate who have not yet signed. Although it is seldom true that the amount printed is, in fact, the amount to be received by the player, the press establishes a caste system within the club by asserting that certain players make, or should make, more or less than the other players.

Vinegar Bend Mizell's reaction to contract discussions was that of any shrewd, hard-nosed Alabama farmer who always got plenty of peanuts for his peanuts and why shouldn't the subsidy remain the same? If the farmer has a bad year on the farm nowadays the government still supports him in the style to which he has become accustomed. "It's a matter of principle," cried Wilmer, according to the paper.

"We're still pretty far apart," said Devine.

"Go get 'em, Will," I thought. "I'm with you."

"You can't win," said Larry Jackson, as he signed just one day before we opened.

"Vinegar probably wants to be traded," went the rumor in the clubhouse. "Left-handers think they got the world by the tail."

February 20—St. Petersburg, Fla.

FROM our rented beach house at Indian Rocks I drove to Al Lang Field in St. Pete, crossing the toll bridge at Madeira Beach. The toll was fifteen cents; round trip a quarter. "Let's see," I figured. "How much will that be before we break camp?" The stomach-tightening of nervous expectation struck me as I added up the ridiculous total of small change. . . . "Got to remember to carry plenty of quarters," I thought to myself as traffic wound slowly through the city. "There must be an easier way to come," I thought. "The first day is always a little mixed-up. Wonder what Mizell is thinking about now."

At the ball park the curiosity seekers were watching the "curiosa" outside the clubhouse. Players walked from the parking lot carrying equipment bags loaded with gloves, shoes, jock straps and high hopes. A huge, almost gross, Negro wearing a dirt-stained Panama hat sat at the gate on a portable camp stool. "Hello, Brosnan," he said. "Horace still likes you, boy."

Dirty Louie! Relic of the Polo Grounds! Even when the Giants weren't drawing flies in 1956, Louie was there in the bleachers every day, yelling at each player who came down the clubhouse steps. The elemental fan!

"Hey, man," I said to him, "wouldn't Stoneham pay your

way to Phoenix this year?" Some players suspected Stoneham hired Louie to agitate the opposition bullpen. Even from as far away as the bleachers Louie could do it. Wonder if he's ever heard about soap?

The first workout was scheduled for ten o'clock. The clubhouse was filled by nine, and we sat around for an hour, anxious to go. But first came the speeches. Spring training has a convocation ceremony that follows strict patterns all over the baseball world. Manager speaks: "Wanna welcome all you fellows; wanna impress on you that you each got a chance to make this ball club." (This hypocrisy is always greeted by an indulgent and silent snicker from the veterans of previous training camps.) "We got a big job to do, and with a couple of breaks I think we can win the pennant. These are my coaches; what they say you can consider it came from me." Solly Hemus was forced to make his opening speech to the club while August Busch, the owner of the Cardinals, sat in the background smoking a pipe. Solly was understandably nervous. His ability to verbalize as a new executive had to withstand both the boss's criticism and the experienced cynicism of the ballplayers. Solly quickly, and wisely, turned the floor over to Howard Pollet, the pitching coach. Howie is a quiet, soft-spoken gentleman, a type not ordinarily given to accepting coaching jobs. He echoed, quietly, Hemus's remarks about each pitcher having a chance to win a job. And he reminded the pitchers that they were not going to impress him by throwing hard during the first three days. "All you'll do is hurt your arms, and make it tougher on everybody. Just be patient and we'll give you a chance to show us what you can do." Actually, most of the jobs on the club had been filled by the time the contracts had been mailed out in January. The pitcher who impressed most quickly was the one who would get first crack at the few positions still left open. Whereas physical performance is the basis of judgment in baseball, verbalizations of that performance often distort the player's value. It isn't always how you play the game, but who watches

14

you play that determines what kind of a chance you get the next spring. The minor league managers, the scouts, and the front office talent judges can cut a player from the roster long before the Florida sun dries the sweat of the first day's workout.

Sitting in front of me listening to the hypocriticism, and spitting tobacco juice into a sand box, was Marv Grissom. Hemus had been quoted as saying old Marvin would be the No. 1 short man in the bullpen. That was my job! How did he get it away from me before the season even started! I nudged Grissom, and asked for a chew as Johnny Keane and Harry Walker, the other two coaches, spoke a few words. They both had managed for years in the minor leagues, and since Solly had already used the typical manager's speech, they had nothing much to say. Hemus brought it all to a close as he said, "Let's go get 'em," and we charged out of the clubhouse into the sun.

February 22—St. Petersburg, Fla.

A SPRING training clubhouse can look like a prison scene—lockers so small they seem like cells, racks of bats stacked like so many wooden gun barrels, lines of sweaty, stinking uniforms and sweatshirts hanging everywhere. It is a barracks into which the manager and his coaches march, barking discipline: "Run around the park, run to the clubhouse, run to the john, sweat till you bleed."

In the batracks you'll find mementos of the past season. The bats bearing names of players no longer with the club are stacked for the last time in a Cardinal clubhouse. The Del Ennis model, fat and heavy, shaped like a billy club; the Wally Moon bat, wispy-thin at the handle to match the skinny Moon legs; the Hobie Landrith models, all of them, the thin-handled, the barrel-ended, the ones with the base hits

15

still left in them, and probably the ones with the holes in them. Since the pitchers would be hitting for the first week, none of the "regulars'" bats were on display. Pitchers use the dregs of the woodpile, whatever has been discarded by the hitters who ordered them from the factory in high hopes that Hillerich & Bradsby could do for them what nature had apparently forsaken. We took the bats onto the field and broke them one by one, as pitchers are prone to do. (Twenty dozen bats are broken each spring in a major league camp.)

Each player drew a slip of paper from the trainer; a date with an X-ray technician. "Only take you five minutes, boys" —which hardly gave one time for anything but the X-ray machine itself. Each day a group rode off to the clinic after the workout. The first groups groused about losing their hard-earned nap time. Succeeding groups went happily, anxious for an eyeball report of the student technician with the good hands and the high bust. "Get your chest X-rayed, indeed." She certainly had hers.

Curiously her titillating explorations of the back and chest were simply in the cause of medical history. Most of the player-patients were pitchers, and it seems that all pitchers are quite a bit more developed on one side of their torsos than on the other. The monotony of the nurse's humdrum occupation was relieved by her quick (but so thorough) examination ("What a body!") and her confident exclamation, "You're a right-handed (left-handed) pitcher, right?" Outfielders and infielders have no such overdevelopment. Catchers, of course, have underdeveloped brains or they would never have chosen that particular job, but X-rays of their heads would probably be useless. Masochists are what they are. A man has to love to get banged up if he deliberately chooses to be a catcher.

Chest X-rays are a comparatively new idea in organized baseball. Ever since Red Schoendienst shocked the Braves' management with his losing fight to tuberculosis, baseball has been anxious to prevent diseases of that type. Hope alcoholism doesn't strike too many players this year. What would Busch do with the pictures taken at the clubhouse door after the notice was posted about free beer once a week? A line of ball-players, each carrying a case of Budweiser on his shoulder, hustling home after the workout. Smiling, thirsty men, about to enjoy life after a hot day on the ballfield. Would anything prevent beer-drinking?

Traffic in the trainer's room on the third day of practice made it look like a receiving room of a Harlem hospital on Saturday night. After the first two days of running in the spring sunshine, a ballplayer's feet look positively leprous, with blisters and lesions covering his aching toes and heels. "I'd say that I tape at least a toe and a half on each pair of feet," said Doc Bauman, as he sadistically swabbed merthiolate on an open sore. "It's all part of the game. A week from now I'll be rubbing sore arms, and massaging pulled thigh muscles. A month from now I'll have everybody in shape, and all I'll have to worry about is cracked skulls from wild pitches, or sliced tendons when somebody slides into second base . . . or maybe a slight psychological depression in the front office. I have pills for everything."

February 24—St. Petersburg, Fla.

I was reading the stock market quotations before the workout when Sal Maglie finally arrived. He walked down the aisle between the lockers, carrying his duffel bag and shaking hands right and left as he came. "Hey, veteran right-hander," I called, "is everything all right?" The sight of Maglie sidling toward me was worth a fanfare. Sal is not a pleasant-looking man—he looks like an ad for the Maffia, in fact—but he has a nature that transforms his face in the light of any friend-ship. If he feels that his troubles also trouble you, he will even listen to you tell them. "How is it, Sal?" I asked, as he loosened an impeccably tasteful tie.

"Well, I tell you, driving down here from Clearwater—that's where I'm staying, with a friend there—I felt my back going stiff on me. Feels like pleurisy, or something. I'm gonna talk to Solly about running too much today. How's everything with you, Professor?"

"Sal," I said, "Grissom was right. He said that you and he got it knocked up down here. Train on your own, and all that. Like, you reach forty and *you* tell *them* how much you run. Is that right?"

"Well, Grissom's a lot older than me, y'know," said Maglie, referring apparently to the number of hours separating their respective forty-first birthdays. "What he says about training wouldn't apply to me too much. He still throws just as hard as he did when Ty Cobb started playing the game. Whaddya say, Griss?"

A splattering of tobacco juice plopped into the floorboards in front of my locker and Uncle Marv stuck a raw-boned ham out to greet Maglie. "Any lies this guy tells I can double," he said, pumping Maglie's hand. The contrast between Grissom's huge, fast-balling meathook and Sal's slim-fingered, curve-ball claw pinched my memory. Many suns had set on pitchers' duels that featured Maglie and Grissom. Finesse and Power. With so many young prospects cluttering up the place these two old gentlemen would add some much-needed balance to the clubhouse picture. There's something to be said for a few less hungry faces staring at you, avid to take your job away.

February 25—St. Petersburg, Fla.

DURING the first week pitchers dominate the scene, working hard to get ahead of the hitters, most of whom report a week later. We work for a desperate cause, however. The rulesmakers were all hitters who hate pitchers as their common enemy, and the percentages have been weighted in recent years to favor the hitters. If pitchers are ever to be ahead of the hitters during this year, that time will end in two weeks.

The pitcher's training day goes like this: Run a while—throw a little to loosen the arm. Run a while—play a little pepper. . . . "Three men to a game, one hits, the other two field. And hit the ball! No lollypopping. That don't do you no good." Run a while—do some pick-ups, twenty the first day, twenty-five the second day. "We'll be doing a hundred before we leave here." (Over my dead body.) John Grodzicki handles the pick-ups. He rolls a ball ten feet to his right, and the pitcher runs after it, picks it up, tosses it to Grodzicki, who rolls it away to his left, the pitcher running after it, and back, and over and over and over.

After the pick-ups, the pitcher asks Hemus's permission to leave the field, and off he goes to change his sweatshirt, drink a glass of orange juice, or coke, or milk—"None of it's good for you," Bauman will say.

"I'm thirsty, Doc!"

"Take a salt pill and some water, and get back out there before they forget you're on the club."

And then you can get down to some serious running.

We run in groups of four, thirty minutes a day, from foul line to foul line. Run halfway, walk halfway. Cleverly I attached myself to a group that included Maglie and Grissom. The two forty-year-old gentlemen run like colts the first day, and creak along at a more leisurely jog from then till September. Assuming his saddest expression, Maglie ambles back and forth, groaning as he runs, talking as he walks.

"This gets harder all the time . . . every spring," he said. "If I didn't have to work to eat I don't think I could take it." We turn at the line and jog back to Grodzicki, who stands at the halfway point counting out the laps.

"Sold my liquor store before I came down, you know. Made a good deal . . . you know what I mean?" We ran again.

"But I'm on the borderline, boys. After you get to thirty-five you only count ahead to that thirty days' severance pay." (At forty-one, Sal could draw more in thirty days' pay than most of the players on the field would draw during the entire season.) Machiavellian Maglie—he might have been the model for a medieval Italian woodcut.

February 27—St. Petersburg, Fla.

OUR offense arrives officially tomorrow. Some early birds are here, taking up precious time in the batting cage. The pitchers naturally have a right to complain as they miss a turn at bat. The only time we get to hit all year . . . one week. No wonder the Cardinals were last in the league in runs scored. (Pitchers tend to talk as though their bats were the obvious salvation of the team's troubles.)

Shagging for the rest of the club would be our job after tomorrow. Baseball's infantrymen we'd be. Doggies! Servants to a bunch of banjo hitters! Broglio, his beard dripping sweat, stumbled over me as I dropped a fly ball.

"For Christ's sake, Ernie," I said, "you'll wear yourself down to a respectable size if you hustle like that all day. I liked you the way you looked in Japan. Fat and full of Black Label."

"Have to keep moving, dad," he said. "Wife's pregnant again. Can't afford to relax any more."

"Your wife here or in Frisco?" I asked.

"Didn't think it was worth it to bring her. The rents around here are fantastic."

"Yeah, Ern, but this is the big time. You gotta go first-class even if it means you go in the hole till June."

Broglio smiled weakly. "I had three kids before I was twenty-five years old. I've been in a hole ever since I got into baseball. This year I'm trying to get out."

20

"Well, Ernie, you only go this way once, y'know." I really wanted to sympathize with him, but all I could think of was how glad I was that I never had his troubles. We were damned lucky not to have any kids for the first three years of our marriage. How we missed I'll never know.

March 1—St. Petersburg, Fla.

"How can you expect me to run with a foot like that, Doc? Look at the length of those nails, and that little blister there. No, no, next to that soft corn. Could you fix me up in time for the workout, Doc? Ordinary man would be in the hospital."

Bauman's eyes were getting pouchy, puffed up, and damn near pugnacious as the stream of complaints taxed his energy. During the latest clubhouse convocation he had said, "I'll be here from seven in the morning, and I'll stay as late as you want me." Augie Busch cheered this loyal devotion to the Cardinal cause. He praised the speech-making of Hemus, Devine, and Bauman on the day the whole squad had assembled for the first time. "Anheuser-Busch must get back up on top again," he cried. "The Cardinals give us a great deal of pleasure when we win, and they cause plenty of cussing and crying when you lose. Now, let's get in good shape and go get 'em this year." His yachting cap looked like a cheerleader's beanie at a student pep rally as he waved his hand to the applause of the conscience-stricken, newly hopeful athletes. At last, we knew what were were fighting for!

Verbal instruction was the first order of the day, and fifty players gathered on the mound. Johnny Keane, the Verbal Instructor, raised his fungo bat (all coaches religiously carry fungo bats in the spring to ward off suggestions that they aren't working), cleared his throat, and said, "Today, we are going to teach you how to run the bases." In a previous

Verbal Instruction, Keane and Hemus ("What I say you can consider as coming from him," said Solly) had taught us how to bunt, and therefore presumably we would know how to get on base. How to Run Bases was the logical sequel. Organization had erred slightly, though. Only the pitchers were in on the "How to Bunt" meeting, and doubts plagued me still—how were the other eight guys going to get to first base?

"Fundamentals are important," said Keane. "Without fundamentals you can't get to first base in this game. We're going to go over things that you should know, and if you were a coach first and a player second, you would know, because I—and Solly would have, too—learned more coaching runners than we, or rather I, ever learned running." Hemus interrupted to say that he had never been a coach, but that whatever Keane said you could consider came from him. . . . Solly: "And be aggressive on those bases, whatever John has to say. Go ahead, John."

(If all of Keane's instructions come in sentences like that last one, I thought, I'll need a tape recorder to take notes. You could get lost among the commas.)

Keane pounded a point into the dirt at the front of the mound with his fungo bat. "Don't keep your eyes on the ball, boys." My ears pointed, twanged, and came to attention. "Don't keep your eyes on the ball!" Why, for twelve years I'd been warned that bodily harm was imminent to the ballplayer who didn't keep his eyes glued on the ball, be it thrown, batted, or lying in the outfield grass. Again, the Verbal Instructor had come up with an electrifying statement. "How is he going to get out of that?" was the collective comment of the suddenly awakened players who gathered more closely around the heretical coach.

"What I mean is," said Keane, pleased at the attention he was finally receiving, "don't watch the ball after you hit. Just watch it till it hits the bat, and then forget it. The bat will do the rest. Your job is to get out of the batter's box and down to first base as fast as you can. You might even get to second base if the ball actually is a base hit. And let me point out right now, that it isn't the beautiful hook slide into second or your blazing speed going from first to second that turns a single into a double or gives you that extra base at any time. No sir! Believe me, I've seen it a thousand times. If you can just concentrate on running as soon as you hit the ball—and the bat will take care of the ball, don't worry about that—you can get all the extra jump you need in the first four steps you take away from the plate. That is where that extra base comes in! Right at the plate. By the time you get twelve feet up the line to first you should be going as fast as you can go, and don't stop till you have to. Round that bag!

"Now, we got you to first base, and we tell you, 'One man out.' Please nod your head, or something. We know you know that there is only one out, but we want to be sure. We want you to be friendly with us, and talk to us down at first. So when we say 'One man out' it is our little way of getting to know you better; besides passing on some pretty useful information to the first baseman or whoever else might be listening. We're going to be giving signs all the time in the coaching box. We know that you have other things to think about, like what the blonde in the third row thinks of your graceful running and all, but the signs we give and the words we pass on to you can help win ball games, and help us do our jobs, because that is what a coach is for. So don't just stand there and wait till we nudge you in the ribs before acknowledging a sign or a word we pass on. We have the responsibility, you know, to make sure you know how many are out, and whether or not the hit-and-run is on, and things like that.

"You're on first base, now, and the next hitter hits a ball in the air between the outfielders. We don't want you to stand halfway down to second admiring the scenery and waiting until the outfielder catches the ball. We want you down at second ready to tag that bag when he drops the ball, or can't get to it. That is, unless the guy has a poor arm, and the ball is way out there, and you think that you can get back to tag first after the catch and still get to second base before he throws you out. It would be smart, boys, to know what the outfielder's name is, and how well he throws the ball from the outfield, and even what he eats for breakfast, or how much he had to drink the night before, because if he can't get the good jump on the ball the next day you can take that extra base on him every time and that is what wins ball games, boys. This is your business, boys, and instead of studying the stock market you ought to be studying the fielding statistics of the outfielder, who might not be able to throw you out if you only knew that he had a bad arm. Get yourself a copy of the *Sporting Guide* and see how many runners that guy threw out last season. And you could even watch him throw before the game although I know you have to change your shirt, and have a coke just before the game starts so you are probably going to be up in the clubhouse instead of down on the field watching the outfielders throw, like coaches usually are. If you know that guy might not be able to pick up the ball very well, or has trouble throwing, you can take that extra base without our help, which is the way it should be since this is a split-second game and every second counts. If you don't listen to us you can sometimes get away with plenty just by keeping your eyes open and not just listening for the coaches to tell you something."

Hemus broke in with "and you don't have to wait till the outfielder catches the ball before you tag up. Cheat a little bit, especially at first and second when you're going to tag up after a fly ball. The umpires will never call it on you, and sometimes they won't even call it at third if you leave a little early, although you never can tell when one of those hard-nose bastards is going to be checking on you. So just before the ball hits the outfielder's glove, make your break and take off running.

"And another thing. When you're on first and the next guy hits a ground ball, there's only one thing you should have on your mind. Knock that shortstop or second baseman down. Don't let him make a double play. Get to him and knock him on his ass. He's only ninety feet away and he has to catch the ball, tag second, and worry about you hitting him and he might not ever make that play. When you slide into second keep that front foot up in the air. You don't have to cut him, mind you, but sometimes that's the way it goes. Your job is to break up the double play."

March 3—St. Petersburg, Fla.

CUNNINGHAM still holding out . . . Best fielding first baseman on the club and the best hitting prospect . . . and I guess he knows it. How's he going to get that good money, though, when there are five other first basemen on the roster? . . . Wonder if they budget salaries by position? . . . They've got Musial out in left field, which is a poor joke, but at least he adds a lot of financial balance to the outfield . . . good thing for Cunningham that Stash finally got out of the infield. Spread that money around the ball park, I say. Give those outfielders some responsibility and maybe they'll bear down a little when they're not hitting. Some of them are lost when they haven't got a bat in their hands.

Poor Bauman. With the whole club in camp, business in the training room is booming.

"One of these days, Doc, you should get up a list of all the ballplayer's ailments you're treated—real and imaginary," I told him, as I held up my right arm for a massage and a coating of warm Vita-oil.

"It'd take a whole book," he said. "Some of these guys got complaints even before they hit that door. Why, I could fill a ten-hour day just listening to you guys bitch about how tough it is to play baseball!"

"But, Doc," I protested, "this is Old Broz you're talking to. Do I give you any trouble?"

"Your pills are in that little plastic bottle on the shelf, Boom-Boom. Now, go pitch batting practice and rest your brains. I got work to do."

March 4—St. Petersburg, Fla.

YESTERDAY my new roommate for the '59 season arrived . . . I think. Usually it takes me forever to make up my mind whether or not I like a man. As a ballplayer I've found it's smart to take my time in selecting somebody to eat with, talk with, and live with, more or less constantly, on the road. A good roomie is hard to find. (It took twenty-two years for me to find my wife.)

My first impressions of Phil Clark were reasonably soul-satisfying. Phil is a Georgia boy with a pleased-to-give-you-the-shirt-off-my-back personality. Just by showing up he's already solved two problems for me.

We were rich in beach houses, having two of them, neither irreplaceable. The one we live in is too expensive; the cottage is too small. The big house has a screened porch facing the Gulf, tall shade trees lining the beach, and spotlights hidden in the trees to light up the surf at night. ("Daddy," the kids say after supper each evening, "turn on the moon, please." And I do it, too.)

Damn the expense, then! How can I turn down the chance to play God the Creator for six weeks? You only come this way once, man. (My facile rationalizations must cost me a grand a year.)

Clark drove to the beach to look at the cottage, and declared it perfect for his family. Since he had a station wagon loaded with a three-year-old girl, a puppy dog, a sewing machine, a television set, and enough fishing equipment to frighten the sharks back to San Juan, I thought the cottage might be a bit stuffy if he ever unpacked his car. But a traveling man learns to adapt himself to the discomforts of shoe-box-sized living quarters. "Phil," I said, "you and Gay take the cottage, then. And, if you're willing to split the driving each day, all of my present problems will be banished."

Phil nodded his head. "The wives will like having a car while we're gone every day." He neatly speared the core of my problem. I do like a man that understands me, instinctively. Do all wives want to know why they can't have the car? Clark helped crack open a case of Budweiser. "Looks like it's gonna work out fine. Ah sure am glad we got settled so fast. Anything we can do for you, now, you just let us know, hyah?" Man, if baseball has a language of its own, it has a Southern drawl! I've never had a *roomie* from Dixieland, though. Except my wife. Well, lightning won't strike twice, I guess.

March 5—St. Petersburg, Fla.

EVEN the most indifferent baseball fan seems to want to know, "Why can't pitchers hit?" Because I've blushed in answering that question too many times in the past ten years, I find myself taking the question seriously. (Actually, no professional in his right mind would think of taking my hitting seriously.) Since it applies to the whole pitching profession the question has insulting overtones that constantly put me on the defensive . . . with a bat in my hands.

Now, *why can't pitchers hit?*

I can answer, as I often have, "We just don't get the necessary practice." Or: "Pitchers bear down harder on other pitchers because it's embarrassing to let an 'out' man get a hit off you." Or: "Who says I can't?"

Serious meditation on the question has led me to the some-

27

what galling conclusion that the answer lies not within me at all. Nor within the subjective consciousness of any typical nonhitting pitcher. If you don't hit, you can't hit, probably. Good God, it might really be true!

Shaken by this horrible possibility I rushed out to right field seeking the truth. At Lang Field, St. Petersburg, there is a plot of ground seventy-five feet long, fifteen feet wide, completely enclosed by a mesh of three-ply cord. At one end of this cage stands a pitching machine roughly the height of Whitey Ford, with flat tires, guts of iron, and a motor in its rear. This is Iron Mike, and he throws rubber baseballs in the general direction of a plate sixty feet away, much as a flesh-and-blood pitcher does. Some of the pitches go directly over the plate, somewhere in the strike zone. (The Cardinals paid another bundle of money for Iron Mike on the Bonus Baby Theory that someday he would improve his control and become a pitcher.) Many of Mike's pitches are *near*-strikes, close enough for pitchers, at least, to swing at. It is here that pitchers take their batting practice. When a pitcher dares ask Hemus, "Are we gonna hit today?" Solly says, "If you guys want to hit, go get in the cage," his manner suggesting that pitchers just don't belong at home plate with a bat. Unfortunately, taking batting practice from a mechanical apparatus that throws rubber baseballs lends a synthetic, disenchanted feeling to the whole operation.

The only human element in this training procedure is Paul Waner, an ex-wizard at hitting major league pitching, and the object of my search for an authoritative opinion on the question, "Can Pitchers Hit, or Not?"

"Why not?" said Paul. "Let me see you swing a bat."

Waner looks like a gnarled gnome, the figment of a wild Irish imagination. At his best playing weight, 140 pounds, he could have passed for an ex-jockey sidling up to tout a favorite horse. Yet, Fred Fitzsimmons, the pitching coach when I was with the Cubs, said Waner hit the ball through the box harder than any other hitter that Fitz had faced in the major leagues.

"He'd stagger up to the plate with that big bat of his and you'd swear you could throw the ball by him. Zip! He'd snap a line drive right by your ear."

"Frankly, Paul," I said, as Waner racked up a dozen balls in the pitching machine, "if you can make a hitter out of me, you're worth more money—both you and Iron Mike."

"Let's see you hit a few first, then I'll see if I can help you. You might remember that Lew Burdette was one of the worst hitters you ever did see a couple of years ago. He'd go up to the plate, wave at three pitches and laugh all the way back to the bench. We taught him a couple of things and now he can hurt you if you give him anything too good to hit." Waner waved me to the other end of the cage and plugged in his pitcher. For the next few minutes the only sounds to be heard were the hum of the electric motor, the swish of my bat, and, occasionally, a few plops and plinks as the ball and bat connected haphazardly.

"You're lounging at the ball," said Paul.

Perhaps he meant "lunging," but then I might just as well have been lying on a chaise longue, criticizing Iron Mike's control, a subject on which a pitcher might speak with more authority.

"The first thing you have to try to do," said Paul, "is *bellybutton*. Then, you got to really *block* when you block. You're hitting the bottom half of the ball, and you should be trying to hit the top half. You got to wait for the ball to get right up to the plate, and you gotta pop those wrists when you swing. You're not doing any of those things. That's why you're lounging at the ball. Now, we'll take up breathing," he added, "as soon as I fix this thing."

Breathing I was relatively familiar with, so I decided to go along with the rest, and resumed my position at the plate. Waner worked on Iron Mike with a pair of pliers. (Some of Mike's pitches were going over my head as well as over the plate.)

"Now, wait for that ball till it gets right on the plate. Then, *belly-button!* Get your stomach out front as fast as you can, and that means you can't step first, then turn. It's all one movement. Snap your hips around and the bat will follow up naturally."

The crack of the wood sounded so good as I swung that I thought at first my hip had popped out of place. The batted ball whistled by Iron Mike, getting no reaction out of the machine but pleasing Paul, who said, "That's what you call belly-button! After you've pivoted on that front foot to start your swing you block your hip so it won't turn any further. The smaller a step you take, the quicker you get your belly button around and your hip blocked. The longer you wait for the ball to get to you, the faster you have to block and belly-button, but you cut down lounging at the ball and you won't have a lazy bat.

"I guess I never could stomach those pitchers before, Paul," I said, happily. My well-intentioned pun whistled by his ears, and he proceeded. The next pitch was at my head. Iron Mike hasn't much of a sense of humor either, I suppose. "When you swing at the ball," Waner went on, "try hitting down on the ball, right through it, like. When you hit the top half of the ball, she'll rip through the infield like a scared rabbit. You won't be popping the ball up, or hitting those easy fly balls."

"I thought a hitter was supposed to keep the bat level when he swung, Paul." I said.

"Well, that's what they say, 'cause that's what it looks like, but it's just an optical illusion. What you do is roll your wrists so you can cut into the top of the ball, so you can't have the bat level, really. When you see the ball right there—" he pointed to a spot two feet in front of him, belt-high, just ahead of his front hip—"you move. Block that hip, snap that belly button around, cut down on top of the ball, and watch her go."

The timing was the tough part, waiting for the ball till it got "right there."

"Take a deep breath just before the pitch starts coming," said Waner. "Then, hold your breath till you start to swing.

That makes you relax and wait." I had visions of myself turning blue in the face waiting for a slow curve, and collapsing. If any of the batting feats of the great hitters ("All the good ones do like I been telling you") are hereafter described as breathless, I will view them as literally so.

If Waner was right, and he certainly made it sound logical, some of my most cherished, traditional theories about batting were about to be destroyed.

"You really don't hit the ball out in front every time. Only when you're trying to pull it down the line.

"You have to forget about swinging level at the ball.

"Hit down, and through. Hit the top half of the ball."

I can't quite get used to the idea that I should try to hit just part of the ball. It has always been hard enough to see all of the damn thing and to hit *any* part of it. "Paul," I asked, "did you have any trouble when you started wearing glasses and had to play under the lights?"

"No," he said. "I believe I even saw a little better. The ball looked whiter, or something. I could see that top half right out there waiting to be hit."

("Did you ever try clipping individual stitches?" I wondered to myself.)

We gathered the balls from all over the cage, and racked them up for another session. Usually a pitcher is limited to one basket load at a time, but no one was waiting in line. My hands were forming tiny blood blisters as I swung my Wally Moon model at Iron Mike's pitching. But all I could think about was the way the balls sounded when I hit them. A pitcher learns to tell by the sound whether or not a ball is hit well or not. From the mound you quickly put the three sensations of sight, feel and hearing together, and you know for sure that the ball is gone, man, gone. You watch your pitch go just where you didn't want to throw it, with not quite as much stuff on it as you wish—and . . . what a vicious sound a line drive makes!

Why can't pitchers hit?

Just call me Tiger, dad.

March 7—St. Petersburg, Fla.

"HAVE you asked Hemus yet what he intends doing with you this year?" my wife asked me.

"Yes. As a matter of fact, I talked with him today." I was stirring the gin gently with a vermouth-soaked spoon. "We more or less had it out this morning during the workout. Devine obviously goosed him about that blast I made when Solly said I'd be a long man in the pen this year."

"Why you always want to make managers mad at you, I don't know."

I had no such intention when Hemus called me in. (In fact, I never intentionally make anybody mad at me . . . it just happens.) Hemus asked me how my arm felt after throwing for a few days. "I'm planning to use you as long man this season," he went on, "and we want that arm strong and ready to go."

My bowels began to roar as Hemus confirmed the press report. "Why long man, Solly? I don't want to sound like a troublemaker, but, hell, I was a long man for my first three years. By now, I think I'm ready for a better job."

He donned his best diplomatic attitude and said, "Now, Professor, don't get mad. If what you're worrying about is money, and how much you're going to make being a relief pitcher, don't worry about it. We've got the kind of pitching staff where you're gonna be more valuable as long man. And what's good for the club is good for you."

"Well, yes," I said, "but my experience has been that pitchers who win, or save, games get the most money. Last year I think I proved that I could do both. Now, as long man, I won't be getting much chance to do either. Or doesn't *long man* mean the same thing to you as it does to me?"

"Look," he said, "I've got four starting pitchers. If one of them goes bad, and I take him out when we're still in the

32

game . . . say, one run down, or we're tied, or still ahead . . . then you come in. Whether it's the third, or fifth, or eighth, or ninth. You can go long and short. We know that. You stop 'em for a couple of innings and we get a chance to come back. Then I got Grissom and Kellner to pitch an inning or two.

"As for making more money. If you do the job I'll see you get what you want. Relief pitchers are becoming more and more valuable every day. You gotta have good ones who can pitch every day, or damn near it."

His plan made my arm sore.

First of all, if he thought he had four major league starting pitchers I'd like to know who in hell they were. And "if one of them had a bad day," I wouldn't be surprised if all four got bombed four days in a row. And, if he thought I, or any other pitcher, could stop major league hitting for three or four innings four days in a row. . . ! As a master plan, it looked great. You could almost work it out with an IBM machine. Now, if I had a plastic arm . . .

"Solly, you gonna be my agent next spring?" I asked, smiling partly to myself, partly in resigned agreement to his wishes. Even if I didn't quite understand him completely, and even if I didn't agree with what I understood, he was offering me the prospect of steady employment. Considering the high cost of good living, there is plenty to be said for opportunity. Only I wish to hell he'd find a better title than "Long Man"!

March 9—St. Petersburg, Fla.

HEMUS called a meeting for the last workout before the start of the exhibition season. "We're going to use the same signs in these games as we will all year. So let's pay attention." He turned to Johnny Keane. "John?"

Keane jumped onto a bat trunk waving his ever-present

33

fungo stick for quiet. Broglio murmured to me, "I think he sleeps with that goddamn bat."

"These are the signs we're gonna give from third base. Solly will be on the bench." Keane waved his bat, relegating Hemus forever to the dugout. "You pitchers get together with the catchers later and work out your own signs. These are for the hitters, and we don't want anybody missing signs, 'cause it just messes up everybody, including the guy who messes it up. Now, then, we're gonna have an Indicator, signs for bunting, taking, and hit-and-run. We're gonna have a take-off sign, and a sign for the squeeze play.

"The most important sign is the Indicator. When I rub my hand over the Cardinal on my shirt, that means a sign is on. You see me rub the bird and you watch my right hand . . . right hand only. Forget I got a left hand. With my right hand I'm gonna touch some part of my uniform or body. One touch . . . it might be my cap, or neck, or pants, or arm sleeve . . . one touch, and you're taking. Two touches and you're bunting; three touches, hit-and-run . . . on that pitch, 'cause the runner is going. Those are the three signs you gotta look for when you go up to hit.

"Now, when you're at the plate, look down at me on every pitch. Maybe I don't wanna give you a sign, but I may be pulling at my pants leg, or rubbing my ear, or tugging at my cap, anyway. They will be looking at me, too, trying to steal the signs, so I'll be trying to confuse them by doing the same things when I'm *not* giving a sign as I do when I am. Get me? *Only* when you see me hit that bird do you know something's on. And when I give you the Indicator, count the number of touches that follows. Maybe I'll give you more than three signs! Maybe I'll give you four or five! I'm just doing that as a decoy, in case they start to pick something up, or we suspect they might. It only means something if I use one, two, or three touches after the Indicator."

Keane had the earnest manner of a second lieutenant outlining the intricacies of an espionage detail. All major league

34

clubs use Indicators, decoys, and signs for everything but nose-blowing. The passion for disguising these signs defies reason, although it does give the players on the bench something to do. (The manager will say, "Try to get their signs, boys.") Yet, 90 per cent of the time, the situation determines the strategy, and an experienced player knows who will bunt or when the batter is taking. Even more predictable are the steal and the hit-and-run, since there are only a few men on each club that can do either one. What's more incongruous, although mathematical progression makes it improbable, I've seen the same sign used by two different clubs in the same game!

"The steal sign," Keane went on, "will be given to the runner only after the batter gets the *Take*. We don't want you hitting when that runner is trying to steal. If we did we'd give the hit-and-run. The steal sign is either hand gripping the opposite elbow. It's a figure 4, and that's *for* stealing." He grinned. Nobody seemed to get it. "Let's not be missing the steal sign. You don't have to go on that particular pitch, if you don't get a good jump on the pitch. If you slip in starting, or don't think you can make it, stay on first. The only time you *have* to go is the hit-and-run, 'cause that hitter is swinging at the ball no matter where it is. If you don't go, you penalize the batter for no good reason. We're gonna run a lot this year 'cause we got a running club . . . that right, Solly?"

Hemus nodded. "Whatever John says you can consider it came from me."

"Now, there's the squeeze. We have just one squeeze play. Suicide! You gotta bunt the ball! So you gotta know the play's on, and we gotta know you know it. So with a man on third base I rub across the bird, and touch my pants leg. One touch after the Indicator! You're bunting. You answer me, telling me you got the sign, by showing me the palm of your hand. Don't wave your hand at me. Pick up some dirt, look the other way, and rub the back of your hand across your back pocket. Then I see your palm and I know you got the squeeze.

"Now, I yell to the runner on third, 'Make the ball go through!' and that's the sign to him that he's going in on the next pitch. Got that, you runners? If the batter answers the sign by showing you the palm of his hand you still gotta wait for me to say, 'Make the ball go through!' "

Keane cupped his hands at his mouth as he described what he would do during a squeeze play. His fungo bat slipped to the floor, its clatter echoing in the tense silence. The squeeze play commands breathless attention from ballplayers. Actually, major league clubs don't use it but twenty times a year, and it works only half the time, but the great importance of the squeeze is vividly impressed on the mind because of the depth of managerial despair at its failure. "That'll cost you fifty bucks, Brosnan! For Christ's sake, all you gotta do is bunt the ball!"

Coach Ray Katt whispered to Julio Gotay, the nineteen-year-old Puerto Rican phenom who was to open the exhibition season at shortstop. Julio's command of English was giving him a stomach-ache—his vocabulary was not equal to ordering a decent meal—and Katt was translating Keane's instructions.

"Do you understand, Julio?" asked Keane.

Gotay shook his head.

"Well," Keane frowned, "we'll go over them again tomorrow."

March 12—St. Petersburg, Fla.

SOME players who go to spring training know they have the club made. Others think they do. Half of those invited only hope to. They don't have a chance.

Some players are just making too much money to be optioned out, even though their work in the spring deserves demotion. Many players are full of promises from the front office, the press, and the coaches, who assure them and the world, for instance, that "Julio Gotay is the greatest prospect ever seen in a Cardinal uniform. He can do everything." Except make the team. His chances of running Grammas off short wouldn't find takers at a hundred to one. Except, perhaps, in the southeast corner of the clubhouse, where the rookies have their lockers. They really believe that "everybody has a chance to make this club!"

This hypocrisy undermines the morale of many players. The young kid who is on the roster only because the club had to protect him from the major league draft; the experienced player who just had a pretty good year in the high minors; the veteran who just had a bad year in the majors and hopes to hang on for one more season; and, perhaps the most tragic emotional victim of the cut-down, those "good guys to have in the organization, who will be the backbone of your triple-A ball clubs." These are the pitchers with not quite enough speed; the good power hitters with a just-big-enough weakness to which major league pitchers can throw; and the good glove men with the weak bat or the fair arm or the slow foot. Makes you shudder to think how easily you can be put in your place before you even get a chance to play in a major league park.

So often it's a question of slight degree of ability! Between two pitchers it may be the way one holds a runner on base that determines whether the negative vote of a front-office talent judge has doomed his chances. (I can thank my good Fortune that I got *my* final chance with the Cubs. They needed pitchers damn bad!)

Some players are just on spring vacation, exercising daily, fishing and golfing for a couple hours a day, and waiting for the season to start.

We split the opening games with the Yankees. They are loaded again. You'd have to be a DiMaggio incarnate to make

37

Stengel raise his eyebrow. Obviously the Yankees can hardly wait for the bell to ring.

March 15—St. Petersburg, Fla.

THE papers had it first: "Cunningham Signs With Cardinals!"

"Is everything all right, Professor?" he greeted me, beating me to my own typical Brosnan salutation.

"Everything, Joey, is all right," I countered. "Have you found your shoes, yet?"

His expression was blank at my question, but his grip was firm as we shook hands. Then, his memory rang an Oriental bell, and the Cunningham smile broke open his customarily somber face. "Ah, so," he said. "Ask Blazer."

He turned suddenly and sprinted off across the outfield. Cunningham has an all-business attitude whenever he walks out of the clubhouse onto a ball field. He may rush up to a conversation and insert a wisecrack that breaks everyone up, but then he'll suddenly dash off as if his conscience had reminded him, "Hustle!" In this spring of 1959, having held out for several weeks, he was constantly on the move, racing from infield to outfield to cover all of the positions he would probably have to play during the season.

Even during the Cardinals' tour of Japan in the fall of '58 Joe roared around the ball parks as if some Nipponese first baseman was hot after his job. He epitomized the Cardinal spirit that excited Japanese baseball fans. Off the field, however, Cunningham lived it up as if the Orient were going out of style. He and his roommate, Don Blasingame, were out to "see everything and do everything." On the last night in Tokyo, with a seventeen-hour plane trip ahead of them, Joe and the Blazer decided to redo one of the more memorable sights. "We can sleep on the plane, Blaze, all day."

"We ain't slept for two days now," groaned Blasingame,

38

who sometimes pretends that he really doesn't like to live it up a little.

The fascination of the Japanese inn had provided more than one of the Cardinals with pleasant reveries for the cold wintertime. Early morning sight-seeing—like one A.M. early-morning—was a not uncommon venture. Invariably the young Japanese guides that worked at night were able to find a secluded and peaceful—almost discreet, you would say—hotel to visit. Unlike the usual tourist, the ballplayers were not as anxious to be seen as they were to see.

At night, the typical Japanese inn is displayed by indirect lighting that suggests moonlit retreat, even in the incessant rain that comes in the fall. Rocks, carefully arranged, suggest mountains; shrubs suggest trees; the Oriental-wooden architecture suggests rendezvous. Here, suggests the host (or hostess), you forget past and future.

"What I like is the service," says Joe. "You go in, kick off your shoes and put on slippers. One of these dolls puts your shoes in a rack by the entrance. Then she smiles, and bows. Next thing you know you're all taking a Japanese bath." His grin becomes subtly suggestive, almost a leer. "The tub is sunken below the floor and is about four feet deep. You drink a beer while the water steams up, then step down into the bath, sit back, and relax. Everybody smiles. When you're ready to wash up, you step out of the tub, get lathered, rinsed off with a bucket dipped into the tub, and back down you go for another R & R—that's rest and relaxation, man. You're snickering."

The Japanese bath is an unusual custom for an Occidental to enjoy, but it is an easy habit to get into. If it's not the first thing to do after you land in Japan, it may well be the last before you leave. Especially after a night of sight-seeing, which occasionally includes a bit of carousing—perhaps a strenuous exercise or two. Cunningham and Blasingame, in their anxiety to do the right thing by the Japanese as well as themselves, absorbed a maximum of Oriental culture on the last day and night of our stay in Tokyo.

The rising sun found them padding quietly and contentedly through the lobby of the Imperial Hotel. Sleepless, perhaps, but loose as a goose, like they say. The wild, frenetic activity of our Sayonara was still an hour away. Packing bags, exchanging currency, paying bills, dragging through customs —some tourists find these things exasperating. Blasingame and Cunningham took them in stride—or shuffle—having dissipated whatever frustrating impulses they might have found disturbing.

They sat, or reclined, on a bench at the airport, waiting for the call to board the plane to Honolulu. I asked Cunningham if everything was all right, even though I could see it was. He grinned and opened one eye halfway. Suddenly, his eyelid jerked wide-open, trembled consciously, then sank slowly into his cheek. He nudged Blasingame and said, "Hey, Blaze, I forgot my shoes."

March 20—St. Petersburg, Fla.

FIVE consecutive days of rain! Let's go back to Arizona.

No one can work out. Gloom has saddened the sweet natures of the coaching staff. They can't even run the pitchers in the outfield. The water soaks right into the ground, though. If the rain would let up for a few hours we could throw a little, anyway. This whole state is like a sieve; pretty soon that water will be sloshing back up out of the sand. Can't be much more room to run off.

The best thing about rain during the season is the bridge game that helps kill time. Only three bridge players on the club this year, however: Cimoli, Jackson and I. Pollet could give us a fourth, but he won't play. When he and I trained together with the Cubs, he played every night. Guess coaches and players aren't allowed to mix socially. All we're after is a nice, sociable game! (Jackson and I played for five yen a point in Japan. Lost twenty thousand in a three-hour train ride. Rained there, too.)

Finally scared up a foursome. Had to play on the table in the pressroom. Only dry surface in Al Lang Field. Hemus gave interviews to New York sportswriters while we played. "We're going to score more runs this season." (Christ, we looked as bad now as we did all last year. What's he call "more runs"—three a game?) "Blaylock and Broglio ought to win 12-15 games apiece." (He's out of his mind, and the bell hasn't rung yet.) "Jackson and Mizell have looked good. Brosnan's been excellent." (Sweet guy, that Solly.)

"Better make this the last hand, boys," Pollet interrupted. "We're going to fly to Cuba."

"Yes, we are," said Cimoli disdainfully. "Two no-trump."

Jackson passed.

"The Reds tried to fly to Havana yesterday," said Gino. "They sat on the runway for an hour and a half. Then they went home. It's too wet to fly, or anything else. What do you bid, partner?"

Pollet circled the table, looking at all four hands. "Gino, if Bing can find us a ball park down there we're going. Cincinnati took off an hour ago. They're playing the Dodgers tonight."

"Bet it rains in Havana," said Nunn. "Three no-trump."

March 21—St. Petersburg, Fla.

OUR sunset is back! An old beachcomber told us that the weather would break only when the evening winds shifted. The weatherman, obviously an employee of the chamber of commerce, has made hourly predictions that the weather would change any minute now. The sun finally broke through at five-thirty this afternoon, and as we toasted Old Sol with a glass of chilled gin, the western horizon lit up like a big log fireplace. Scudding dark clouds cover most of the sky, and the surf is pounding what's left of the beach, but we knew the rains had to go. "Daddy will be here tomorrow," my wife said. "The weather just had to change!"

"I talked to Hutch yesterday," I said.

Fred Hutchinson had driven from Tampa to say hello to the people he worked with in 1958. As Cardinal manager then he had been well liked by most of his players. After his experience with our offense he must drool at the power of the Cincinnati club working out in Tampa. Even though Hutch is working with the Reds as the manager of Seattle, with his luck he'll probably end up with a bunch of .225 hitters. Baseball is a game of ruts, many of them discouragingly long.

"The Old Bear told me he's happy at Seattle," I said. "He sure recovered fast from the screwing he got last year from Busch."

"Don't use that word," she said.

"What's wrong with 'Busch'?"

My wife glared at me. "Did Hutch say anything about that letter you wrote him at Christmas? You sounded so grateful. Why? You didn't *owe* him anything. You did a good job for him, besides."

"A ballplayer always owes a good manager a debt. I learned things from Hutch and I thanked him. He gave me a chance to make more money for one thing. It was on his recommendation that they traded for me. And he gave me confidence in myself when the most I might have expected was a good chewing out. It's not just winning for a guy that shows you like him, anyway. As a manager, maybe, yes. But I think it's just as important, for player and manager, that there be mutual respect, man-to-man. I've never been able to do really good work for a manager that I thought was a first-class ———. Nor for a manager who obviously thought I was one."

"Don't use that word," she said. "There are so many people in this world you have to work for that are first-class . . . Oh,

42

why do you talk like a ballplayer all the time?"

"It's not only me. You don't know how many guys I've talked to who say the same thing. If a manager treats you like a dog, bite him. Eye for an eye, and all that. The manager has a certain responsibility to you, too. His job depends on you doing good."

"You're going to cut your own throat one of these days," she said.

Turning this logical truth over in my mind, I poured the last of the martini into my glass. At least the managers I like will know it, and those that I don't will, too. Why make this life complicated?

March 25 — St. Petersburg, Fla.

SOME days I can remember clearly, everything that happened. Some days in baseball are not easily forgotten. Some days I'm certain that I'm really not losing my memory at all, just some friends. Baseball friendships are mostly transient affairs; ballplayers come and go. You don't know from year to year whether you'll be congratulating a man for hitting a home run, or knocking him down with a fast ball so he won't. In spring training you see them leaving every day.

Sal Maglie has gone down the drain.

If he was to tell about it, he might say that he pulled the plug himself. He was pitching to Dave Philley, with the bases loaded. Philley hit a high pitch over the right field fence to knock Maglie out of the box, beat us a ball game, and crush any hope that Sal might be helpful in the 1959 season. He said, "I had him set up all right for my pitch. I meant to get the slider in on his hands. You know what I mean? I just didn't get it in there, and—you gotta jam him. You know that."

Some days I can remember clearly, but this particular day ended right about there in my mind—that one pitch stopped

43

the clock. By twelve-thirty one workout was already over. Those pitchers that weren't working in the game had run for thirty minutes, staggered into the clubhouse and sat, sopping wet, in front of their lockers. Maglie, sipping soup from a paper cup, sat on the rubbing table agitating each player as he went by. "Atta way, boys, sweat it out. Best way to get in shape. Right, Doc?" Bauman laughed.

"How in hell you gonna get in shape then, Sal?" yelled Broglio, mopping his face with a towel. "All the running you done here is from your mouth."

"Kid, I've run more miles in this game than you've thrown strikes." Maglie tossed the soup cup away and picked his glove up from the table.

"Hey, veteran right-hander, you pitching today?" I asked. "If you are, I'm not going swimming at the beach. I'm going to put my uniform back on, and watch from the bench. Because you are such a wonderful example to us young pitchers."

"Maybe you ought to try learning something instead of poppin' off, young man." Sal walked out of the clubhouse as the loudspeaker started to blare out the lineups. Since he was the second pitcher of the day, Maglie had to sit in the bullpen till the sixth or seventh inning. Pollet had decided to permit his pitchers to throw seventy-five pitches, now, before he took them out. (Or did Solly do it? It's hard to tell just who is running the pitching staff.)

I showered, put a dry uniform on, drank a cup of soup, took a pack of gum and a bag of chewing tobacco from the trunk, rolled up my sleeves to get a sun tan on my biceps, and joined Sal in the pen. Grissom was there, and Phil Clark, too. We had decided to agitate Maglie since this was the first time he'd be pitching in a game all spring.

"Veteran right-hander, I was beginning to think that you were down here just to pitch batting practice this spring." I smiled at him as I shoved a handful of tobacco into my mouth and settled back to enjoy the game.

"It takes a while," he answered. "My back's been a little

44

sore, and my arm's just getting to feeling good, now. I'm a little bit older than you, y'know, Broz."

"You're a little bit older than everybody, Maglie," said Marv Grissom. "They're makin' me stay out here today just in case you get in trouble and I have to come bail you out. And I could be fishin' too!"

"Could be worse, old man," said Sal. "You don't have to walk as far to get me as you did at the Polo Grounds. Who in hell you callin' old, anyway! That number on your back is damn near right. Forty-two. No, it's shy a year."

Grissom aimed a stream of tobacco juice at Maglie's shoe, spraying my sock as Sal jerked his foot away.

Pollet cut the comedy, asking, "Sal, how long you need? He's going two more innings." We scored two runs in our half and led the Phillies by three as Maglie stripped off his windbreaker and said to the catcher, "Let's go, son, gotta warm up my little dab. Shut up, Grissom."

I walked up to the dugout for a drink of water, and sat next to the fountain where I was almost in line with the mound and home plate. In order to criticize and appreciate a pitcher's work, you have to see it the way the catcher does. Any TV camera that shoots from directly behind the plate may get too broad a view of the umpire at times, but *that* picture shows the fundamentals of the game, also: *Where is the pitcher throwing the ball and why?* The game starts there—all that follows is figured in percentages.

Sal got a big hand when his name was announced as the pitcher. But he was hanging his curve, and Bouchee hit one over the centerfield fence. Two men were out, though, and, after a walk and a single, Sal got 'em out in the seventh. "Can't get my rhythm," he said on the bench. "I'm wild high, can't get my breaking stuff where I want." Little balls of sweat popped and ran down the hollowed cheeks of his unshaven face. He looked like he'd already pitched seven innings himself, and the tension of tightly strung nerves was showing. When a pitcher starts doubting his own stuff, he prays for an easy inning. He needs one.

There was no easy inning left for Sal. Philadelphia quickly loaded the bases. Sal was not the smooth, smart pitcher I love to watch. The evidence of his true craftsmanship was not there. He was trying, though, mixing his stuff—a curve, then a wasted fast ball; a slider on the hands, or a slow curve for a strike; a brush back, and a change of pace. They were hitting the strikes as if they knew what was coming.

Dave Philley was announced as a pinch-hitter.

"Come on, big man," I yelled.

"Make that good pitch here, now," I said to myself.

He didn't make it. Maybe he couldn't do it. Maybe he *is* too old.

We walked to the parking lot together, Sal getting into his big spotless Cadillac. "I need more work," he said. "I have to be sharper than that. Think I'll ask Solly if I can pitch some batting practice tomorrow."

He drove off slowly.

I wondered to myself, "Will he ever pitch anything but batting practice, any more?"

March 26—St. Petersburg, Fla.

THE Gulf is calm enough for us to go swimming. When Anne Stewart came back from a morning dip in the surf, I'd finished my coffee.

"Think I'll go in early and agitate Doc," I said. "He's been working his ass off all spring. There's an article in the paper about some doctor who's going to cure pitchers' sore arms by changing their diets. That oughta slay Bauman!"

It's a moot point in the baseball world whether doctors who take care of ballplayers should be fans or not. If he is not a baseball fan, the doctor thinks the player is just like any other

46

male. If he is a fan, his professional opinion seems to be colored sometimes by heroic regard, or wish fulfillment. . . . "You got to go out there and give it your best. We need you!" There was a physicist, I recall, who said it's impossible to throw a curve ball. Ha! (That guy was a frustrated pitcher, no doubt, who probably had trouble with his fast ball, too.)

Bauman was adjusting the diathermy machine over Grissom's back as I entered the clubhouse. "Doc," I said, waving the newspaper clipping, "do you have any of these foods that 'enable a pitcher who tires after seven innings to go nine or even more with little effort'?"

"What got you up so early, Brosnan? You pitching today and your arm is sore?" Bauman was hiding his smile.

"No, I'm serious now, Doc," I said. "Did you know that the eating habits of horses, dogs, canaries, and goldfish are supervised, and ballplayers are not, so therefore Grissom is lower than a goldfish?"

"I read the article, yes," Bauman said. "And I agree with that doctor—what's his name—Fredericks. Ballplayers eat nothing but junk!"

"Only the higher-priced junk, though," said Grissom, as he relaxed on the rubbing table. "And in the better places, too."

"Doc, no wonder us young pitchers can't get worked on," I said, tossing the clipping into the trash can where it belonged. "Look here, Kellner's getting ultrasonic, Marv's getting heat. Who's the needle for?"

Bauman held up a ten-inch hypodermic. "Dr. Middleman is going to give Bob Blaylock a shot of cortisone for his hip. Maybe we can break up the inflammation."

I shuddered at the thought of that needle going in. "That may break his hip, too, huh, Alex? I've seen shorter line drives than that thing."

Bauman uncapped a bottle of Decadron, and counted out a three-days' supply of pills for Alex Grammas, whose arm was sore.

"Doc," I said, "with all of this junk you got around here, there shouldn't be any sore arms in camp." I waved at the machines, the massage tables, the boxes of pills.

"You should be glad I've got these things," he retorted. "But you're right about sore arms. There shouldn't be any in the spring if you guys would take care of yourself, eat right, and exercise a little. When you start training, like I said in the meeting, for the first few days walk around on your heels and reach for the sky! Stretch those muscles out! After ten days of running and throwing—why, there's no good reason why a ballplayer in reasonably good physical condition should strain himself to the point where it hurts!"

"Well," I interrupted, "it's maybe like that doctor says. We don't eat the right junk. You gonna order some of these pills that will make me 'go nine with little effort'? You want to keep in step with modern medicine and all that jazz, Doc."

"Listen, I'll do my job. You do yours, Professor. Obviously you don't need any Dexamyl to get you through the day, today. Get your sleep last night, did you?"

"Doc, you know I always get a little sleep each night."

March 28—St. Petersburg, Fla.

"I TALKED with Bob Elson the other day," I said to my wife, as we walked along the moonlit beach. "Guess he broadcast our game with the White Sox back to Chicago."

"Oh, good," she said. "Wonder if anybody we know heard the game. You pitched pretty well, didn't you? Wish I'd seen the game. Seems you never pitch when I'm out there."

"You just get nervous watching me, anyway. I talked to Turk Lown before the game, too. Omar says his arm is a little slow comin' around. He should play handball during the winter. You moaned 'cause I came home tired every night last winter. It was the handball every noon that did it, of course.

Sweating instead of eating takes a lot out of you. But it made my job a lot easier for me this spring."

"I'll never complain about anything again as long as you keep pitching the way you have so far," she said.

For two years in a row I had come into spring training with my arm muscles already stretched out. Handball had been responsible as much as anything for my early success. All I needed was a chance to throw and I'd be in midseason form within ten days. At times during a ball game I might wish for a little black handball to pitch instead of the bigger baseball that sometimes felt like a basketball. But every pitcher has his bad days.

In the game with the White Sox I had relieved in the sixth inning and finished the game as we won. In the sixth, seventh, and eighth innings I had thrown no more than ten pitches per inning. That was my goal for the season. Never waste a moment on the mound. Ten properly placed pitches should retire the side, if there is enough stuff on each pitch.

"Those White Sox sure got a bunch of banjo hitters," I said to my wife, shaking my head as I thought of the ninth inning of the game. "Nothing can get me madder than to have a couple guys hit good pitches like they were using a paddle instead of a bat. And get base hits yet! They've got a kid they're hoping will hit some home runs, but I don't know. He missed a couple pitches he should have hit."

"Who's that?" she asked.

"To tell you the truth, I can't think of him—left-handed hitter. Funny, when you're pitching to these young phenoms that get a lot of publicity, you work more carefully than you do on a big star. Then, if the kid doesn't live up to his headlines you tend to forget about him."

The ninth inning had started well, the first two men failing to hit. Nelson Fox was the only White Sox player between me and a cold beer. I had thrown hard for three innings but I felt strong enough to cut loose with everything I had for three final pitches. Fox fouled four pitches in a row—two fast balls,

49

a slider, and a curve. He simply punched them back of third base, exasperating me.

"Swing the bat, you little squirt!" I mumbled as I put all I had into an overhand curve ball. It broke perfectly, but Fox blooped it into left field. I blinked at him as he stood on first, chewing tobacco. How could he do that to me! A perfect pitch!

Jim Landis lunged at a slider and topped it down the third base line. I had no play; Boyer had no play. Landis beat out a hit, and the White Sox threatened my streak of five straight scoreless games.

I cursed my luck on the mound. "You bunch of Punch-and-Judys!" I said to the Chicago bench, muttering almost loud enough for them to hear me.

The next batter half-swung at a good, low change-of-pace and lofted the ball toward left field, just as though he were playing badminton. I threw up my hands in disgust, then relaxed as I saw the ball would not reach the outfield grass, and Boyer would catch it for the final out. I didn't think it would ever come.

"Thank God we don't play them this summer," I said to my wife. "They'll drive a pitcher batty."

March 30—Bradenton, Fla.

IMAGINE playing the Braves to decide the league standings! What we did today probably determined seventh and eight. Not that the Grapefruit League is earth-shakingly important. And last place is hardly worth fighting for. But what an omen for the season! Wonder if Solly is daydreaming: "Sept. 25— Braves And Cards To Decide Pennant." Hoo boy!

Poor Broglio. He reads in the morning paper that he has to go at least seven today to prove he deserves a starting job. It rains so hard all morning they just about decide to call the game, and Ernie relaxes a little. Then the rain stops so they decide to play it anyway.

Meanwhile the entire Braves front office has been taking turns chewing out their ballplayers for being last in the league, so they are out for blood. Broglio falls down on his first pitch, because the mound is muddy. He loses his normal stride, gets wild and throws everything high, especially to high-ball hitters. Finally, Aaron hits one 450 feet and they have seven runs in two innings.

Is Ernie excused from pitching? Hell, no. He's going seven! Have to prove something. All he proves is he can't pitch high to high-ball hitters in this league. What we're supposed to be doing is trying to win, I'd think. Maybe Hemus is trying to prove to himself we can win by following a script.

April 3—St. Petersburg, Fla.

"You going to Miami, Marv?" I asked Grissom as we stood in left field during batting practice. We had all looked forward anxiously to a weekend in the Big City.

He tore the top from a package of Beech-Nut tobacco and smiled. "I haven't made a trip yet this spring, have I? Why break a new record? . . . Bauman still thinks I ought to take whirlpool and diathermy every morning. My back is just as stiff now as it was when I hurt it."

I grabbed the tobacco before he could get it back into his pocket. "I owe you another chew. Listen, when you and Phil are rowing that boat out to sea to feed the fish, doesn't your back bother you?"

He grinned at my dig. "Jim, when I'm fishing, nothing bothers me. I know you don't do much fishing. But you oughta try it when you want to get away from a problem. Give me a couple of beers, a good rod, and an even chance to land a fish . . . there's nothing in the world going to bother me."

51

"Your back really bothers you though, doesn't it?" I asked. "Seriously, I mean."

Grissom turned around to stare at the boats sailing in the bay behind left field. "It's going to come around, I know it will. Every year since I hurt it originally with the White Sox, it's bothered me some. Last spring in Arizona with the Giants, I had trouble just like this. One morning, Bauman—Frank, Doc's brother—was popping my back and I heard it snap into place. And everything was all right from then on. I didn't pitch much last spring at all, but I came around once the season started. And I didn't make any bus rides out there, either!" He laughed as if he had pulled something on the rest of the pitchers. Who cared if he never made a road trip? The lucky bastard.

"You've made a few in your time," I guessed. "How long is it now, Marv?"

Hemus trotted past us to shag fungos. Solly was constantly moving around the park, running from foul line to foul line . . . setting example or trying to get in shape? What's with you, Solly?

Grissom nodded in Hemus's direction. "I've seen a lot of those guys come and go." He laughed softly, to himself. "There was a piece in the paper about Warren Giles today. You know, when I first came to the majors with Cincinnati, Giles was running the Reds. He took a look at me in a work-out and called me into his office. He told me to forget about baseball and go back home and find a job. That was almost twenty years ago." Grissom spat some tobacco juice. "I even outlasted Giles. They booted him up to president of the league and Gabe Paul took over."

"Who was the best man you ever played for, Marv?"

"Leo!" he said, emphatically. "Durocher had them all beat. Nobody could touch him when it came to getting the best from a ball club. I could talk about him as a manager for hours."

"You'll have to save it," I interrupted. "Here comes Howie."

52

Pollet came walking toward us down the foul line, motioning for us to meet him at the bullpen. "Howard would like you to do about a hundred pick-ups, Marv," I said.

"He's not waving at me, I'll tell ya. None of those things with my back." Pollet threw a baseball at us, and Grissom grimaced as he bent over to pick it up. "I think I'll go see Doc," he said, and we both headed past the bullpen to the clubhouse. I didn't quite make it. Pollet grabbed my arm and said, quietly—too quietly—"Let's do a few pick-ups, James."

"Okay, Howie, just how few do you want us to do?"

"You start it, and I'll finish it," he promised, as I groaned into low gear.

"Easy now, Coach," I said. "My back's killin' me."

There were some heads missing on the flight to Miami. The ax had fallen for the final time this spring, ending the suspense for at least ten players, five who stayed and five who were sent to the minors. Only twenty-eight men can be on the opening day roster and all the players who wore Cardinal uniforms at Gran Stadium, Miami, will open the season at Busch Stadium, St. Louis. As we drove from the beach to the airport in St. Pete, Clark said he was relieved to hear he was at least making the trip back. "I'm startin' to wonder why they're taking me, though," he said. "Ah haven't pitched in two weeks!"

Those dog days at the end of spring training ruin many a ballplayer's sleep. The pitcher who had a bad inning; the shortstop who messed up a double play; the hitters who couldn't get their timing right away, and who then pressed, and tightened up, and lost their chances. "Why in hell don't they let us know, anyway?" Nerves grate, tempers explode for no good reason. "If only they'd give me one more chance! I know I can make this lousy club!" The manager and his coaches and anyone connected with the front office are verbally ripped in the bull sessions of those players who suddenly get that feeling they're about to be left behind.

Then that cut-down day comes. You report to the clubhouse as if it were any other day. The clubhouse man—the guy who takes care of the bags and shines the shoes, the fellow who orders the bats and hangs up wet jock straps to dry—stands at the door with a list. He may smile halfheartedly if he liked you, or he may just thumb you on your way. But his spoken word, "Skip wants to see you in the office," can unleash the torment of harassed, frustrated ambition. "I won't go. I'll quit first. To hell with this goddamn club! *And* baseball! I've had it. I quit! . . ." And you go, quietly.

At the airport the club assembled in the lobby, startling little boys who ran after pens and pencils squealing, "There's Stan!" This was the Cardinal team that would play 154 championship games in the 1959 National League season. It looked suspiciously like the same club that had finished fifth in '58. Oh, add a couple young pitchers and four new first basemen. But youth has so much to learn in this league, and only one first baseman can play at one time.

Everyone was smiling again. Freedom reigned. This was the first overnight road trip. Husbands were rid of wives, kids and nerve-racking domesticity. The single men were anxious to see new places, try new pleasures, play new games. (Why is it we end up playing the same old game?)

My eyes prowled the book racks. Finally! I had read that Bruce Catton's book *A Stillness at Appomattox* had been published in a pocket book edition. Such a saving! Since my wife is from Virginia, I have heard both versions of the Civil War, as taught in the public schools. Somebody's lying. Having been misled on many things in my childhood education, I don't know who it is. Catton may not have been there during the war but he makes it sound as though he had. Fascinating history! Beats games.

Leo Ward didn't room me with Phil Clark after all. Big disappointment. Traveling secretaries usually have an uncanny sense of knowing who should room with whom. Maybe Leo is just off to a bad start this season. He certainly was in a slump in '58 when he roomed me with McDaniel. About the only thing Lindy and I had in common was the same doorkey. Come on, Leo, shake yourself. Let's everybody have a good season and we'll finish sixth.

Alex Kellner will be easy to get along with, though. All I need to do is learn to like Westerns on television, "because that is what we're going to watch," he said. I had to read my book with a pillow over my left ear, a pillow beneath my right ear, and just enough light to see the larger type. No wonder I have to wear glasses. Since Kellner has the reputation of roping mountain lions for a hobby, I'm not going to plump for Jack Paar.

April 5—Miami, Fla.

BALTIMORE won the Grapefruit League championship by beating us twice. That gave us the cellar to romp in all by ourselves. Hope it is as incongruous for us to be last in our league as it is for the Orioles to be on top in theirs. What a ball club! Paul Richards should get an Academy Award for best direction in a dramatic presentation. Any manager who can win fifty games with that crew is an awesome genius. Of course, by the time Richards gets through demonstrating the various arts of pitching, bunting, sliding, the hit-and-run, the pick-off plays, catching, coaching, and how to sign a check, every player who ever saw him is willing to concede his glove, bat, job, and checkbook. If he's not the best, then there isn't any best . . . just a few better-than-average managers. But, dear God, how can he weave a pennant without material?

April 8—St. Petersburg, Fla.

SLOWLY swelling waves of the Gulf lapped softly at the sand on the morning of our last day in Florida. I carried all but one of the deck chairs from the patio to the porch, stacking them next to the door, and just a few feet away from my own luggage. The big house was empty. My kids were gone, my car was gone, Anne Stewart was on the road again. Wife! You should have married an Army man, like the Colonel planned. "But I didn't like the thought of all that moving from one place to another," you said. Ho, now, babe!

I walked through the house, upstairs and down. The dresser drawers were empty, the closets were clean, the kitchen cabinets were bare. In the refrigerator I knew I'd find two cans of beer and a half-empty jar of pimiento. We set a new record! Just one jar for the ants, or the landlord, or whoever gets the relics of our habitation.

The beer was mine, of course. Taking a can opener from my shaving kit, I walked out to the beach, picking up the last beach chair from the patio. Plunging the chair legs into the sand, I sat back, happy with the immediate moment, regretting the soon-to-be-reminiscent spring training of 1959, apprehensive about the future season. It had been a cold winter in the North, I remembered. St. Louis was north. I could feel the cold already.

The St. Petersburg *Times* said, "Fair and Warmer Wednesday." Already, the morning sun was making my beer can sweat. I picked up the razor blade to cut out the sports page headline: "Brosnan, Mizell, Hal Smith Brightest For Cards." (Carefully I preserve these artifacts of an expiring career. Those inches of print that measure relative success. You doll! You bum! I collect them all.)

Hemus had said, "We'll win more than we did down here. It rained a lot. But it wasn't the fault of the weather. Everybody is in pretty good shape, and we've had some pleasant surprises."

An uneasy feeling gnawed at the pride I felt from reading the headlines. Everything has gone so well this spring. Physically I have been loose and healthy, mentally I've been content. My mistakes haven't cost me—those sliders that hung, most of them were popped up in the air. Could it be that I've been granted custody of the Golden Arm for 1959? Is the good lady, Luck, on my side this year. I pinched my right arm to see if it was real. It hurt. It is human. What a damn shame.

"This is the time of the year you can afford to experiment, and make mistakes," Hemus had said. "We're in a little slump, now, as far as runs are concerned. But we'll come out of it. And what better time than now!"

What better time, indeed, to drain the last suds from a can of beer, and throw the can into the waves. Give that Budweiser a good start and it may go all the way! I watched the sun gleam upon the surface of the water-tossed can until the Clarks' car horn beeped a summons. Gay Clark had volunteered to drop us at the airport on her way back to Georgia. A sweet girl. A veritable queen.

I gathered my luggage, locked the doors, and headed north to open the season.

April 9—St. Louis

"THE night before" is one of those peculiarly personal phrases that frequently repeats itself in a man's memory. It can refer to a wild time, or to a sad moment, or to the traditional misty haze of dim reckoning. For the professional ballplayer, the night before Opening Day is full of extreme nervous tension. All of winter's fond hopes and daydreams, all of the spring-training trials and successes, all of the promise-filled publicity focuses eyes, in the baseball world, on the players. There's no more time to think and dream, to plot and scheme, for this is it ... the championship game. Only the first of 154, perhaps, but to eight teams it's the only chance to be as good as any other team in the league for one whole day. You may have won every game in spring training, hit 1.000, or pitched perfect ball, but you're no better than the next guy when the first pitch of the season starts on its way.

It usually rains, it seems to me, the night before we open the season. It did in '54, I recall, and again in '57, and '58. It's raining now, which is another good reason to go to bed at ten o'clock, to try to sleep, and then to read, and then to write a letter. Perhaps it would be better to talk it out, letting the sound of words soothe the nerves. If I was simply worried, and nervous about how badly I might bungle the job tomorrow, I would prefer to talk it out. But I feel only a mysterious concern for the security that my successful spring has given me. Perhaps the Law of Averages *will* punish my pride the next time out. In this game you have to do it over and over again . . . the better you do, the more you are expected to do. Pride's price, and it is sometimes cruelly exacted by that insidious Law.

It's better to write about it. Let the sight of words console my nerves. (One reason I married my wife was to have someone to console me. She was three hundred miles away, but I could write about it as easily as I could talk about it. I took out my pen.)

DEAREST WIFE, AND LOVER, ETC.,

With the spring training season ended, and my ambitious efforts rewarded as handsomely as possible, I would not have surprised my ego had I grown peacock feathers as we flew in from Florida. Hemus, noting that I haven't given up a run in three weeks, and only three all spring, has made me No. 1 —publicly hailed, or branded, me as such. Long Man, indeed!

No peacock, I though. Truthfully I'm slim-hipped, loose-armed, flat-bellied . . . and featherless. Certainly I've had a successful spring. Surely, the bell rings tomorrow, and we start from scratch. If I start to give up runs now, I'm a bum again. Success breeds a maggoty fortune that needs constant replenishment and refurbishing.

Still, there's the sun, just eight hours away. And here I am, and here's nervous bowels, and here's the issue—win, or lose everything. The prestige of my position must be upheld by the act of triumph; and every pitch must be impressive. And then, there's the next game. Success breeds also a feeling of insecurity. Where can you find a comfortable spot to relax, at the top? It's a definite problem of balance, for there's no hand hold above, and damn little support to lean on. Besides, when you climb to the top of the ladder, the Achilles tendon is exposed, almost indefensibly. Eight other guys want this job. If the knives start to jab they may hit this heel if it's left carelessly unprotected. I'm trying to remember, here in the rain, if I made obeisance to the proper gods. Will my unguarded rear go unscathed? Let's face it, I can be had. The black forces of despair have made it with me before!

It's another year. You'll have your sorrowful, pining days as before, waiting behind, never any more sure than I am that I can do it. It's harder to sit, hopefully, on the bench than to play the game. But this man's ready to start a new season, and we're the team that can take it all. . . . You and I. Not the Cardinals, probably. Hemus is optimistic about *his* chances; but I'm confident about ours. So let's round those bases, and have fun, and love, for the long season ahead.

I Love You, etc.,
MEAT

Rereading, folding, sealing, and stamping the letter took just as much energy as I had left for the night. I turned out the light and slept.

April 10—Opening Day in St. Louis

EACH and every spring, a veteran ballplayer, retired and reminiscing, reads the prologue before the curtain rises on the new season. In the spring of '59, Tommy Henrich said it:

"No matter how long a man remains in baseball he always hankers and looks forward to opening day, and believe you

59

me, it takes a young player a long, long time to get over those opening day butterflies and discover finally that he really is an old pro."

Butterflies come in many shapes and sizes. The larger ones lie supine in the stomach most of the day—be it Opening Day, or Debut Day, or World Series time. Occasionally the younger, less experienced butterflies flutter restlessly during the first conscious stirring of the morning. As the years go by, and those days pass nervously into memory, the stomach muscles learn to tighten early on the butterfly wings. In that way the twitch is controlled, and only when the tension has mounted to its peak does that thump rattle the stomach walls. The most jaded old pro has his emotional weak spot—the first "Star-Spangled Banner" of the season; the catcher's peg to second base that signals the end of springtime playtime and the start of business; the sudden realization that from this moment on, everything goes into the record book.

I get nervous before I eat on Opening Day. Just thinking about putting something in the stomach serves to agitate my nerves. As if subconsciously I've held a tight clamp on the obvious seat of nervousness; and then to think of adding to the job! It's too much. But I eat, anyway. Proper, as it says in the book. A rare steak, a green salad, tea and a dish of ice cream. An unusual breakfast, perhaps, but then it's an unusual day . . . every year.

From the George Washington Hotel to Busch Stadium in St. Louis it is a twenty-minute drive in a car, a thirty-minute ride by bus or streetcar, and at least an hour's walk. Once, after losing a game, I walked all the way back. So I know. Most of the ballplayers who live during the season at the George Washington have never walked all the way. Most of the time they drive, in a car or a cab. The cab fare is $1.50. For any number of reasons—like I want to be alone with my nervous self—I take the streetcar. The fare is a quarter.

When I got to the clubhouse on Opening Day, there was no line at the ticket office. It not only looked like rain so that a box office queue was easily discouraged, but Hemus had asked everyone to come early—three and a half hours early. Last-minute strategy? Had he forgotten something? Come now, Solly, everyone else is ready. Nervous, maybe, but ready to play. Managers, of course, also get nervous before the game. This puzzles me somewhat. In the majors the manager's job is virtually completed by the time the umpire says "Play ball!" It's really up to the players then. If they do their job correctly and efficiently, the manager might just as well take a nap, as much as he'll be needed.

Most of the players were already in the clubhouse by the time I arrived. Even Larry Jackson was there, quietly waiting for the warm-up ball, soft-spoken for the moment. Nervous, Larry, about starting the game? You? (Such a cool cat, that cocky Jackson. You wouldn't think . . .)

Everyone else on the club took batting practice. The pitchers ran. The Giants streamed onto the field, sun-tanned from Arizona, big and cocky and dreaming about the pennant. (The West Coast writers insist!) The Giants loosened up in pepper games while waiting impatiently for us to get off the field. Finally the buzzer sounded just as a pitcher pounded past the dugout chasing Pollet's last long throw. "We'll have a meeting," Pollet said as he came off the field. "Everybody upstairs."

Each locker in the Cardinal clubhouse has its color-matching, three-legged wooden stool before it. A three-legged stool is not very comfortable—stools are for milking, or standing upon. But we sat, uncomfortably, while Hemus conferred with his coaches, picked up a pencil, score card, and loose-leaf folder, and finally gestured for attention.

"We're gonna go over the hitters now, and on the first day of every series. Just to decide how the infield and outfield is gonna play them. Everybody will sit in on these meetings." He held up the loose-leaf folder. "This is gonna be the book for the pitchers to keep. We'll have one on each club. The starting pitcher for the next game will be the one who keeps

61

the record. Here, Ernie, ask Nunn how it works; he kept the same type of book for Walker last year.

"Now, we're gonna record every pitch made to every batter. You guys may think you know how to pitch everybody in the league, but this record will give us some proof. And you might just learn something, too, so don't be afraid to look at the book when you're gonna be pitching. After we're through in here, going over the hitters and how we want to play them, then Pollet will take the starting pitcher, the catchers, and the bullpen into my room and we'll decide how we're gonna pitch everybody."

Hemus handed Jackson a score card. "Tell 'em how you want each hitter played. Never mind how you're gonna pitch to 'em right now."

"Davenport!" said Jackson, reading from the starting lineup. "He's a pull hitter and a fast-ball hitter . . . and an inside hitter. I like to play him to pull all the way, infield and outfield. He'll bunt, too, Ken."

Boyer nodded and asked, "How you gonna pitch him?"

Hemus interrupted, "Let's not worry about that right now. He's a dead pull hitter no matter what you throw him, anyway."

"Okay, Solly," said Boyer, "but if we're gonna pitch him away, he might decide to go with the pitch. He can hit to right if he wants to."

"No, he can't," said Cimoli. "He never hit a thing to the right of shortstop all last year against L.A. And, man, he musta hit .500 against our pitching."

Jackson raised his eyebrows in doubtful agreement with this report of Davenport's prowess. "He's not a very good breaking-ball hitter, and I'll probably be throwing him sliders all day. He can hit to right, but he's a better pull hitter, so you gotta play him that way. In case I make a mistake on him."

Jackson looked around the room for any further comment on Davenport. "Brandt's hitting second. I like to pitch Jackie down, and try to make him go for the curve ball. He'll chase it once in a while."

"How do you want him played, Larry?" asked Hemus. "He's got pretty good power."

"That's right. Let's play him straight away. Alex, you can shade him a little into the hole at short. And, he'll bunt, too."

Cunningham mumbled something to Blasingame sitting next to him.

"What's that, Joey?" Hemus yelled. "Let us all in on it, Joe."

Cunningham flushed slightly. "I was just saying that he guesses a lot. That right, Blazer?"

Blasingame grinned. "Don't ask me, Joe, I play second base."

"You can give him the line in right, anyway, Joe," said Jackson. "Mays is next."

"Don't let up on him!" Three pitchers said it simultaneously.

Jackson frowned to himself. "I'll go in and out with Willie. You can play him to pull in the infield, but straight away in the outfield. He'll run."

There is no one way to play Mays, of course. Just as there is no one way to pitch him. The phrase that marks a good hitter is, "Pitch him in and out." Sometimes, if he is a smart hitter, too, you add, "And don't give him the same pitch twice in a row." Later in the season, you add, "Knock him down once in a while." And, if he is especially hot, "Don't give him anything to hit if he can beat you the ball game." Mays's name in a meeting commands brooding, respectful attention.

"Cepeda." Jackson scratched his head. "I've had my best luck jammin' him, but his best power's up the middle, so you gotta bunch him in the outfield. If he does hit the inside pitch, we'll have to give him two bases."

"Does he bunt much, Marv?" asked Boyer.

Grissom, who had played with Cepeda the year before, shook his head. "Only when he's not hitting," he said. "He's a swinger."

"Kirkland. Play him to pull. I'm gonna jam him with everything. He can hit the ball a long way to left center, but I won't throw him anything out where he can hit it that way.

"Rodgers. How'd he look this winter, Nels?"

Chittum started to rise as if the question had startled him. "Well," he said, slowly, "I threw him a lotta curve balls. So did everybody else, I guess. He didn't hit much in the Dominican. 'Course, they gotta big ball park down there. Ask Smitty about him. He and Rodgers had a big fight."

"Yeah, I know," said Jackson. "But he's still a low-ball hitter, then, right? You can fist him, I remember."

Harry Walker spoke up from the back of the room. "He hit a ton in Arizona this spring. In that light air. But he don't like anything off-speed. And you can get into him good, like you said."

Hemus nodded. (As if what his coach said had come from him, I guess.) "You skipped Spencer, Larry. You want Rodgers played to pull, is that right?"

"Oh, yeah, Spencer." Jackson looked up at the ceiling, as if trying to remember some peculiar fact about Daryl Spencer. "He tries to go to right in this park. He can hit that screen, too, if he gets his pitch. I'm gonna try and jam him. Play him straight away. He likes to hit-and-run, Blaze."

Jackson looked up from the score card and asked, "Is Schmidt catching, or Landrith?" Then he continued without waiting for an answer. "They're both pull hitters, anyway. Hobie's a better low-ball hitter, and Schmidt's a high-fast-ball hitter. Curve 'em both."

As Jackson calmly, confidently disposed of the Giant hitters, I tapped the burned-out tobacco from my pipe. Half-listening, I recollected the admiring opinion I once felt when I attended major league meetings. They make it sound so damn easy, I'd thought at the time, ignorant of the soon-to-be-experienced fact that these positive opinions were based on ideal percentages. Who would hit What Where! That depends, son, on how you pitch him. If you jam him, or change up on

64

him at the right time, or keep the ball low, he will hit the ball where you expect him to . . . most of the time. And if your defense is where you expect it to be, and the batter doesn't top the ball so that he can outrun the throw to first, or doesn't break his bat so that the fly ball drops in between the correctly placed defense . . . well, man, it's conceivably possible to control the game calmly and confidently from the mound. But don't cry when your best-laid plans go down the drain.

"Brosnan," said Hemus, suddenly interrupting my thoughts, "you and Nunn and Blaylock come with Howie into my room and we'll go over these guys the way you ought to pitch 'em."

The meeting—another first for the year—was over. Everyone but Jackson, Pollet, Hemus, and the bullpen was headed for the door. "Five minutes till infield!" cried Keane, as he looked for his fungo bat. "Wait till I get some cigarettes," said Jackson, as we walked back to the manager's office. Hemus had his private double locker, and a desk, but not enough room for us all, as we crowded in to sit on the floor, and on the desk, to hear it all over again. How To Pitch the Giants!

You can say how you're going to do it all right. But can you throw each pitch where you should? There's the bitch! Even a veteran, successful pitcher like Carl Erskine says, simply and humbly, perhaps, but truthfully, no doubt, that Sal Maglie and Preacher Roe were the only two pitchers he ever saw who could do with every pitch just what they said they could.

Hal Smith, the Opening Day catcher, said to Jackson as Larry came into the room puffing on his last pregame cigarette, "When I give you the fist, that's the pitch-out, just like last year. And when I take my cap off and scratch my head, that means I'm lost. Or at least I'm thinkin'." Everyone grinned at his bald head.

"We haven't got too much time, now," Hemus said. "There's going to be a ceremony before the game. You all will have to line up along the third base line. Not you, Larry, you'll have to start warming up by then. Now, how you want to pitch these guys?"

"If I have good breaking stuff I'll use that mostly—slider and curve. They're a fast-ball-hitting club, mostly. And, except for Rodgers and Mays, I guess, they're a high-ball-hitting club." He paused, grinning. "And if I don't have my good breaking stuff, we'll all play deep and cut across!"

"Well, you're gonna have good stuff," said Hemus, "don't worry about it. You gonna jam Cepeda, then?"

"Last year," Smitty said, "we had good luck with him throwing curve balls down in the dirt. Especially when we got ahead of him. He chased them a lot. 'Course you gotta get ahead of 'im first."

I coughed, clearing my voice to ask, "Is there any other way to pitch Kirkland? I keep throwing him sliders and fast balls on his hands and he keeps knocking them right out of the ball park."

"Ever since he came up, that's the way we've pitched him," said Jackson. "He never gives me any trouble."

Hemus added, "That's how we pitched him over at Philly, too. Up and in, and slow up on him once in a while. He's got good power to left center. You don't want to pitch him away."

There didn't seem to be much room for argument. "Everybody seems to agree," I said. "I'd be willing to pitch him away and let him hit that way, if he would. The bum thinks he's Josh Gibson when he sees me out on the mound."

Pollet said, quietly and seriously, "What you must remember is that when you jam him, make sure you get in there good. Make it your best pitch, and have confidence in it. I've never seen Kirkland, so I can't say whether you have to or not. But your slider is just like Larry's. If he uses it, no reason why you can't."

I didn't want to sound as if I were afraid of Kirkland. Perhaps it sounded that way. It certainly was in bad taste for me to say so, of course. Pitchers should look and sound confident even when they are bewildered, unhappy, or sick at the thought

66

of repeating a mistake simply because there seems to be no other solution. It would be even more embarrassing, if not mutinous, if he hit a fast ball off the left center field wall. I had practically received orders not to throw that.

Maybe I wouldn't have to worry about it. Jackson might go all the way. Doubtful. Nobody pitched a complete game all spring, except me. Against the Yankee "B" team, most of whom were now at Richmond in the International League. Well, I know how to pitch all of *them*, anyway. Zipping my jacket, I walked out to the third base line as Charley Jones, the public address announcer, introduced the 1959 St. Louis Cardinals.

Four hours later I sat at a table in Thompson's cafeteria, stabbing ham and eggs, drowning my burned-up pride with cold milk, and salting, slightly, the lower lids of my angry eyes. How in hell can you get into such a sad position? How can you fall so far so fast? One minute you're a hero; four hours later you're a bum!

I can't stand to be booed. Some people say I'm being childish; most ballplayers say you get used to it. I can't believe that they really hear those boos; they turn off their ears when the ugly noise begins. Desperately, I try to do the same; inevitably I manage only to turn up the sound, and it rings and reverberates for hours after I'm gone, the crowd's gone, the game's gone.

When twenty thousand people applaud as you walk out to do your job, it should be an inspiration. It should make you feel good. (Applause is what you play for, too, as well as money.) When those same twenty thousand cry, "Ptui, you let us down," you have to feel bad. Most of the fans probably didn't open their mouths; many probably sympathized with me when the booing started; some, reasonable critics, probably said, "Guess he didn't have it tonight."

"Didn't have it! The bum blew it!"

Even in the clubhouse I could hear the final smattering of

boos as Charley Jones announced the results. "Here are the summaries. Giants, 6—Cardinals, 5. Winning pitcher, Antonelli. Losing pitcher, Brosnan." Boo! Like an echo. Like the tardy, final twist of the knife. It hurts. Don't let them tell you it doesn't.

On this cold, nervous Opening Day, the Giants wasted some chances and gave us two runs, but they scored three off Jackson in the first seven innings, and led by a run when Cocky was lifted for a hitter. We then scored two more runs and I was in there, ready or not.

What do you mean, ready or not? This is your job, boy. He gave you the ball, and he gave you a run to work with. What more can you want? You can't go up to him and say, "I haven't got it today, Solly. I don't feel up to it. I don't want that ball. It's cold and I'm shivering, and I was enjoying the game from the bench."

No, you can't back out. You take the ball and the signal for a fast ball, and you throw five straight pitches at Cepeda's fists, and he finally strikes out. The rhythm starts to beat in your mind. The winning beat—a simple co-ordination of movement. Bend for the sign, glance at the hitter, grip the ball for the selected pitch . . . whoa, now! This is Kirkland. That's a slider you called for, Smitty. I don't think I can get him with it. (Kirkland hasn't hit a slider all day. That's the pitch to throw him. Make it a good one. Try it one time.) Here it comes, then . . . up, and in . . . right on his . . .

Kirkland hit it on the roof. It was gone all the way. I didn't even look. Maybe it went over the roof. I watched Willie run into the Giants' dugout, where Antonelli waited to shake his hand. The game was all tied up. Off the hook again, aren't you, John?

Spencer hit a fast ball through my legs for a single. . . . I didn't get that pitch into him far enough, either. Have to go for the double play, now. Keep the slider away. And down . . .

Damn, it hung. Right in his eyes. Rodgers is a big, powerful man. His eyes lit up as he swung, and the ball went deep to

68

center. A high fly? Maybe Cimoli can catch up to it. No, it's carrying. . . . Breaking balls carry so damn much farther when they're hit well.

Spencer scored. Rodgers had a triple. Schmidt hit a high fast ball ("He's a high-ball hitter. Keep it down") to Cimoli, who threw Rodgers out at the plate. I was backing up home, and walked quickly to the dugout when Barlick called Rodgers out to retire the side. But some alert fans spied me. "Boo!" they called. And they were so damn right.

However, Grammas tied the score a few minutes later, lining Antonelli's high fast ball ("He's a high-ball hitter," the Giants had said in their meeting, I knew) into right center field. Antonelli was tired. Rigney came out of the Giant dugout to talk to him. Whoever was going to hit for me would face a relief pitcher. I looked down toward the Giant bullpen to see who was throwing, when Hemus, who had been standing on the dugout steps thinking to himself, suddenly decided against better judgment and said, "Come on, Jim, hit for yourself."

Good Lord, Solly, let's not carry this too far, now! I walked slowly up to the plate, barely conscious of the booing that greeted my appearance. What the hell do I look for from this guy now?

Antonelli pointed out to Rigney that I was hitting for myself, and Rigney decided to leave John in the game. There were two out and, with Antonelli the first hitter in the ninth, it would be almost a waste of pitchers to bring in someone to pitch only to me. A likely prospect considering my past record as a hitter.

But, wait now! Had I not spent hours in the cage in the springtime, learning how to hit? Hadn't it looked easy? Just breathe deep; hold it; wait till the pitch is right at the plate; belly-button; block! I grounded weakly to short and we went into the ninth.

Speake batted for Antonelli and I walked him. (No sliders this time, I decided. Be careful. Make him hit the curve.) I couldn't get the damn thing over. I watched Hemus, in the dugout, stare at his bullpen down the left field line, then stare at me on the mound. What the hell's wrong with you, Brosnan?

Davenport bunted but he hit it too hard and Speake was forced at second. There's a break. Brandt took the first slider low and just a bit outside. Good pitch if he'd only go for it. Then I hung another one.

". . . time of the game—two hours, forty-six minutes." It doesn't take very long, really, to lose your confidence. To embarrass yourself, jeopardize your position, maybe lose your job. Hemus went a long way with me. He could have taken me out. He should have taken me out! I grinned ruefully to myself.

("What the hell, man, forget it. Anybody could see you didn't have it. Hemus asked for it, the silly dope. If a pitcher hasn't got it you get him out of there before he blows it. Right?") What a second-guesser, my ego! I climbed aboard the streetcar, and went back to the hotel.

April 11—St. Louis

WHILE reading the newspaper and digesting the printed disappointment of the Cardinals' (and my) failure, I poured coffee into my sore head. Why make it a twice-told tale of misery and woe? Why do I read about it? How can I help myself!

Also, I read: "Snow Cancels Cubs' Opener." First thing I look for in the morning paper. Did the Cubs lose? Since they were the first team ever to trade me I get a vicarious thrill out of seeing them get beat. (It was like being kicked out of my own home!)

Poor Anderson. Scheffing had him down for the opener in

Chicago. Andy's nervous by nature. Wonder if he's bitten his nails off, yet. The longer the game is put off, the worse it will get for him. Wonder if Doc Scheuneman bought any new sleeping pills for the Cubs. Or tranquilizers. That's it. "Loaded with Equanil, the young Chicago right-hander posed with a snowball." Stay cool in Chi, man. Those Los Angeles writers were indignant for sure. Imagine having to tell California readers that a baseball game was called because of snow.

Crumpling the sports page in my mad right hand, I walked to the bookstore. I maintain a small library in my locker in the clubhouse. Nothing like a book to keep your mind from thinking. I walked down Olive Street, past Cunningham's apartment. Past tornado-damaged buildings, half-wrecked, wall-crumbled apartments, staggering down the hill like crippled refugees. Joe's place still was intact. "Blew in some windows. Knocked me off the couch," said Cunningham. "There I was, two in the morning, reading the Bible . . . !"

Yeah, Joe. Mary Bible. When was it, now? Early spring. You were still holding out for more money at the time, right? Did you think it was Devine wrath, Joey?

The bookstore had been blasted, too. Everybody in St. Louis is catching hell this spring. Have to find a humor book. I don't dare laugh for a week after last night's performance. Nothing wrong with tickling my mind, though. I can read with a sober face, and laugh inside. If my face gets desperate for a relaxing smile, I'll blame it on the book when Hemus frowns.

No Thurber, here. No DeVries. Ah ha! Here's the book. *Sub-Treasury of American Humor*—E. B. White. Now there's a good psychiatrist for you. But, then, he probably hasn't been booed.

It was a long day in uniform. We paraded from the park to downtown St. Louis. There, in a simulated dugout we sat while a thousand kids walked by, shaking hands with the Cardinal team. Perfect gimmick. A pretend dugout. All kids love to play pretend. The basic appeal of baseball. Fans see themselves in big league uniforms, making the sensational play, hitting the long ball.

"What was wrong with you, yesterday, Brosnan?"

Little punk. Here you are, kid, have an autographed picture. Hang it over your bed. Pray to it each night. Maybe you too will wear one of these monkey suits someday. What an ambition!

Back we went to the clubhouse. Four more hours till the game starts. Run with the pitchers? Too cold, Howard. Too stiff to run. Too damn much trouble. Why should I get loose, tonight? He sure as hell won't use me again so soon. That first exhibition was probably traumatic, believe me! Broglio started. His first big league game. It was hard to tell whether he was sweating more outside or inside. Constantly wetting his lips as he stood on the mound waiting for the sign. He walked four men and hung one curve in the first inning. Got out of it, though. Only two runs scored. Cepeda ripped the curve for his third double in two games. Got to flip him next time he comes up!

Bauman wrapped an electric jacket around Broglio between innings. Like sticking him in an incubator. Precious, fragile talent is a pitcher. Ernie went six. That's less than hoped for, more than expected for the first time. Too bad we had to lose.

Sad Sam took his job seriously for a change. Best pitcher St. Louis had in '58. Terribly hurt when he was traded. He said, in St. Pete, "Just let that Hemus hit against me one time!" Hemus walked in the seventh. Sam never came close to him. Injured pride utters idle threats.

Two straight for Frisco. Their writers are demanding the pennant already.

Two straight for Hemus, Anyone for the cellar?

April 12—St. Louis

Sunday.

Day of rest.

In the next life perhaps. Or at least in the next profession. Sundays on which ballplayers rest from their labors are either cold because it's winter or miserable because it's raining and the scheduled game, or games, had to be postponed. Most of the time ballplayers work harder on Sunday . . . like the schedule says. "Get your rest, boys. Double-header tomorrow." The only thing worse than working on Sunday is not being able to relax on Saturday night.

A car horn honked at me as I left the cafeteria where I had eaten breakfast. "Been to church, Jim?" asked Pollet as I climbed into the front seat next to him.

"Hello, John," I said to Keane, who was in the back seat. "Yes," I lied, "just came from there." Not really any of his business whether or not I go to church on Sunday, but if he thought I should, I would . . . pretend to, anyway. It's all a big pretend game, isn't it? How can I be properly reverent on the day of a game? How can I promise not to take the name of my Lord in vain: I don't know ahead of time whether we'll win or not. Be glad to exchange promises, though.

There is a regular Babel of religions on the Cardinals. Mostly Christian. That looks like the best creed—even the Japanese ballplayers are buying it. One of their big-name sluggers crossed himself each time he stepped up to hit. Worked twice. But two for thirty-one! Hell of a poor percentage.

Catholics predominate on the Cardinals. They should. Great organization. Here, we have the coaching staff, Musial, Bauman . . . that's the core of the ball club! Wonder what the fine will be for lying about going to church? Two more weeks in Hemus's Limbo? Only way to get out is pitch your way out. But how can you do that when the only place to pitch is outside Limbo? Besides, all of the pitches are taken. Maybe there's a new one in Frisco. I treasure novelty "isms" like the beatniks. Now, there's a pitch. I'm susceptible. I already feel beat.

Blasingame hit the second pitch to him down the left field line for a double. In three days he had hit more balls to left than he had during the last month of the '58 season. "If you learn to hit to left, you'll become a .300 hitter, Blaze," said Hemus. And Harry Walker and Stan Musial and Fred Hutchinson, etc. For years, day in and day out, they had been saying it. Looks like he finally heard the message. Couldn't happen to a nicer second baseman.

Cimoli and Boyer also got base hits, and Rodgers booted another ground ball—five errors in three games—so we had three runs in less than twenty minutes. Another Cardinal first for '59! Looked like those prayers had reached the front office. But Vinegar had forgotten to petition the Lord to forsake Cardinal errors for one day. Two ground balls were messed up and Mays hit a curve ball off the center field fence to tie the score. Willie has always been a pain in the E.R.A. for Mizell. Used to be customary for Mays to reach third a good deal of the time when he hit against Wilmer. All he had to do was get on first—by walk, or error, or single. Then he'd steal second and third. (It would have been smarter for Mizell to hit Mays in the knee with his curve ball. That would keep him on first. Maybe.) Willie picks his spots when he attempts to steal bases. Certain pitchers, or catchers, but mostly pitchers are ordinarily incapable of preventing Mays from taking an extra base if he so desires. "Not this year. No sir!" said Mizell in the spring. "You all will see." Bravo! Hold him to triples this season, Will, and he'll never lead the league in stolen bases.

Musial returned to first base in the starting lineup. End of experiment. Stan has an amenable, sometimes adventurous, spirit. He went along with Solly when the suggestion was made that left field was easier to play than first base. It isn't. Never was. There's less action there, but it is more strenuous.

Musial made it look dangerous. Damned subtle of him. He stumbled and tumbled off the left field wall once in each of the first two games. Hemus quickly tore up that page of his script and told Bill White to exchange places with Musial. That weakens two defensive positions. Still a good move, though. The life Hemus saves may be the Man's.

Mizell pitched the first complete game of the season, with some woolly-headed managerial faith sustaining him. In the ninth Cepeda tripled home the tie-breaking run with two men out. The next four batters were right-handed, a baseball fact of life that doubly discourages tired left-handed pitchers. Having given up twelve hits and faced forty-one batters already, Wilmer was obviously tired. He could have used some help. Alou proved it by hitting the first pitch to him out of the ball park to make the score 6-3. Spencer then lined out for the Giants' last try, but dinner was over. We hadn't smelled a run since the first inning, and Worthington mopped up the ninth with eight pitches.

Where was the bullpen? Warm and anxious. Hast thou lost confidence in us already, O Hemus? That's our job. Isn't it?

April 14—Los Angeles

Sixty thousand people saw us win our first one. That's what we needed. Inspiration. Most of the opening day crowd came to root for L.A. But they switched over when Smitty hit a three-run bloop over the Coliseum's left field screen. After hitting nine shots right at the Giants' defense in St. Louis, Smith might have been excused for cursing his luck. If he cursed. Which he doesn't; although he said "bird seed" once, I recall. In '57, I think.

McDaniel picked up the win. My old roomie! Phil Clark asked me, on the bus, why I hadn't asked to room with him, like I had said I would. "In fact," he said, "I haven't hardly seen you since we left Florida. Don't you like me any more?" Since I hadn't spoken to anybody for three days, my apologies were haltingly muttered. "When I'm not going good, I don't get along with myself, even. Don't let it bother you."

If I seemed unfriendly it was merely a thin crust of my opening day embarrassment. Ever since I'd found the *Sub-Treasury of American Humor* I'd been laughing to myself in mind-tickled pleasure. A stewardess on the plane that carried us from St. Louis had been visibly disturbed at my nervous giggling. I was reading Mark Twain's wildly funny criticism of Fenimore Cooper's Literary Offenses. The stewardess, young and pretty, stopped pacing up and down the aisle (lust-filled eyeballs irritate the best of them) and asked, "What in the world are you laughing at?"

I read to her:

> Cooper's art has some defects. In one place in "Deerslayer" and in the restricted space of two-thirds of a page, Cooper has scored 114 offenses against literary art out of a possible 115. It breaks the record.
>
> There are nineteen rules governing literary art in the domain of romantic fiction—some say twenty-two. In "Deerslayer" Cooper violates eighteen of them.

Like (I said):

> They require that the personages in a tale shall be alive, except for the corpses, and that always the reader shall be able to tell the corpses from the others. But this detail has often been overlooked in the Deerslayer tale.

And:

> They require that when the personages of a tale deal in conversation, the talk shall sound like human talk, and be talk such as human beings would be likely to talk in given circumstances, and have a discoverable meaning, also a discoverable purpose, and a show of relevancy, and remain in the neighborhood of the subject in hand, and be interesting

to the reader, and help out the tale, and stop when the people cannot think of anything more to say. But this requirement has been ignored from the beginning of the Deerslayer tale to the end of it.

They require that when a personage talks like an illustrated, gilt-edged, tree-calf, hand-tooled, seven-dollar Friendship's Offering in the beginning of a paragraph, he shall not talk like a negro minstrel in the end of it. But this rule is flung down and danced upon in the Deerslayer tale.

They require that the author: Say what he is proposing to say, not merely come near it [and] use the right word, not its second cousin.

I glanced at the stewardess to see if she could take any more without breaking up. She stared back at me, politely, but without the least hint of a smile. She must get her kicks some other way. Or maybe I told it wrong.

When we deplaned in L.A. Marv Grissom took right off for his home near San Francisco. His back is still hurting him. The cold weather in St. Louis didn't help any. "All I have to do is throw for ten minutes, and the next day I can hardly get out of bed," he said. With Kellner limping on a bad leg, and Hemus scared to trust me on the mound, the bullpen crew is a disorganized rabble.

As if the Coliseum wasn't enough to rattle a pitcher's nerves. The first impresion of that monstrous screen, twenty-five feet or so behind the shortstop, invariably causes the comment, "What the hell are they thinking about? They're making a joke out of the game!" And the joke's on the pitchers, of course.

Actually, the impressions soon wear off and you find that the best way to pitch in L.A. is the best way to pitch in any other ball park. It helps to have a good sinker ball, or some special pitch that is consistently hit into the ground. McDaniel has a good sinker . . . sometimes. Didn't have it last year, but he had it today. Had his appendix removed this spring.

So let's all work on the sink ball. Bob Turley said it: "One fast ball isn't enough nowdays." Admission of that fact is the mark of a maturing pitcher. When you have a good fast ball and have mastered the curve and change of pace . . . add another pitch or two. The rules will probably be changed to hobble the pitching delivery. Those hitters must have a powerful lobby working for them.

At the Dodger Dinner, a formal affair that opened the Dodger social season, baseball was belabored by the wits of Hollywood, such as there are. Everyone was there! An interminable dinner hour. Even Joe Garagiola, the Cardinal broadcaster, spoke, in quips and starts. Joe is considered something of a humorist, and, like Mark Twain, is from Missouri. The resemblance is strictly residential.

April 15—Los Angeles

SPRING nights in Los Angeles are cool, not quite chilly; too warm for heavy jackets in the dugout, but too cold for thin cotton sweatshirts on the field. Pitcher's weather. Warm enough so that you can work up a comfortable sweat— "There's nothing like sweating," says Al Scheuneman, illustrious and wise old trainer of the Cubs. "A pure gift of nature. Be glad you can sweat, boys." However, on some days you can sweat so much on the mound that your shoes get soggy. That's not pitcher's weather. (That's Cincinnati weather.)

Don Drysdale is a pitcher. He seems to thrive on cool, spring nights. "He should, the big bastard," say the hitters. "When he's right he'll knock the bat out of your hands. And when the weather's cool, your hands can feel it for days!"

Drysdale's fast ball is "live." It "moves." It rides in on a right-handed batter. When the hitter sees the pitch coming into his "wheelhouse"—where he hits the ball best—he starts to swing too soon at the spot where he thinks the bat will meet the ball. And if that ball rides into him far enough, it saws off the handle like a bullet clipping a tree branch.

When Drysdale is fast—on some days a pitcher throws harder than on others—his fast ball pops the leather of the catcher's mitt. Like a sledge hammer slamming a fence stump. The very sound can numb a batter's hands, even before he gets out of the on-deck circle. "Got to get out in front—got to be out in front on the pitch," he says to himself. Of course, Drysdale also throws a fast curve ball. If the batter sets himself to get way out in front on the fast ball, and the pitch turns out to be a curve ball, he may suffer the embarrassment of looking like he's chasing bumblebees with a butterfly net.

Drysdale was fast tonight. Very embarrassing to our side. Can't win without runs in this game.

Gene Green didn't catch, of course. He was the No. 1 catcher on the Cardinals when Hemus took us to Japan in the fall of '58. But Gene married when he returned, and now he's No. 2 catcher. Sometimes it's hard to adjust.

"Greenie," I said, as we sat on the bench, watching Drysdale and sniffing the late-blooming smog wafted from City Hall, "you've hit against Drysdale. And you've caught me—and hit against me, too, in winter ball. How would you compare our fast balls. Is mine live like Drysdale's?"

"Well, no, can't say it is, Jim," he said. "His comes in to me and yours sails away from a right-hander . . . sometimes." He grinned as if the erratic nature of my best pitch was something to laugh about.

"Would you say I was as fast as Drysdale?"

"Uh-uh," he shook his head. "You got a sneaky fast ball, though. It doesn't look as fast as it actually is. Or maybe it looks faster than it actually is." His sense of humor about my talent was choking me. Right up to here.

"Drysdale throws a heavy ball, I understand. Not that I give a damn about your ribs, but if I were to pump one into your side, it wouldn't be the same as if he did it, would it?"

"Can't say it would," he said, still smiling. "Your stuff

doesn't sting my hand like a guy who throws a real heavy ball. In fact I don't mind catching your fast ball at all. Naturally I'd want to have a glove on in case you might be having an especially good day."

All of these answers were depressing, but I'd heard them for years. We all of us wish for the bigger, better body—the greater talent. I'm disappointed daily to wake up and find that I still have the same old tired right arm instead of a powerful and glorious new one with which I could truly do wonders! That's all I need to win twenty, Solly. New equipment.

We had a rally going in the sixth. Musial was on second when Cunningham hit a shot through Drysdale's legs. Demeter charged the ball and made a nice one-hop throw to the plate. It looked like Stanley was going to slide under the tag, but Dusty Boggess said no. Dusty shook his head first, then raised his right arm to signal that Musial was out, and he took a lot of time about the whole operation. By the time his arm came down, Musial had changed his satisfied smile to a growling frown, and the frown broke up in a string of suggestions.

Suddenly, Musial bit off a choice word, shrugged his shoulders, dusted himself off and trotted back toward our bench. He passed Hemus, who was running with his mouth open, screaming at Boggess. Solly kicked dirt on the umpire's pants, blew smoke up his nose, threw his cap on the ground, and was given the thumb in a most cursory dismissal. Another first for the Cardinals. Boggess has a splendid sense of humor, and is often willing to let anger have its moment just to see if anything funny will happen, but hat-throwing is against the rules.

Hemus had always had a reputation, as a player, of being a crybaby. His respect for the umpire—baseball's representative of law and order—was meager, even for a juvenile delinquent. "He better be a good boy from now on," an umpire had warned, when Solly's appointment as manager was confirmed.

And he had been. This was his first eviction. And he had a

legitimate complaint. The play was very close. It looked like Stan might be able to get in there. But he didn't, said the umpire. Amen.

April 17—San Francisco

ANOTHER Cardinal first last night. In fact, an all-time Cardinal first! A major league record, yet! It took twenty-five men to lose a nine-inning ball game. Which is certainly giving everybody a chance. Or wasting a lot of manpower. Considering the way this club is being run, you might call it bureaucratic inefficiency.

The committee on pitching—Pollet and Hemus—decided to let me work, after five other guys had toiled for seven innings and seven Dodger runs. It was just like old times, mopping up when our side was three runs down in the last inning.

Demeter was my first opponent. He is burning up the league. Hitting pitches he isn't supposed to hit. When he first came up to the majors, carrying a big bat full of minor league home runs, he showed a marked weakness for the breaking ball, especially sliders. He soon tried bending over the plate in order to follow the curve ball more closely. However, he then couldn't hit the fast ball on his hands! But he swung at it, almost desperately, it seemed. Eventually he was having trouble with both fast balls and breaking balls and was put out to pasture as a defensive outfielder who came into the game in the late innings. Duke Snider's caddie is what he became.

Now, however, he's laying off the high-tight fast ball, and waiting for pitches he can handle. Like hanging curves, or inside sliders (a fatal form of pitching madness). Such lessons are learned in the spring, tra la, but soon are forgotten again. He could be expected to seek his own level before July, and start swinging at those pitches he can't hit. But even now the slider low and away for a strike is still effective—to him and anybody else you care to mention. The trick is to throw it right there. So I did. Thrice. Demeter, too, was denied.

Neal looked at a third strike and Hodges popped up, so that was that. When we loaded up the sacks in the ninth, I envisioned a tie game, at least. Mayhap a three-run rally and a possible win for Old Broz! Glory. Kellner, who can't run yet with his bad leg, but who swings a big stick, was summoned to hit for me, just in case Tate walked, or was hit by a pitch, or somehow drove in the tying run. But he grounded out. We might have set an unapproachable record for large-scale futility. If Kellner had hit for me, then McDaniel would have pitched the last half of the ninth. I even spied Keane looking fondly at his fungo bat in the bat rack. Just in case, eh, John?

April 18—San Francisco

WE FLEW from Los Angeles to San Francisco hoping for some revenge after the three defeats the Giants had handed us to open the season. San Francisco's ball park is another pitcher's hell. The prevailing winds blow fly balls into the seats in left field; the wind frequently prevails, even against the most clever and well-executed pitching. Don't, by God, make any mistakes on that mound!

Mizell made only one. Cepeda hit another home run. What a habit! But our first four hitters had shelled McCormick as if he were just another bonus baby, and Mike went home without retiring a man. That's the worst way. A pitcher hardly gets a chance to see what his stuff is really like.

Before the game started Kellner joined us in the bullpen. The visitors' dugout in Seals Stadium is built for little league teams, and can't accommodate any extra pitchers. So we finally all got together—Solly Hemus's bullpen—critics, bo-bos, and just plain pitchers. When we noticed that the breaks were clearly going to go our way all through the game—Mizell actually got a base hit!—Kellner and I went behind the stands back of the bullpen. There, the grandstand vendors take their coffee breaks, eat hot dogs and other delicacies, and read newspapers, *Playboy*, and such stimulating fare. That is, they do, if they can find an empty chair. *Kaffee klatsching* is an old bullpen custom. Vinegar Bend got along very well without any help from us, thank God. Pitching with a bellyful of sugar doughnuts, neither of us would have been an artistic success, probably.

Well, you can't lose 'em all, I guess.

One of the more pleasant aspects of Seals Stadium is the smell. Walking from the hotel to the ball park, you pass by a bakery, which dispenses the scent of sugary rolls and freshly brown-crusted bread as though from a huge atomizer. The visiting team clubhouse overlooks this bakery. The windows cannot be opened in the clubhouse without causing immediate hunger pangs to twitch athletic stomachs. Especially in the morning, before a day game. San Francisco is a nighttime wonderland. There's so much to do and see after a night game that breakfast time usually comes too soon to be properly attended. (In fact, baseball games interfere seriously with the visiting ballplayer's social life in San Francisco.)

However, the clubhouse man in Frisco does keep a pot of coffee hot, and somehow you can manage to get through the meeting and dash down the steps, through the runway and into the fresh air. Only there isn't any. The brewery behind the park advertises its product by wafting vast clouds of freshly brewed beer fumes over the left field grandstand into the visitors' bullpen. There's nothing quite like the smell of new beer in the morning after a night on Frisco town.

Occasionally—rarely, to be sure—the wind blows *in* from left field *before* the game. (Stoneham has God switch air currents in the last of the first inning, to favor Mays and other right-handed hitters.) The breeze from San Francisco Bay brings fresh cool draughts of foggy, foggy dew. Mixed with the odor of sea-gull droppings and sewage, this unpalatable, but peculiarly intoxicating sea-broth actually leaves droplets of moisture on the face. You can sniff at your leisure when batting practice begins.

As our thirty minutes of hitting flew by, we ran—we pitchers—for fifteen minutes. Pollet chased us by artfully demonstrating how not to allow a man to catch a thrown ball. He tosses the ball just far enough to give you hope, but too far for you to get to it. And he learned it all in just three months as a coach! (As a pitcher, of course, he had moaned for fifteen years about the way the coach ran him.)

"Jeez, this air is hard to breathe. Don't you think?" asked Nunn, as he staggered back into the single file of pitchers waiting turn to run. Nunn's sweat band, circling his forehead above his glasses, was already soaked with hard-earned, expensive perspiration. "Is the air always as heavy as this out here?" he asked. A sudden spurt of fumes from the brewery convulsed him. Hard to tell whether he enjoyed it or was being nauseated. "Man," he laughed, "what a way to keep a glow on."

When the game started Blasingame walked while I was preparing my chewing tobacco. First, I take a piece of gum—Wrigley's Spearmint, of course. The agency for which I work services the account—and I chew it rapidly, sucking the sugar coating till the sweet taste is gone. The gum isn't supposed to add taste or flavor to the tobacco, just hold it together, for a longer, chewier cud. Meanwhile I tear the outer paper of the gum wrapper into thin strips, separate the silver foil from the inner paper, tear that paper into strips, and cover the shredded paper with a small mound of dirt. This routine is a daily ceremony with me, and I don't consider a game started unless I've done it.

The tobacco package is unrolled next. There is a special way to curl a partly empty package of chewing so that the tobacco stays fresh. Since I chew half a pack a day, it doesn't have much chance to dry out on me, but one must pay attention to the ritual. As I shoved three fingerfuls of tobacco into my mouth, Blasingame stole second, causing me to spill some tobacco shreds on my uniform. This is not strictly part of the ritual, but I often do spill tobacco. I have the Bad Hands, especially in the cool weather . . . before day games . . . in Frisco. (Used to be New York before the Giants and Dodgers moved west.)

Sanford was the Giants' pitcher, and he just couldn't get the ball down for a strike. Blazer had ducked under four straight pitches, and Sanford was three and one on Cimoli when he decided to try throwing the other direction. And he picked Blasingame off second. Sanford used the "San Francisco pivot" to accomplish this most embarrassing gambit. Landes, the umpire, ignored Blazer's complaint that Sanford wasn't playing fair, and had, in fact, balked.

In working their pick-off play, Giant pitchers use a gimmick to modify an otherwise typical maneuver. The shortstop (or second baseman) signals the pitcher that the play is on. The pitcher acknowledges the sign, takes his stretch, looks at second, then to home, and begins counting, one . . . two . . . three. The infielder also starts counting when he sees the pitcher turn his head toward the plate. On two, the infielder darts toward the bag; on three the pitcher turns to throw. If the timing is perfect, the play occasionally succeeds. If the runner is alert, and he usually is after seeing the Giants work one or two pick-offs ("Goddamn it, I don't want anybody picked off second base," storms manager Hemus, Haney, Scheffing, *et al.*), the play is close, and lovely to watch, and . . . so, let's get on with it, man.

The Giant pitchers, however, have added a wrinkle, a plus—an illegal one, perhaps, but brand-new, so that the rules-makers haven't had a chance to legislate against it. Just before the pitcher wheels to throw, he dips his back knee, the leg that is on the rubber. This movement is a customary one for a pitcher. Everyone does it. Gives you a chance to push off as you start your forward motion. *As you throw to the plate.*

However, Giant knee-dipping occasionally precedes a turn-

and-throw to second on the pick-off play; an unexpected maneuver that prevents a runner from getting an early jump on the pitch to the plate. If the runner is just a bit anxious, he's a dead duck.

Now this is clearly deceitful on the part of the pitcher. It circumvents the rules. It enrages base runners. A presidential directive, no doubt, will come from Giles's office to the chief umpires, warning against such immorality on the pitcher's mound. The rules imply that any movement of the pitcher that tends to deceive a base runner must be called a balk, and all runners get an extra base. *Deceive* is a most ponderous choice of words. What in hell do they think a pitcher is doing when he throws a curve ball? If deceit is, in truth, a flagrant violation of baseball morality, then the next logical step is to ban breaking balls, and let the hitter call his pitch.

Blasingame slammed his helmet against the iron railing when he returned to the dugout, and Cimoli walked. Blasingame then kicked the helmet another ten feet. Cunningham also walked, and Boyer was hit by a fast ball. Blasingame hid in the runway so Hemus wouldn't kick *him*.

Sanford was still throwing everything up. I'd never seen him so wild. Finally Rigney walked out to the mound, frantically washing his hands as White came up to hit. Rigney doesn't use soap and water, of course, as he stands with his pitcher on the mound. He simply goes through the motions of purging himself of any associated guilt, as if he certainly had nothing to do with such a miserable pitching performance. Rigney sweats a lot during a ball game.

White hit a fly ball, and Cimoli scored, but Flood grounded out. And that was our attack for the day. Two more men reached first. Musial lined a single to left in the seventh for our only hit, and Rodgers booted a ground ball. Another one, that is. He already has made more errors than McMillan will make all season. And it's not even cut-down date yet.

"He's pressing," said Pollet. "Just like a pitcher will. When you're not making good pitches, you tighten up. Your arm

86

doesn't follow through all the way on the pitch. You change your style of pitching and make more mistakes.

"Now, Rodgers is letting the ball play him instead of him playing the ball. He's lost confidence in his hands. He won't charge the hop, and throw. He waits for the ball to come to him, then he has to hurry his throw. So he's making it twice as tough on himself."

Sanford finally relaxed after his wild start and pumped his fast ball inning after inning. With a no-hitter going, a pitcher tends to stay with the pitch that has been successful all through the game. For the most part, Sanford used his curve and change as waste pitches. Which isn't really "pitching," but craftsmanship has little to do with pitching no-hitters.

"For Christ's sake," moaned Hemus, as we trooped into the clubhouse after the game. "He didn't throw anything but fast balls all day. Got one guy out on a curve. Let's bear down up at the plate. He's not that good."

In the ninth, Hemus, too, struck out on a fast ball.

April 20—En Route to Chicago

MONDAY is traditionally an off-day in Organized Baseball. It is a ballplayer's custom to go golfing, or swimming, or picnicking with the family on Mondays. Once in a while Monday is packing and traveling day, for managers tend to cut their rosters on Sunday night in the spring. They also like to announce trades then, too, so that on Monday the players can move to their new clubs. Ever since the Giants and Dodgers moved to California, however, Monday has lost some of its bright, cheery color on the ballplayer's calendar. Eight Mondays a season, we spend eight hours on an airplane. A hell of a way to enjoy an off-day.

When airplanes were first discovered by baseball traveling secretaries—about five years ago—there was a minor revolt on some ball clubs. There will always be a number of people who think the best way to keep their feet on the ground is to stay out of airplanes. An extraordinary number—percentage-wise—seemed to be making their living playing major league baseball. At first, these nonfliers were able to make their own way, from baseball town to town. But the shift to California forced them to revaluate their convictions. "If you want to play major league baseball now, you learn to fly. Think it over."

The soul-searching led one pitcher, Don Newcombe, to a psychiatrist, who apparently convinced Big Newk that flying was better than working for a living. Even Sal Maglie accepted his fate, although he frequently voiced objections to satisfy his conscience. "One close shave like this," said the Barber, "and I hang up my jock," as he exhibited clippings indicating that near-collisions between planes are a daily occurrence. Such morbid preoccupation with fatal accident statistics is food for idle gossip, and not worthy of a cool customer like Maglie. Moreover, trainers now carry tranquilizers to make plane-life bearable for the fly-shy.

You can sleep on the plane all day—it's easy to stay up the night before, on the Coast. Expensive, but pleasant. Or you can play cards. There's always a poker game in the back of the plane, and gin rummy is a popular, if monotonous way to pass the time. Occasionally, a bridge game is started, but that takes a lot of concentration, especially for a heavy head. United Airlines provides a rack full of popular magazines—*Mademoiselle, Harper's Bazaar, National Geographic,* etc., any one of which will put you to sleep in a hurry.

One consolation on the trip east is the thought that the plane flies faster coming back than going out. Because of the jet stream, or prevailing winds, or something. It proves, of course, that the wind can help as well as hinder the major league pitcher. On Sunday, in Frisco, the helpful aspect of the Seals Stadium wind was the topic of conversation in the Cardinal bullpen.

Howie Nunn was working on his knuckle ball, a pitch with erratic behavior in calm weather. When Nunn throws it into the wind, its fluttery movement is so unpredictable that it delights the pitcher as much as it confounds the catcher. Gene Green caught as many of Nunn's pitches on his knee as he did in his glove.

Most of the pitchers had already thrown, to loosen their arms, to work on control, or to practice a new pitch. It is customary during the middle innings of a ball game for the bullpen crew to talk shop about the pitching trade. "It never hurts to work on another pitch," say the veterans. And since many of the pitchers are in the bullpen because they weren't successful with the pitches they already were throwing, it becomes a brainstorming classroom. Bullpen sessions have produced some odd experiments.

"Where in hell did you come up with that pitch?" asks the manager the first time a new pitch fails. "Well, shove it under your hat, and forget about it." End of experiment.

I, personally, like to work on my spitball in the bullpen. The spitball is illegal, of course, although it's quite popular in the National League. (Also, the International, Texas, Pacific Coast, and most other leagues I've worked in.) It's not an easy pitch to control and requires constant practice. Most practitioners in the National, International, Texas, etc., leagues throw their spitballs most of the time they're pitching. Many of them are quite successful, and I've often wished that I could get away with spitballs, myself. However, there's a knack to it. I, personally, need a good stiff wind blowing straight out from the plate in order to get anything on the pitch.

As B. G. Smith was announced as a pinch-hitter for Larry Jackson, in the eighth, I felt greatly encouraged by the lump on Green's shin. My last spitter had just caromed off Gene's leg, as the bullpen bench laughed in appreciation. Pollet, who had feigned indifference to my illegal practicing, suddenly shocked me by saying, "You're in there, James. You ready?"

89

What ho! Jackson had pitched seven good innings, and we were behind by just two runs. Had I been promoted back to No. 1 relief once more? Four other guys had been shelled the night before, so it was really just my turn. I tried to forget my new, sensational spitter—it was no time to experiment on the mound during a game—and I pumped up a few fast balls as B. G. flied out to end the inning and force me into the game.

Ten minutes later, I had the bases loaded, with just one out and our bullpen was working seriously. In the Giant dugout, Rigney reached back into his memory, recalled one of my previous appearances in Seals Stadium, and sent Leon Wagner up to hit for Andy Rodgers. The crowd roared its approval as if they, too, had remembered.

In 1958 I started a game against the Giants and threw three home run pitches in four innings. One of the homers, hit by Wagner, had cleared the back wall of the right field bleachers, at the 425-foot mark, causing sportswriters to go dashing out of the press box with a tape measure. Leon hit the ball against the wind and into the trees . . . across the street. A goodly blast. I had reason to be proud of that one, if I viewed it in a purely objective manner. Which I try to do. Give the batter credit, I say. If he is better than you, make him a true giant among hitters.

Wagner is not, ordinarily, a good curve-ball hitter. The pitch he clobbered into the trees had had all the appearances of a pretty good curve. It was big, it broke down, and it was low and away. Perfect pitch, you say? I thought so when I let it go toward the plate. When Wagner golfed it out of sight I could only conclude that I really didn't have very good stuff that day. Fred Hutchinson, the manager, echoed my sentiments, exactly, and removed me for a relief pitcher.

So lightning doesn't strike twice, does it? I'd been taught to believe it. "Wagner can't hit a good curve ball," Jackson had said in the pregame meeting. Smitty signaled for a good curve, and I stepped back off the rubber to think. "Ten days ago I threw a similarly unlikely pitch and everyone in St. Louis encouraged me to regret it. What other choice do I have? He's a good fast-ball hitter. My slider is not working very well. These guys on the bases proved that. . . . When in doubt, curve him. . . . It's in the Book. Well, he sure can't hit the curve any further than the last time. Or, can he?"

I shrugged my doubts away and wound up, in one continuous motion. I threw the good curve . . . same place . . . low and away. Did he hit it out again? He did not. He tapped it right back to me, like a good little boy, and we had a double play to retire the side. We still lost 3-1, but instead of being a bum, again . . .

"Nice going, Broz. That's the way to pitch."

Yes, sir, that's the way I did it last time. This game will drive you batty.

April 23—Chicago

IN Chicago, as the plane taxied up the O'Hare runway to the United Airlines ramp, I saw my wife at the gate. A wife looks good at the end of a two-week road trip. I asked the stewardess if I could pick up my bags before they were unloaded into the delivery truck and taken to the hotel; and I worked on my homecoming smile.

For two weeks I hadn't had much to smile about. No one on our ball club had had much reason to be gay. The lethargy and dull despair that accompany a losing streak can't be dismissed completely except by winning. A ball club that lies last in its league is in a depressed mental condition. However, any blues song contains some happy notes. If I couldn't win at the ball park I knew I would make out at home.

After playing two years for the Cubs I had decided to make Chicago my winter home. The Cubs traded me down the river to St. Louis just six months after I'd bought a home in suburban Morton Grove. This dastardly and underhanded maneuver (the first time is always the most painful) fulfilled a hoary maxim in baseball: buy a home in the town in which you play, and you'll be traded before your first lawn blows away. So it was, and I cried, not realizing that misfortune is only 30 per cent bad.

Since Chicago is the hub of National League baseball, I soon found that I could spend a good deal of time "at home" if I played elsewhere than Chicago. Not only did I get a chance to enjoy a summer home in St. Louis, but every time the Cardinals made a trip to Chicago and Milwaukee I could commute to work from Morton Grove. County Stadium in Milwaukee is just ninety wild minutes from my garage. What could be more relaxing and restful before a game than to drive on tollway roads? So, thank you, John Holland, for treating me as a negotiable asset rather than just a normal human-type business employee. (All us big league serfs got happy days to sing about.)

Throughout our plane trip from San Francisco Hemus and his brain trust had shuffled papers, ideas, and frowns as they wrestled with the ponderous responsibility of the Cardinals' sorry showing so far. I walked past them to the men's room to tie my tie and practice my smile. They sat, red-eyed and glum-faced, lost in momentary pessimism. Phooey on top-level discussions of baseball policy! If the bottom level is at fault, why talk over the heads of the people responsible? Why not have the ballplayers discuss the problem? Maybe we didn't know what mistakes we were making on the field. I shook my head and bid adieu, subconsciously, to the intra-mural life. Turning on my smile, I grabbed hold of a bound-to-be-more-pleasant domesticity.

"Baby, you look too dressed up just to meet an old husband. What's the story?"

My wife usually dresses well, even for breakfast,. but she had perfume behind her right ear, a sure sign of party-going. "We're invited to the Studts' for dinner. I had to have a night off from the kids. I hope you don't mind."

Since that hardly would make any difference anyway, I immediately canceled dreams of a slipper-pipe-and-brandy evening at home. Having just come from the Club Hangover in San Francisco, I was well tuned for a night at the Studts'.

"There's no better place for us to rid ourselves of modern-day tension. And all that jazz. How are the kids, anyway?"

"Timmy has taken over your job," she said. My own son after me, too! "He came up to me today after I'd told him you were coming home and he said, 'Daddy can sleep on the couch downstairs can't he, Mommy?' nodding his head as if it was all settled. He's been sneaking into our bed every morning lately."

"You know that's against the Gesell commandments," I said. "What do I do now, sneak upstairs after he's asleep at night? And, then, crawl back down before he wakes up in the morning? My marriage license gave me more freedom than that, it seems to me."

She tried a tentative smile, herself. Evidently it agreed with her disposition, and she laughed out loud. "Meat, you're crazy as a crab!"

Life already seemed more agreeable and with each martini laugh lines loosened the cynical and bitter tensions of the first ten days of the season.

Wrigley Field crowds greeted the Cardinals with the dignified reserve typical of mature, knowledgeable fans. After the first day, in fact, they stayed at home to enjoy the games on television. (We had drawn a larger crowd at the airport when we left San Francisco.)

The Cubs played it cool, to match the weather and the fans' reception, by winning two out of the three games. On Tuesday, Glen Hobbie almost pitched a perfect game. He had one till two were out in the seventh, when Musial hit a curve ball down the left field line for a double. That was our only hit— the second ignominious offensive failure within four days.

The wind blew from the lake, a stiff, cold breeze that stopped fly balls in mid-home-run flight and dropped them into outfielders' gloves. Wrigley Field can be the best park in the league for a pitcher. (It can also be the worst in the league when the wind turns around, which it does too, too often.) Several of our stouter batsmen smashed Hobbie's fast ball better than the results indicated. Banks had to retreat a good ten feet behind shortstop to haul in the longest drive.

Between innings, half of the ball club was under the stands stoking a fire with broken box slats and stolen rake handles. We might as well have used our bigger bats. Harry Walker joined the crowd, and after he had stamped his feet and blown on his fingers he smiled broadly and talked incessantly. Walker is likely to do that whenever he is awake. The Walker grin had all the ear-to-ear marks of a Cheshire cat's contentment. The managerial plum about to fall, eh, Harry? Speculation was rife that Walker was anxious and ready to substitute for Hemus. Considering his relative wealth, Walker doesn't fit the mold of yes-man-type coach. Having had notable success as a minor league manager he might well be pardoned for second-guessing an inexperienced, albeit clever, young newcomer like Hemus. Pity the poor manager's plight when his team is losing. He's all alone, even if he has trustworthy assistants.

Cunningham hustled back up the runway to the fire can, thrust his hands over the flames, and moaned, "Ain't they got any pitchers in this league that don't throw a heavy ball? First we get Drysdale, then Sanford, and now Hobbie. My hands feel like they've been asleep for a week."

Maybe that was our trouble in Chicago; too much sleep.

April 25—St. Louis

As a healthy, American adolescent I dreamed of mighty and glorious feats of athletic skill. In the spring and summer I played baseball; in the fall I played football, and in the winter

94

I even tried basketball. My daily efforts seldom resembled my nighttime dreams. When it came time for a professional career I had little choice, but I am ever thankful that I play baseball, a gentle sport compared with most others.

Occasionally the game gets a little rough. Like yesterday. Ordinarily my ego frowns at bodily contact (on the ball field). Yet, I have attempted the rock-'em, sock-'em type game—like yesterday. This necessarily graceless incident over with, I have now collected my wits, a sore back, a set of perfectly normal X-rays, and a puzzled expression on my mind. What possessed me to try such a mad stunt?

It was a hot Saturday afternoon following a cold, exasperating Friday night game in which I'd worked with no distinguishing merit. Hemus, hoping perhaps that I'd learned something, shoved me right back on the mound when the Dodgers knocked Blaylock and Broglio out of the game. I proved to be no noticeable improvement. Before I retired three batters I had given up the tie-breaking run. (We were scoring runs as fast as the Dodgers.)

Hemus let me hit for myself, however, and I walked to the plate cursing myself, and wondering for the thousandth time why I didn't find an easier, less embarrassing way to make a living. With one mighty swish of my bat ("Belly-button! Block!") I hit a line drive through shortstop and all the way to the fence, for a triple. There I was on third base with the tying run that would take me off the hook. I was mad at myself, sweating and tired from the heat, and foolishly intoxicated with sudden new strength. Wouldn't it be nice to plow into somebody, now, and growl, and tear up a storm!

Johnny Keane cautioned me to "let the ball go through" the infield before I headed home. His words were the verbal part of the sign for a squeeze play. I looked in to the bench to see if Hemus had gone mad. With nobody out we had a chance for a big inning, and a squeeze bunt just wasn't reasonable at all. It was only the fourth inning and already nine runs had been scored in the game. It looked like a hitters' day. Keane yelled at me to look at him. He rubbed his hand across his shirt, a negative sign that probably meant there was no play on. I was still panting from the unaccustomed excitement, anyway, so I waited, four feet off third, while Blasingame walked.

Now, I had no choice. I had to try to score even if the ball was hit right back to the pitcher. "Ball hit on the ground you gotta go," Keane reminded me. That was the play. By forcing the Dodger infield to make a play on me at the plate I could prevent a double play. If I managed to get caught in a rundown, and eluded a tag until Blasingame got around to third, and Jablonski, the hitter, got to second, we would have two men in scoring position with only one out, instead of two outs and a man on third. It is an ideal play and occasionally works, if the runner on third is a hell of a lot more agile than I am.

It was just too hot for me to be dashing back and forth between third base and home plate. They would get me, anyway. "I'll run into him and try to knock the ball out of his hands," I thought. My adrenalin glands started to pump and I suddenly felt like a young, healthy, college-type fullback. "Gimme the ball, Coach, and watch me run right over that guy." I looked in to the plate at Roseboro, the Dodger catcher. He waited, well equipped, for head-on collisions, with shin guards, chest protector, steel-barred mask, and redoubtable stubbornness. He's not a very good catcher, but Roseboro has a lot of guts. Just getting back there takes plenty of courage.

"Okay, Rosie, here I come," I thought. Unhesitatingly, Jablonski topped a ground ball to Gilliam at third and in I went, just like I had told myself. Even when I got to within a stride of Roseboro I still felt young and healthy and full of college-type spirit. Strange? Odd behavior? You're not just bird-turding there, man! I'm a professional coward when it comes to physical violence. If I can't talk my way out of a fight, I'll sneak my way out.

When I could no longer stop the inevitable collision, I frantically hoped that the ball being thrown by Gilliam couldn't reach Roseboro till I did, and Rosie would hardly have a chance to defend himself by ducking and flipping me over his shoulder. But the ball did, and Roseboro did, and I did . . . go head over heels over head over the plate and into the dust. Whomp! I played dead, artistically, according to the Associated Press photographs.

That was enough for me, and though I faked a game try by limping to the mound to start the fifth inning, I couldn't see working any more with a malfunctioning brain. So Kellner warmed up for the first time in the season and shut the Dodgers out for five innings to win the game. This happy result pleased the X-ray technician who welcomed me at the hospital. I didn't feel any too good about it, myself, till I'd drunk a bit of Black Label as a medicinal tonic. Made my back feel much better. It beats rubbing alcohol.

Attendance for the Sunday game was announced as 12,345. Charley Jones is just kidding, I thought to myself. He's trying to add laughs to the farce on the field. (We lost 17-11; L.A. made twenty base hits; and a grandstand vendor was hit by a foul fly ball, right in the middle of his "Hot . . . dogs!") The net total crowd made up a unique combination of numbers, perhaps, but this series had seen a number of unusual combinations. Hemus presented a lineup card on Saturday to the umpires that raised quizzical eyebrows all over the ball park. Dascoli, the umpire-in-chief, would have been excused had he questioned the legality of speculative experimentation during a championship game.

"Like, is he serious?" asked a fan sitting behind the bullpen bench.

Boyer, a superb third baseman, moved to shortstop and Hemus, a fair second baseman, replaced Boyer at third. White and Cunningham, both excellent first basemen, went to center and right fields, respectively. Crowe, a fine pinch-hitter, started the game at first base. This unorthodox (to say the least) defense ran from the dugout on to the diamond to begin the first inning. One St. Louis sportswriter blinked his eyes in amazement and muttered, "Let's hurry up and lose this game, too, so we won't have to look at this lineup again."

Blaylock started on the mound but his nerves were not quite able to stand up under the thought of what would happen if a ball was batted past him into the confusion. He didn't get a man out.

Change for change's sake was one excuse that came to mind as White misjudged a fly ball. We hadn't been able to win with the old lineup, despite the fact that defensively it was the best and most likely to succeed. Unfortunately, defense starts with the pitcher and the pitchers, unfortunately, were humanly capable of giving up several runs per game. (Or maybe this should read, the pitchers were not superhumanly capable of pitching shutouts daily.)

Our best defense, however, was inhumanly conservative about scoring runs, or even getting base bits. The combination of no runs for our side and a couple runs for their side made the Cardinals last in the league in games won. Therefore, the question arose in the managerial mind: Shall we sacrifice defense for punch? Can we give up even more runs per game yet overcome this deficiency by scoring many more times per game? Do we have the material for such a radical alteration of accepted professional strategy?

Most of the professional answers to these questions were "NO," but it no longer seemed fitting, or even safe, for Hemus, as manager, to expect improved results from the daily exhortation—"Stay with 'em, boys. Keep swingin' those bats. I know we're gonna start hitting soon. You guys are better than you've shown. The balls just aren't falling in for you, that's all."

The balls weren't being hit far enough or hard enough to fall in, actually. The most optimistic eye had to see this evident truth sooner or later. The awkward manner with which Hemus handled the finally convincing evidence indicated that he still had reservations. He still had faith in Blasingame, and Boyer, and Hal Smith, and Cunningham. None of them were hitting much. (Blasingame was back to pulling the ball instead of slapping it to left.) But all of them were capable, historically, of better performances.

So, the spectacle of wholesale changes in the lineup was instinctively felt, in the bullpen, to be a whim of the manager, not to be taken seriously. Not to be commented upon with cynical disparagement—"I'm going to work out in center tomorrow, Howard. Anything would be better than this!"—or to be viewed with exasperated alarm—"What the hell do we do when a fly ball goes to center? Back up the plate or run out to second and be cut-off man for the relay? That outfield couldn't throw my grandmother out if she tripped and broke her leg halfway to the plate!"

Pitchers are constantly convincing each other that they could play the outfield better than the assigned outfielders, who, naturally, think they could outpitch most any man claiming the job and title and responsibility that goes with being a pitcher. The unhappy results that attend any such switch in jobs are usually slighted as unfortunate experiments. Hal Jeffcoat, a born-and-raised center fielder, took the idea seriously one spring. He weathered the scorn and laughter of both his fellow outfielders and competing pitcher teammates, eventually earning a position that kept him in the majors several years longer than he might have expected, considering his meager talents as a hitter. (When he finally forsook hitting for pitching, Jeffcoat became a better hitter. Of course, he probably had visions of greater prowess as a pitcher than he actually achieved, also. But therein lies the dilemma of unobjective personal evaluation. When you aren't exceptionally able, you don't dare see yourself as others see you.)

"How many people you guess are here?" I asked Nunn as we stretched out on the bullpen bench.

"I don't know," he said. "I guess about fifteen thousand, maybe. I'll say 14,792."

"Bet there's between eighteen and twenty thousand," I said.

He looked around, myopically estimating through his thick safety lenses. "Hell, there isn't that many, I know. What d'ya want to bet?"

"Bet a buck. I say there's between eighteen and twenty thousand."

"You're on," he said, sticking out his hand with an I-can't-lose assurance.

He couldn't win, either, because the announced attendance of 12,345 *was* between eighteen and twenty thousand.

"You think you're so damn smart," he said. "You think that's fair? Hey, you think that's fair, Greenie?"

It wasn't fair. And it wasn't very smart. But it did pass the time till the phone started ringing. Hemus wanted to change his lineup again. But with obvious good reason. None of the pitchers he called on seemed to be able to stop the flood of runs. Thank Giles the Dodgers are leaving town.

April 29—St. Louis

"Doc, did you get a cigar from Grammas?" I asked Bauman as he hosed hot water into the whirlpool tub. Despite the off-day we were all at the ball park to work out. It is a tradition in baseball that a losing club shall exercise lightly for an hour on the off-day to indicate that they are not complacent or satisfied with losing or some such reason. The workout seldom amounts to anything; a short batting practice, a sermon from the various coaches, and a fifteen-minute running session for the pitching staff. But it creates a guilt complex or at least a guilty feeling, in the group morale; this often enables one or two members of the team to play over their heads for a day. I could think of no better time to have some physical therapy for my aching (for publication only) back.

"Umph," Bauman grunted.

"Doc, remember all that jazz about Dr. Fredericks and ballplayers eating junk all of the time, and all that? Well, I read in the paper where this same Dr. Fredericks—I guess he's the same guy—has decided that 16 per cent of all Americans in the age group from twenty-one to thirty-five are sterile 'because they eat junk.' His very words! Do you think that's why Cincinnati let Grammas go?"

Bauman's attention antenna sprang into prominence. "What does Grammas's baby have to do with his being traded?"

"You know Alex had been married for ten years and that this was his first child. On the Cincinnati club if you don't have at least three children you're not even average. Some people doubt your virility, then, and it's only one step further to doubting your ability. My conclusion is fairly obvious, isn't it?"

"No," said Bauman as he turned up the heat control dial to live steam hot. "Brosnan, you haven't even stopped by to say hello for two weeks. What's been eating you?"

"Bo, you're evading my serious question. I want to know whether or not you agree with me that this is a good sign— Alex finally having a baby? Certainly, you're not for sterility, and against intercourse during the season!"

"You sure you don't feel good enough to work out?" asked Bauman. But a grin started to crease his jowls. "Where'd you see this on Dr. Fredericks?"

"I read it somewhere," I said. I tried to dismiss the subject. "Doc, where do you think I'm going?"

Bauman glanced sharply at me as I lowered myself into the whirlpool bath. "What makes you think you're going anywhere?" he countered.

"Things, Doc, just things. I'm not long for this clubhouse and you know it."

Bauman capped a bottle of vitamin pills, placed the bottle back on the shelf where it belonged, and walked over to the rubbing table next to the whirlpool tub.

"Listen," he said. "If you think they're going to give up on a guy with your ability, you're nuts. You may give up on yourself, but they won't quit on you. What you gotta do is shake yourself a little bit."

I could have said that I didn't understand Hemus, and he didn't understand me, and never the twain should meet. But I didn't. Major league trainers (Bauman is one of the best) have an instinctive knowledge of their ballplayers that often transcends any understanding that a manager can achieve. Still, the trainer's job is to maintain the health of the team, and any physical or mental ailment that upsets the team (or the manager) requires quick, sometimes unsympathetic, correction. I could see I wasn't going to get any sympathy from Bauman, so I sloshed around in the whirlpool a bit and said, "Doc, this thing is too hot. Can I get out?"

Bauman sniffed at my abrupt (obvious?) desire to change the subject. "You stay in there till I tell you to get out. I guess you're not interested in working out today, right?"

I wasn't.

April 30—Milwaukee

"For Christ's sake, Philip, forget it, will ya? You'd think that was the first game you ever lost."

I felt cornered by the reasonable, though distasteful, plea of Phil Clark, as he described for the seventh time how badly he felt about losing the game to L.A. on Sunday.

"You think I deserved it?" he asked. "You think the way they hit me, and the way they hit Mizell, that I deserved to lose the game?"

I couldn't, reasonably, decide one way or other. Rules are rules. If you're the pitcher of record in a ball game, and the winning run is scored via two bloops and a misjudged fly ball—why, what difference does it make that another pitcher —preceding you—had been shelled every time he threw a ball over the plate?

"Phil, you've been pitching pretty good ball," I said, trying to temporize without being too sympathetic. "But the breaks have been going against you. They'll even up."

"Yeah," he said, wryly, "but will they even up before I get sent out? That's the question."

I could easily extend reasonable sympathy to Phil since he'd had more than his share of bad breaks. Nothing discourages a pitcher more than to see good pitches go to waste. The percentage sometimes goes against you. Clark, being a good pitcher and knowing how to pitch, had made so many good pitches only to see them turned into handle-hits, bad hops over the infielders' shoulders, bloops to the outfield and squibs through the infield, that a sympathetic observer, like a wife, could almost cry in desperation.

But, man, that's the way it goes in this game. You make your pitch, and if it's the right pitch, it works . . . most of the time. If it's the wrong pitch, you find out soon enough, and they tell you soon enough, also. If you don't believe them, they send you somewhere else so they don't have to listen to you; and so that you can ponder by yourself the misfortune that has struck you. Etc.

"Phil, forget it. They're either gonna cut you or they won't. You got two weeks to not worry about it. Relax."

If they had any intentions, in the first place, of keeping him, they'd discount his bad luck and bank on the fact that he knew how to pitch and the breaks would soon start coming his way. If the committee on pitching couldn't determine—couldn't rationalize—*my* troubles as a temporary loss of form, though . . . how could they be so optimistic as to assume that Phil Clark's failure was obviously bad luck? He had a bitch, but then so do we all.

The seniority system is unreasonably operative in organized baseball, it seems. Especially in the major leagues. The human errors of the veteran ballplayers are so readily excused whereas the same errors of a rookie are savagely condemned. The percentage of bad breaks is the same for both rookie and veteran.

And just so long as the professional game is analyzed by percentage, so long will the errors be common to all players.

Why not judge the players by mental mistakes, then?

Why not say, "If you can't learn, and use, what we tell you from our experience, then we'll send you out to gather your own experience. If you do what we say, then we can't blame you for the bloops and the squibs and the bad calls behind the plate. Or, at least, we won't judge you on those universal—we had them, too—misfortunes."

Brooding about Clark's fate was not conducive to the contentment that life in the Milwaukee bullpen should bring. The bullpen in County Stadium is 450 feet away from the dugout . . . and the manager. Distance lends enchantment, at best; contentment, at least. Let's get on, then, with relaxation. The ninety-mile drive I had from Chicago tired the eyes.

"Talking about losing jobs," I said, as I lit a match for Green's cigarette, "did you see where Bill Norman got fired at Detroit?"

"Yes," said Pollet, as he stuffed three baseballs into his jacket pocket. "That was a shocker. There's a guy who does nothing but think baseball every minute of his life, and yet he couldn't figure out how to get his club out of a slump."

Clark nodded his head. "Norman was in our league last year. He sure can chew that tobacco. Bet he uses a pack and a half a day, anyway."

"There was a quote in the paper the other day," I said. "Right after Narleski had lost another game in relief for Detroit. Norman said, 'I'm going right down the line with Ray. He's my best relief pitcher.' What he meant was, he was going right down the drain with Narleski."

"It's tough on a manager when he's gotta rely on one man when that guy isn't doing the job," said Pollet as he stood up and walked over to the low fence that separates the visitors' and the Braves' bullpens.

"What's he trying to say, Philip?" I asked, laughing . . . at myself.

"You know," said Clark, "there's sure been a lot of relief pitchers hurtin' this spring. Narleski, and this Hyde over to Washington. And Muffett—he's back in the minors already. Coupla years ago, the Cardinals thought he was gonna be terrific. We were both pitchin' at Houston that year they brought him up. It was to be him or me. And Harry Walker decided he'd rather have me and send Muff up to the big leagues. Awful white of him, wasn't it?"

"Forget it, Philip," I said. "Muffett did get off to a real good start, I remember. Maybe they built him up too much. He's a pretty good pitcher, but Harry Caray made him out to be the greatest relief pitcher in Cardinal history. Caray sounded like a Cardinal press agent instead of a radio broadcaster."

"Your wife says he's been blastin' you, I hyah," said Clark.

"Yeah. Well, there's nothing much good to say about the way I been goin', but Caray should keep his remarks to himself. He blasted Smitty last night when he relieved you. There was no call for that. Here it was the kid's first appearance of the year and Caray has already given up on him. What's more, his opinion encourages everybody within two hundred miles of St. Louis."

Caray, in solemn vocal tears after Mathews had greeted Smith with a single to drive in the ninth run in a 9-3 loss, had said, "How can anyone expect Solly Hemus to produce with material like this?"

One dozen ill-chosen words, and Smith was skewered on the barb of public opinion. It was an uncalled-for criticism in the first place. Mathews had hit a good pitch—hit it just good enough for a single to right. To suggest that Smith was a symbol of Hemus's failure so far as a manager was to undermine Smitty's chances of keeping his job. Publicity, especially bad publicity, attaches itself like mold to a ballplayer's name.

"Old Blabber-mouth," I went on, "ought to do his sponsor some good and go soak his fat head for an hour in a barrel of Falstaff beer."

"The only thing that would do is kill the taste of the beer," said Green.

"How about that for a good blast, Marv?" I called out, looking around for Grissom. "Hey, where's the Veteran Righthander?"

"He didn't even make the trip, Brosnan," said Clark, shaking his head. "Marv's gone on the disabled list. Where you been for the last two days?"

"Shh!" I cautioned him. "I been commuting to Milwaukee from Chicago every day. Don't tell my roomie, though. McDaniel probably thinks I just never got in last night. How about that Hemus lifting the curfew? What did you do last night to relax, Philip?"

Clark laughed at the mention of the curfew-lifting. Hemus had called a short meeting after the Braves had clobbered us 9-3 on Wednesday. He spoke softly, in a resigned tone, about how we obviously were all tensed up, and pressing too hard, and why don't we all stay out all night and really get loose. Forget about baseball for a couple of hours. (The inference that we thought of nothing else but baseball after leaving the clubhouse was a subtle compliment, at that.)

"Solly oughta try that more often," said Broglio. "Did you ever see such a bunch of relaxed ballplayers?"

We watched Warren Spahn pitch to the rested, tension-free Cardinal lineup. Three up, three down. Spahnie no longer throws aspirin tablets like he once did. He's gone modern. For nine innings he threw tranquilizing pills, and our side ate 'em up. We lost again, 1-0.

And that's no way to relax. Kellner started, and pitched seven innings. Aaron hit a home run off him in the fourth, and that's how it stood when I was waved in. The walk from the bullpen to the mound at County Stadium seems nearly as long as the drive from Chicago to Milwaukee; but I soon got over that tired feeling when Mathews hit a line drive between my legs. That's a frightening experience. Just one year ago, Gus Bell had hit one at me that didn't quite get by. It broke the metal cup inside my supporter. No memento of my career is more treasured than that split cup.

A batted ball that whistles past your thighs is by you before you can react, of course. The most sensitive-minded would, if time allowed, assume the position of the Maiden Surprised at the very thought of a batted ball rifling straight at . . . Gives me the shudders.

Aaron, however, bunted, and I was more than grateful. About the only way I know to get Henry out is with sliders away from him. And that's asking to have the ball hit right back up the middle. Adcock then slashed a ground ball back at me, and I had no time to shudder before the ball plunked into my glove. Unconscious, you say? Hell, man, with these hands? Just great reflexes, that's all.

Mathews, who had started to third, suddenly froze in disbelief when I wheeled around with the ball in my hand. I ran right at him, like the Book says. If I could tag him without any additional play having to be made on him, Adcock would have to stay on first. This would remove a man from scoring position, theoretically. The way that the balls were coming back at me, I was willing to take a chance on a long fly, though, even if it meant a possible double or triple.

Mathews stood motionless until I was arm length away. Then he darted back to second. I tagged nothing but air, recovered my balance, and flipped the ball to Blasingame. Blazer was forced to chase Mathews toward third base, and he finally ran him down; but Adcock had meanwhile reached second, and I was embarrassed. Here I had a chance to make a good, albeit unconscious, play, and I blew it. Blew it just as awkwardly as a man could, without rehearsals. Hemus disgustedly waved for me to walk Covington, and Crandall stupidly popped up a high slider that he should have hit out of the ball park. Saved by the Law of Averages! (I make a mistake, they make a mistake.)

May 3—Pittsburgh

(PITTSBURGH's not a bad town.)

Being a creature of habit I try to adjust my life on the road during the season so that my wife knows pretty well where I am, at night . . . after a ball game. In case she wants to call me. (On our first wedding anniversary she tried to call me in Montreal. She tried to reach me at midnight, and on the hour after that. She didn't know where I was. Whenever I was in Montreal I never did, either.)

In Pittsburgh I usually go to Danny's after a ball game. Danny serves good food, and good booze. Danny is personable, friendly, intelligent, and generous. Danny's is just across the street from the hotel in which we stay. I can make it safely to bed no matter how tired I am . . . of good food, good booze and conversation. On Friday the first of May—or Saturday morning, to be exact—I was happy about all that.

On Friday night Dick Stuart hit a home run off me. Although his home run had nothing to do with the outcome of the game, it monopolized baseball conversation for hours afterward. When the ball hit the bat, I knew it was in for a long ride. The sound shattered my composure. It was an ugly sound. The crowd responded with awe-filled, delightful cooing that ended in loud hand-clapping. There was some snickering, also, it seemed to me. I stood on the mound, mentally measuring the distance the ball went. The last I saw of it, it was sailing over the light tower that rises 120 feet above the ground to the left of the scoreboard, 405 feet away. The ball wasn't coming down, it was going up. Where it landed nobody knows.

When I was a daydreaming pre-teen-ager I played a game with rocks and a broomstick. We lived near a small woods. I would fungo rocks into the trees and listen for the sound of the rock striking a tree. If I heard rock-on-wood I'd credit myself with a base hit. If not, I'd call it an out. Each time I swung the broomstick-bat I was a different major league hitter. Within two hours I could play a double-header.

So I relived an adolescent pastime as Stuart's home run sailed ever onward into the night. If that ball struck a tree I was going to credit Stuart accordingly. But sound, though it travels swiftly, carries only so far. Not as far as that gopher ball, I think. (I'd swear they're doing something to liven up the baseballs this year.)

We won the game, which should have been worth a comment in itself. But no.

"That's the way to pitch, Broz. Make 'em hit the ball and you got a chance!"

"Thanks, Perfessor," said Mizell. "Gave 'em a thrill, didn't ya?" I had relieved Mizell in the eighth, and saved his win.

"Wonder if they're getting any signals yet at Cape Canaveral. That thing's gotta be in orbit."

By the time I reached the noisy sanctuary of Danny's I was so self-conscious of my new fame that I was ready to change my name. Max, the piano player, grinned at me and said, "Congratulations," which was enough to start the bartender laughing. Danny, however, stuck out his big right hand and said, "Jimmy, boy, let's sit down here and we'll talk about Barcelona. Steve, bring my boy, Jimmy, a drink."

Danny knew, too, I knew, but his Castilian sense of tact prevented him from acting like a curious fan. Danny ate while I drank, and we talked about flamenco dancing, and Spanish wines, and the bullfights. But Danny soon left to care for customers and I was reduced to helping Steve empty a few glasses . . . mine.

Suddenly I heard Max say, "Here's the guy who threw the pitch." I turned to see a new customer who bought me a drink and shook hands in one continuous, friendly gesture.

"You'll never believe this, Bronson, but as I was coming into the airport on an American Airlines plane . . ."

That was too much. I staggered off to the latrine, mumbling, "He didn't hit it that well."

By the time Danny returned the sad night had ended; also

several hours of the next morning. I was soon back in the bull-pen. Day games follow night games with bewildering and sleep-defying speed.

"You saved a game, Professor," said Green. "Laugh it up a little."

I lived it up as heartily as my half-shut eyelids would allow. The target for the day was a small paper cup. Green and I filled that cup with tobacco juice, to the squeamish disgust of the other sun-worshipers in the bullpen. It took us one whole pack of tobacco, and seven innings of chewing and spitting—expectorating sounds better—but we filled it. Right to the brim, bubbles of brown spittle popping over the cup's rim there at the end. Hoo boy! It was no mean feat, at that, considering the one-inch diameter of the cup, the nauseated groans of Howie Nunn who watched with red eyes and thirsty throat, and our own gradual dizziness as the tobacco, heat and competitive tension took their toll. (We were betting not only that we could fill the cup before the game ended; but we had a pool on the inning in which the cup overflowed. "The winner," I decided, as I explained the contest to Nunn, "gets to drink the cup. You're a betting man. You want to get in?" He ran off behind the scoreboard just then and I never did know whether or not he picked an inning.)

Actually, Howie was warming up when our bullpen party broke up. Kellner squashed a broomstick into the barely filled cup, spraying tobacco juice all over the bullpen. And eventually Nunn got into the game long enough to help Pittsburgh win 2-1 from McDaniel. The only part of the game that I remember is the last of the ninth. With one out and a man on first for Pittsburgh, Haddix batted for himself. He'd pitched well all day, but I didn't think they'd let him hit in that situation. "He has to be bunting," I thought aloud.

Haddix faked a bunt on the first pitch, which was a ball. Through my mind went a hunch—"He's gonna swing on this pitch." Cunningham started in with the pitch. Joe was play-ing first and he wanted to get the bunt and force Virdon at second. But just as I'd sensed it, and even before I could say it out loud, Haddix swung at the fast ball (which McDaniel just laid in there figuring Haddix actually would bunt like the percentages indicated he should) and grounded the ball by Cunningham down the first base line for a double. Had Joe been playing back, of course, and had McDaniel thrown a breaking ball, as he probably would have if the bunt wasn't obviously in order . . . we might still be playing.

It's just as well, I guess.

Today was still another double-header; which should never happen in Pittsburgh on Sunday. The blue laws are still on the Pennsylvania books, a fact of law that reflects on every serious and sensible baseball-loving senator and representative of the Commonwealth. (And which one of them will dare deny he's a baseball fan!)

The combination of the curfew and Eastern Standard Time, which suspends play at six o'clock in the spring, prevents completion of most second games in the Sunday double-headers. (When daylight time goes into effect, the law is changed so that the curfew hour is seven o'clock. Why isn't this man-made change legal precedent enough to have the curfew boosted to nine o'clock?) In July, when the suspended games are completed, they sometimes list players no longer associated with the participating clubs. It is more than likely that some members of either our lineup or the Pirates' will be missing when we complete the game that was halted today in the seventh inning. Conceivably, a Cardinal who started to-day's second game for St. Louis may be playing for Pittsburgh the next time St. Louis comes to town. This possibility was the subject of a "Knotty Problem" about baseball in the *Saturday Evening Post*. In the theoretical problem I was the Cardinal, Haddix was the Pirate, and we were exchanged in a trade soon after a game was suspended in which I, as a Cardinal, was winning by one run. In the completion of the suspended game after the trade I, as a Pirate pitcher now, became the winning pitcher for Pittsburgh when Haddix, who started the day losing the game for the Pirates, ended the day losing the game for the Cardinals; making the starting pitcher for one team the losing pitcher for the other team. Or something like that.

Anyway, a magazine reader in Johannesburg, South Africa, noticed the name *Brosnan*. She wrote the editor of the *Saturday Evening Post,* who forwarded the letter on to me. The letter asked if the baseball player, Brosnan, had any relatives in Africa. The letter-writer's name was Brosnan, also, it seems. And would I send her an autographed baseball if my name really was Brosnan like it is in Africa. I wrote back saying that my name really was Haddix, and I didn't have any balls. I mean that's a long way to go to ask for a baseball.

But that has nothing to do with the "fight" theme of the day. As we rode the bus to the park an argument broke out between Jackson and Cimoli as to what was the best way to pitch Burgess. Since Burgess was murdering any and all kinds of pitching, Cimoli assumed that the pitchers were not bearing down on Burgess. Since Cimoli had to play center field in the vast open spaces of Forbes Field, he didn't want Burgess hitting the ball that way and making him, Cimoli, run too much in the hot sun.

"You gotta keep the ball up on him!" said Gino, as wrong as he could be, but so loudly positive about it that even Burgess might be inclined to agree with him.

"Listen, Gino," said Jackson, "you let me do the pitching, and you chase my mistakes."

"That's all I been doin'," moaned Cimoli, causing the fight to break out in the mind of every pitcher on the bus. "That damned Dago cries so damn much he's gonna drown in his own tears if we're all lucky."

The temperature rose on the field, too, and even I was beginning to feel a bit logy in the tenth inning. In the first inning I could hardly feel any pain at all. (Pittsburgh is really not a bad town.) In the seventh inning I relieved Jackson on the mound.

Hoak led off the tenth with a single, hitting a change-up

that he had no business hitting at all. Had he been fresh, cool and strong, as he usually thinks he is, Hoak would have swung viciously at the ball before it got up to the plate. Then he'd have stepped out of the box, cursed me for fooling him, jumped back into the batter's box, and taken a third strike fast ball right down the pipe.

But he was too tired to swing hard; he just pushed the ball into center for a base hit. If I hadn't been feeling so good on the mound, I'd have considered it a bad omen. When a hitter doesn't do what he's supposed to do, he can upset your determination to pitch succeeding hitters the way you're supposed to. "What if this next guy bloops one in, also?" you say to yourself. "Better blow the ball by him, instead." Frequently this kind of thinking leads to a big inning for their side.

So I shook it off, and threw a slider past Clemente . . . and also past Hal Smith and the umpire. A damn good slider— broke at least a foot instead of four inches as it usually does. Of course, Hoak went to second. Clemente then grounded to Boyer who held Hoak to second as he threw Clemente out. Hemus then had me walk Burgess, a managerial move that I welcomed wholeheartedly. Stuart came up, smiling as the fans roared.

"Put another one in orbit!" yelled a typical bloodthirsty fan.

Two innings earlier I had knocked Stuart down with two different pitches, the first right at his ear—a perfect flip. A truly delightful pitcher's pitch. I mean, that's what you have to do in this game, work on control all the time. Stuart, for-tunately for him, knew I would throw at him so he was on his way out of the batter's box before the ball got there. But that second flip scared him. Ha! Thought we were allowed only one to a customer?

I called Smitty out to the mound to ask him if we should flip Stuart one more time. But Hal didn't want to take the chance that I might throw the ball into the stands. (Or into

Stuart's ear.) So we fed him two fast balls right on his fists, and he popped the second straight up.

With two out, I felt cocky. My glasses were covered with steam and the bridge of my nose was wet with sweat. I started over toward the bench to ask for a towel, and Bauman came out, followed by Hemus, who waved to the bullpen for a new pitcher.

"Hey!" I yelled. "I just want to wipe off my face, Solly."

Bauman whispered to me as he mopped the sweat, "I was praying you wouldn't do this. He couldn't make up his mind till you started off the mound."

Hemus held out his hand for the ball and said, "I was gonna take you out anyway. I want Kellner to pitch to this left-hander."

"Jesus H. Christ, Solly," I said. "Skinner isn't hitting his weight. I can get him out!"

"Well." Hemus hesitated, as he looked at Skinner, then at the third base umpire who was walking with Kellner in from the bullpen. "Nothing I can do, now. He's bringing him in."

I walked away. Here I'd had my best day since the season started, and the first time I get a chance to pitch myself out of trouble he plays percentages.

Even before Kellner walked Skinner, I could feel the game oozing away. Nunn replaced Kellner to pitch to the right-handed hitter, Mazeroski. Maz hit the second pitch to right field, a fly ball that Cimoli, who had been moved over from center as a defensive measure, should have gobbled up. But Gino broke late, then quit on the ball, and it went over his head. The winning run scored from third.

"That jakin' bastard!" I yelled. I ran up the dugout steps and across the field to the clubhouse, cursing to myself.

Hemus was right behind me, and as we rushed into the clubhouse Cimoli shuffled his way through the door. Hemus said to him, "You should've caught that in your jock, Cimoli. You can just rest the second game if you're too damn tired to play."

Cimoli limped over to the rubbing table and mumbled, "I think I pulled a muscle, Doc."

"How can you pull a muscle in your head," I thought, and I smiled to myself. What the hell, even when I pitched well, I lost. It's the breaks. It's been the breaks all along. *I still can pitch, though.* As I stripped off my wet uniform, I suddenly couldn't find anything worth fighting about.

Hemus had just begun to fight, however. In the second game, he started himself at second instead of Blasingame. Solly stuck his leg into a pitch in the first inning. As he trotted toward first he yelled at Daniels, the Pirate pitcher, "You black bastard. . . ," which Daniels promptly resented because he's a Negro. (That's one thing about the All-American game of baseball. Black is never white. If Daniels were Caucasian, and Hemus had yelled, "You white bastard. . . ," there would never have been a fight.)

Daniels charged off the mound and Hemus scampered up to him, fists at the ready. Both benches erupted, as players from both sides welcomed the break in the monotony. Some punches were thrown, indiscriminately and ineffectively. Nothing came of it all. We didn't even get a run.

In the third inning Hemus dropped a double down the left field line to drive in a run. Daniels bore down on Solly, trying to put a little extra on each pitch. He almost had a fast ball by Hemus, but Solly got just enough wood on the ball to loop a little fly ball that fell just six inches inside the foul line. Daniels flipped his glove into the air in disgust as Hemus pulled up at second with a satisfied grin on his face.

Hemus came to bat again in the sixth. Daniels flipped him with his first pitch.

"Get ready, boys," said Katt in the bullpen.

Even before Daniels let the next pitch go toward the plate, Hemus had stepped out toward him and swung. The bat sailed toward the pitcher's mound.

Even before the bat landed forty feet from second base, Daniels and Hemus were wrestling. Both benches emptied again. The bullpen crews charged toward the mound from left and right fields.

Even after the dust had settled, Kellner and I were still sitting in the bullpen, watching and shaking our heads.

"How bush can you get?" I said. "They're trying to make a farce out of the game."

May 4—Rochester, N.Y.

THE Rochester, N.Y., papers said Hemus had tried to put some spark into the Cardinals by engaging in fisticuffs with Daniels. If that truly was his intention he did it as awkwardly as he could. All he proved to me was that little men—or boys —shouldn't play with sparks, as well as with matches.

If he was truly mad enough to throw his bat at the pitcher, then his gaucherie was almost excusable. If pitchers may throw at batters, why can't batters throw back? (Nobody's arguing that pitchers can't throw at batters.) But, at least, let's make it clear before the fight—or game—starts; and let pitchers wear shin guards. Batters wear helmets at the plate. You can hardly get it into their thick heads that they shouldn't dig in at the plate, any more.

I read about Hemus's spark plugging while waiting for a knackwurst sandwich at the refreshment stand. We were in Rochester on our off-day to play an exhibition game. After the regulars played three innings the rinky-dinks took over, happy to get into a game, finally, but a little apprehensive.

"If I look good," said Bill Smith, before the game, "why they may ship me down here at the cut-down date."

"And if you look bad, they may send you even further," said Nunn.

"Hell, man," I said, "if you look bad enough they're gonna keep you in St. Louis. Everybody looks bad on this nine."

"Broz," said Clark, "you're gettin' bitter in your old age."

My age wasn't bothering me till he mentioned it, but that was another reason to be bitter, so I enjoyed it. When a ballplayer reaches thirty, he's just about had it. There are only five more years to what is virtually compulsory retirement. The few players who manage to break through that age barrier of thirty-five seem to be able to go on indefinitely. Injuries alone can end their careers.

The hot dog vendor handed me my knackwurst and a cup of beer. I walked back to the grandstand to watch the game. The knackwurst was delicious, the best I've ever eaten; but the game was terrible. When Green hit a two-out home run to tie up the game in the ninth, I could have puked.

We were due to fly out of Rochester to Philadelphia immediately after the ball game. With luck we'd make it into Philly by two A.M. After a couple of hours' sleep I could take a train to New York for the day; which is what I do in Philadelphia. What else is there?

The game went into extra innings, and I walked back to the clubhouse hoping that the man had shown up with the two cases of free beer. In each town in which the Cardinals play the local Budweiser distributor is required to furnish two cases to the ball club. This kind of employee relations should redound greatly to the credit of Anheuser-Busch. A cold beer after the ball game gives a ballplayer that contented look.

I got lost under the stands, looking for the visitors' clubhouse. My indiscriminate door-knocking led me only as far as the Rochester clubhouse. There, Bob Keegan, an over-thirty-five pitcher, was soaking his pitching arm in the whirlpool tub.

"How's it feel?" I asked. "You been doing real well this year so far, I see."

Keegan smiled. "It never felt better. If I'd only known what to do with my arm last spring I'd still be with the White Sox."

"Bauman told me that you had a pretty bad arm," I said. "He never thought you'd pitch again."

"I never did either!" Keegan said. "At times I couldn't reach the plate. But I used the iron ball all winter, and gradually stretched my arm out. This spring it hurt a little at first. I went back to exercising with that iron ball. Pretty soon it started comin' around. Of course, I didn't have to worry about makin' the club. No pressure on me. I could take all the time I needed. But those exercises did it, I think. Did Bo show you guys how to do them?"

"Yeah. Like Bauman says, stretch it out, huh?" I laughed. "Glad you're feelin' better, Bob. Don't push it, though. They might bring you up with us."

Keegan looked up at me sharply, and said, "Yeah, maybe." I got the impression that he almost added, "You don't know when you're well off, Brosnan."

That's probably true.

May 6—Philadelphia

LORD GOD, will sorrows never cease.

I had just finished my last chew of the night in the ninth as we scored three runs to knock Robin Roberts out of the box. We then led 7-3. The phone rang in the cage next to the bullpen in Philly and Pollet answered it. He waved to me as he hung up and said, "Jim, you might as well get loose in case he needs somebody."

Mizell had retired seven straight batters and I didn't think there would be much need for help. But by the time I'd taken off my jacket, found my glove under the bench, walked to the bullpen mound and stuck a piece of gum in my mouth, Wilmer was just about out of the game. Wally Post hit the second pitch for a single and Anderson slammed a high curve off the scoreboard for one run.

Hal Smith ambled out to talk to Mizell, taking as much time as he could. But what can a catcher say but good-by?

Keane, who had been running the club since the third when Hemus was thumbed, also took his time before calling me in from the bullpen. I heard Venzon, the umpire, yell to me that I was to come on to the mound, but I kept throwing so that he'd have to come down the left field line to get me. I *like* Tony, and all that, but I needed time to get warm. I threw two more quick curves before he got to me to yell, "Let's go, Brosnan. Didn't you hear me call you?"

I was tempted to get smart and say, "You're the one with the rabbit ears, not me," but I like Tony; really I do. Sticking my nose in the air, I walked by Venzon and out to the mound thinking to myself, "I'm ready."

I could have been more ready, I guess.

I couldn't have looked worse, I know.

Willie Jones was the first hitter, and I knew I could get him out if I kept everything away, and wasted maybe one pitch inside. But he hit a pitch that was just not quite far enough away from him. His fly ball fell a foot inside the right field line for a double. Philadelphia was just two runs down and still had nobody out.

Freese bounced a slider back to me, and I felt better. But Dave Philley batted for Hegan and hit a low slider away from him to left field for a single. It wasn't too bad a pitch. Had it broken down slightly instead of staying flat Philley might have hit it into the ground instead of on a line. Then, too, White might have caught the ball in left field had he been an outfielder instead of a first baseman.

Bowman batted for the pitcher and I was trying to decide how to pitch him, when Keane ran out of the dugout, yelling for time. He ran all the way to the mound and said, "We're going to let Jackson pitch to him." I assumed that what Keane said came from Hemus, shrugged my shoulders, and walked to the clubhouse. At this critical moment I was willing to accept anyone's opinion. The Philadelphia fans were roaring. Do they sense disaster, those miserable fans?

Jackson pitched to four men. Two of them singled, and

two of them walked as the Phillies' radio broadcaster snorted and brayed fanatically. As I uncapped the aspirin bottle in the dressing room, the winning run crossed the plate. I swallowed two pills at once, pocketed two for later, and sat down on the table to wait for the explosion.

The tension was thick. The locker room steamed nervously, the damp walls reflecting every player's breath. I heard the clatter of muddy spiked shoes being banged on the floor; and the scratching of matches as cigarettes were lit.

"That's the worst exhibition I ever saw!"

That's all that was said.

There wasn't much anyone could say. I, personally, didn't say anything for hours except "Let me have another one"— at the hamburger grill across the street from the Warwick Hotel.

Eighteen hours later as we dressed for the second game of the series the locker room atmosphere was still somewhat subdued. Usually the professional ballplayer manages to put aside the memories of catastrophic disappointments. He says, "I just won't think about it. You can't win 'em in the clubhouse. That's the way it goes. You win some, lose some, and some are rained out." Eventually he talks himself back into the state of self-confidence in which he performs best. The aplomb of the eighty-time loser is not always complacency. He knows that a certain percentage of games must be lost because the other team is better for certain games. Again, he knows that his team will occasionally give away a game that should have been won. He comes right back, smiling and fighting. (Lose ninety times in a season, though, and it shows in the face. A close-up reveals frown lines, crow's-feet, and an extra tint of red in the eyeballs from too much regretting.)

We had lost many games, but that was the first one we had given away. Hemus's daily preachment—"You lose because you're making mistakes"—had been emphatically demonstrated. The most grievous fault of a ballplayer is to give a ball game away.

Usually a ballplayer replays a losing game immediately afterward. A conversational autopsy quickly spots the blame. Two martinis and a rare steak later, the game is forgotten till the newspapers come out and rehash it. "The worst exhibition (he) ever saw" wasn't replayed by the bullpen till the next game started.

"Well, that's not the last one we'll give away, either," I said, finally.

"Let's try to forget last night," said Pollet in the seventh inning. "We got this game to worry about."

"Doesn't look like he's gonna use anybody down here tonight, Howie," said Green.

Kellner had started the game and had served up two tremendous home runs to Wally Post, and another one to Hamner. We were down 6-4 as the seventh started. Durham batted for Kellner and bounced out. The phone rang in the bullpen.

"Give me Nunn, I guess," said Hemus.

Nunn pitched the last of the seventh and retired three men in a row. He took a shower in our half of the eighth, when we came up with four big ones to go ahead by two. Again, Hemus called the bullpen.

Pollet turned away from the phone, looked over his crew as as if he were the master of ceremonies on "Who Do You Trust?" and pointed to me. "He wants to know how you feel."

"Give me the ball, Coach," I said, and stood up to take off my jacket.

The eighth was easy. As I started out of the dugout in the Phillies' half of the ninth, Hemus reached up to pat me on the back, apparently thought better of it and said, instead, "Let's see you bear down now, big man. Get that first hitter."

I didn't.

That damn Willie Jones, again. He has an odd behavior at the plate. He'll take a hard swing at a pitch, miss it, and look out at the pitcher, his face purple with rage. It's hard to tell whether he's mad at you for making him miss the ball or mad at himself for not hitting it. Or, he'll take a half-ass swing at a pitch, and you swear you had him fooled. But just set him up for the same pitch later and he'll hit it like he knew it was coming.

So, he hit a pretty good slider into right center. The ball might have been caught had Flood been playing Jones straight away. But I saw at a glance that Curt wasn't going to catch up with the ball. I headed toward the Phillies' clubhouse to back up third base. Jones made it, easily; and he scored when Freese hit a long fly to right field.

Bowman batted for the catcher and singled. The Philly fans yelled for an encore of my previous evening's performance. Out of the dugout came Hemus. He pawed the ground, cleared his throat, looked at the bullpen, and said, "Can you get him out?"

I looked at Dave Philley, who had been announced as a pinch-hitter. He had knocked me out just twenty-four hours earlier. I shrugged my shoulders and said, "Hell, yes."

Hemus looked at me for a moment, then turned and walked back to the bench. Cunningham, who had run back to first, wheeled around and ran back to the mound, a slightly mischievous grin on his face. He asked me, "Is everything all right, Professor?" turned and ran back to first base.

I relaxed, took a deep breath, and shook off Green's signal for the slider.

"No slide balls," I said to myself. "Nothing but power this time. I'm going to throw this ball right by him."

And I did.

May 7—St. Louis

St. Louis dripped cold midnight raindrops when we deplaned from Philadelphia. The dark weather symbolized the reception we expected for the long home stand ahead. A last-place ball club can expect to be the target of a particularly nerve-grating type of booing. We anticipated the raucous jeers of the bully-boy fan who gets his kicks kicking underdogs. Already we had rain. There's nothing so depressing as being razzed by a cloud.

The Cubs were due to arrive early in the morning. My wife and children were coming, also, arriving about noon. My family still follows the Cubs closely, although I no longer play with them. All of the Cub home games are televised in Chicago, and one member of my family watches each and every play religiously. This attention could be of great help if anybody in my family understood baseball. Unfortunately, they are simply typical fans, useless in last place, but great at waving pennants.

I pinned the blame on televised ball games one day when Timmy said, "Daddy, when I grow up I'm gonna be a white man, and a catcher." He then walked away, leaving me to explain the statement myself. Tim doesn't say much, even for a three-year-old, but he covers a lot of ground with every sentence. I'm glad he walked away, before I had a chance to comment.

Maybe Tim will be a manager or pitching coach someday. His statement shrewdly mixed common sense with wild ambition. As in the pitching advice: don't walk him but don't give him anything good to hit, and you'll be a winner.

Sure, Coach.

The Cubs lineup presented several problems, none of which were white men, and none of which were catchers. Timmy's careful attention suggested, perhaps, that he focused his ambition on the weak spots in the Cub lineup. McDaniel mumbled something unintelligible while describing how he would like to pitch to Banks. He might excusably have said, "I won't give him anything good to hit. Maybe we can pick him off first."

"Taylor's hitting the ball better this year," said Hemus, when Tony Taylor's name came up. "You used to be able to curve him to death. But he's hanging in there better this year."

McDaniel rubbed his forefinger across his cheek. "I guess I'll try to keep the ball down on him. My fast ball sinks. Even if he's a good low-ball hitter I have to pitch my best pitch against his best. That's the only way I know how to pitch."

It's every man for himself on the mound. Learn or burn, it says in the Book.

"Knock him down the first time he comes up. He won't bother you the rest of the game. All those Puerto Ricans are the same."

"Taylor's a Cuban," said Gene Green.

"Brush him back anyway. These guys want to take your bread and butter away. Let 'em know you mean business out there."

"How about Altman?" asked Smitty. "How does that pitching book say he hit us in Chicago?"

Hemus looked at Altman's page in the pitcher's book. "Stanky's been watching these guys," he said, disregarding the statistics, whatever they were. "Stanky says they've been getting Altman out with slow stuff. Lots of curve balls. He likes the ball away from him."

The meeting had opened with a pep talk. Hemus exhorted us all to "bear down now and forget those games we lost that we shouldn't have. This is a long home stand, and I think we're ready to make our move." (To the International League, sir?)

"Now," he went on, "we been losing games because we're making too many mistakes. Some of those mistakes include missing signs. We thought about changing the signs. Maybe they're too hard. But we decided not to, because we don't think we can figure out any better ones. So you're gonna have to bear down a little harder.

"From now on, anybody who misses a sign, it'll cost him two dollars. This goes for everybody. If *I* miss a sign, or my coaches, then we'll put up two bucks. I don't like to do this, but it's one way to make you bear down and not make so many mistakes."

Who, pray tell, decides when you make a mistake, O beloved and wise leader?

"Another thing. We had a little scrap the other day. I'm
sorry about what I said, but I'm not sorry about the fight.
What's more, the next time we have one of them, I want
everybody to join in. I don't want anybody laying back while
the rest of us are out on the field fighting. Let's all pull for
each other. Anybody who doesn't join the fight can put two
bucks in the kitty.

"So, let's go over the hitters," he concluded.

As boxers, or batters? I asked myself.

Having played with the Cubs and pitched against them also,
I might expect to know what they could hit and where they
would hit. Yet I had as many doubts about my ex-teammates
as I did about any other club. When you play with one team
for a couple of years, you learn what each player *can* hit,
and you watch, hopefully, to see him do it. The usual complaint of a slumping hitter is: What am I doing wrong? and
not: What are they doing to get me out? A solicitous team-
mate can't answer, "They're making you hit the slide ball."

The irritated retort is: "I can see that, dummy. Why ain't
I hitting it though?"

The truth is: "You never will."

But such remarks cause dissension, seldom do they help.

McDaniel read Walls's name from the score card. I cocked
my ears. Here was a personally interesting situation. Both of
them had been my roommates. Walls and I had discussed
everything, including hitting, and I know how he thinks but
not how he hits. McDaniel and I discussed nothing but religion, so I knew how Lindy pitched but not how he thought.

McDaniel cleared his throat and said, "Walls is a high-ball
hitter. He doesn't hit the curve ball very well. He drags a
lot."

Walls used to say, when we talked about National League
pitchers, "McDaniel's got a real good sinker ball. But he
throws me a lot of curves, and once in a while he hangs one."

Walls made three hits in the game, and McDaniel showered

in the sixth, but we won 4-3. Musial hit a fast ball over the pavilion in the ninth off Elston. (Elston used to say, "The way to pitch Stan is low and away. Nothing but fast balls.")

One of the first things Musial asked me after I had been traded to the Cardinals by the Cubs was, "How were you guys pitchin' me?"

Musial makes $100,000 a year.

May 8 — St. Louis

MY WIFE sat next to Marv Grissom during a ball game. Grissom, being on the disabled list, had to watch the game from the stands.

Anne Stewart said, "He made it the most interesting game I ever watched. Why, he plays every play, pitches every pitch in the game. He sees everything that each club is doing right, and he talks about everything that could go wrong in the game. By the time you came into the game Marv was actually sweating."

"Marv's a helluva nice guy," I said.

"Well, you know me," she went on. "When they announced you were coming in to pitch I started to shake. He leaned over and said, 'Don't you worry about him. He knows how to pitch. If they'd just give him a chance. There are plenty of clubs in the majors that would like to have him.' And when that pitcher got the single off you Marv said, 'Now that was a good pitch. Henry had no business hitting a curve ball like that. I tell you pitching will make anybody nervous.' Then he grinned at me and said, 'Believe me, it's worse watching it up here than when you're out there pitching.'

"And then you let Randy Jackson get a triple! Don't you know how to pitch him yet, Meat?"

What's more irritating than a second-guessing wife?

"Yes, dear," I said. "I've been pitching him the same way

for years. This time he hit the ball. A foot lower and Cunning-ham catches it against the fence."

"Marv said you got the ball up and Randy is a high-ball hitter."

"Didn't Marv ever make a mistake?" I grumbled. "So the ball was waist-high instead of knee-high. I had an idea, any-way. Think what Enright's going to write in the Chicago paper tomorrow!" I said. "Boom-Boom Throws Another One!"

"Oh, honey, forget Enright," she said. "You worry more about what that slob says about you than you do about pitch-ing. *He* didn't throw the pitch."

"Whose side you on, anyway?" I frowned. "How would you like it if somebody wrote up your mistakes in the paper the next day?"

She started to flare up, then sighed, "Meat, let's not fight about it. This is supposed to be our night out. Let's not talk about baseball."

I nodded my head and backed the car out of the parking lot.

"Did you know," she said, "Bobby Adams got his release? Marv told me, and, Meat, he had the saddest expression on his face when he said it. He shook his head and said, 'There goes another one. It's too bad.' I thought he was going to cry almost. How long was Adams in the majors?"

" 'Bout twelve years, I think. Marv probably is worried about himself. Whenever cut-down date comes around, you can expect some old-timer on every club to get the ax."

"You don't think they'll let Marv go, do you?" she asked.

"Nope. It looks like Phil Clark, I'm afraid."

May 9—St. Louis

CLARK called our apartment at ten o'clock to see if I would drive to the park. Since the wives had both decided to set up housekeeping in the George Washington they let us use one car to go to work each day. We were sharing the driving again, as we had done in Florida. Philip came by for a cup of coffee, helped me pry my eyes open, and wished aloud that we could all spend the summer together. On the way to the park he commented on the roundabout route I was driving.

"We went the other way yesterday," I said, "and I got shelled in the ninth inning. Got to change my luck some way, y'know."

"Yeah, Broz," he said, "but when we went the other way yesterday it didn't hurt *me*. At least ah'm still on the club!" The tone of his voice was a bit scratchy; the tension of not knowing whether or not he was the one on whom the ax would fall had finally gotten to his vocal cords. It gets so bad, you can't talk about it; but it's so important to you that you can't think of anything else.

"You're not superstitious, are you, Philip?" I asked. "I never thought *I* was till I started to play ball. One week last year I was going so good that I drove the same streets to and from the park every day. I even found myself wanting to eat the same food and to wear the same clothes. Everything like that."

"Ah'm just like that sometimes," he said. "Once, ah decided not to shave till ah lost a game. Almost had a good-lookin' beard, too. But that's when ah was goin' good."

I parked the car, climbed the stairs to the clubhouse, stripped to my shorts, and walked back to the training room. Picking up the vitamin bottle I looked around to see if there was anything I could needle Bauman about. Doc was reading a copy of *Ace*, a fan magazine for handball players. One of the few topics that Bauman and I ever discussed seriously was handball. Most handball players become fanatics about the game, or quit. Doc and I went so far as to agree that my success in the spring training was due to daily winter workouts on the handball court.

"Maybe we should go over to the gym and play a couple of

128

games," he suggested, almost seriously. He handed the maga-zine to me.

"Don't think even that'd do me any good, Doc," I sighed.

Clark came into the training room and asked, "Okay for me to call out on your phone, Doc?" He spoke in a low voice, a crushed-hope sort of tone. I tried to think of something to say.

"Gay," Philip said into the speaker, "come get me, will ya? . . . No . . . Yeah, I'll tell you about it later. Just come get me."

He dropped the phone back onto its cradle, looked down at the floor for a moment, and walked quickly from the room back to his locker. I started to follow him, thought better of it, picked up the morning paper, and went into the latrine to read.

There was nothing I could say to Philip that would help. At cut-down date in organized baseball it's every man for him-self. My first reaction was relief that it wasn't I who had just lost his job. Both Clark and I had been mutually and similarly ineffective. Neither of us had been hit too hard. Yet, it's not how you lose in the spring, but just because you lose that costs you your job. Especially when you're still trying to make the team. If Phil had been the victim of bad breaks, part of the percentages in baseball, then that was just too bad. What they were looking for in the front office was a head for the ax. Any young victim would do.

May 10—St. Louis

It was past nine o'clock by the time I returned from the ball-park. I had left the hotel at ten A.M. full of bacon and eggs and premature fatigue; for we had another double-header. The flagpole quivered in the brisk wind at Busch Stadium. The flag flapped audibly above the center field wall. Like the finger-snapping of a sardonic giant the noise greeted me as I walked up into the Cardinal dugout. One look at the flag pointing straight out over the scoreboard and I collapsed on the bench to rest. It looked like a long and windy day.

No pitcher in his right mind volunteers to pitch on such a day, unless he's a masochist, or wants to go home early. His least mistake is often turned into a fly ball that swiftly becomes a home run. Baseballs became ping-pong balls in the whipping wind. By the grace of a benevolent commissioner a new rule shall someday be adopted by the National League: When the wind velocity exceeds twenty miles per hour the pitcher may throw basketballs instead of baseballs.

Naturally, I was the first man to relieve in the first game. Disgustingly I threw a gopher ball to Thomson (a belt-high fast ball right over the outside corner. Now, Bobby shouldn't hit that ball out of the park!). Morbidly, I cursed my luck. Hungrily, I ate two cups of Bauman's chicken soup. (Doc plays chef on double-header days so that his boys don't lose weight from not having lunch.)

Nervously, I returned to the bench as we tied the score and went into extra innings. Angrily, I helped protest an umpire's decision that ruined our chance to score in the tenth. (Noren was on third when B. G. Smith grounded to Dark. With nobody out Noren headed home and was caught in a run-down. Averill, the Cub catcher, chased Noren back toward third and threw the ball to Dark. Noren suddenly stopped, turned, and ran into Averill who was still moving down the base line. As soon as he hit Averill Noren stopped, cried "Foul!" and was tagged out by Dark. Noren's play, clever as it was, didn't impress Burkhart, the umpire. Noren had deliberately run into a defensive man who didn't have the baseball. Therefore, Averill couldn't make a play on Noren. Moreover, he had no business being in Noren's way. Averill had been right behind Noren, and couldn't stop in time to avoid contact, so that his intention to obstruct—as the rules put it—was hardly premeditated. Bad intentions or not, Averill might legally have been judged guilty and the run allowed. The umpire sympathized with Averill, however. Hemus took it as a personal insult, and announced that he would protest to the highest magistrate.)

Sadly, I watched as Averill, in the eleventh, hit a fly ball that blew into the first row of seats in left field, to win the game for Chicago, 10-9. Singleton was the winning pitcher for the Cubs; McDaniel lost it. Singleton, McDaniel, and I, plus four other pitchers, got into the second game, also. McDaniel won this one and Singleton lost it. For seven hours we played to a virtual draw. It's an ill wind that blows straight out from home plate.

May 12—St. Louis

WHEN I reached the sixth floor of the George Washington I had to put the box down before I could open the elevator door. I knocked on the apartment door with my elbow. Anne Stewart opened the door, looked at me with dismay, and said, "What's in the box? You been released?"

"Fat chance!" I said. "No, this is full of books from my locker that I've already read, and fan mail for you to answer, and some publicity pictures and clippings. Look at this one." I tossed her a clipping from the sports page of the Chicago *American*.

"Meat, you didn't go out and buy a Chicago paper just to see if Enright called you names, did you?"

"No, that's just a clipping. See? One of my agitating friends from Northfield sent it. No comments. Just the clipping. He's got a great sense of humor."

"Hmm," she read to herself. "This isn't too bad. Enright's gotten on you worse than this." She tossed the clipping back onto the table. I showed her an Associated Press photograph taken when Roseboro flipped me over his back.

131

"Oh, God," she laughed. "You look like you're dead. Does your back still bother you? Poor baby, come give Mommy a kiss."

"Let's have a drink first to get me in the mood, huh?"

"Funny boy!" She picked up the clipping again and smiled. "Old Boom-Boom. Enright really pinned one on you, didn't he? Do the fans in Chicago ever call you that during a ball game?"

"Yeah, sure. They even came down here to yell Boom-Boom one night. If Harry Caray ever gets a hold of that name, the St. Louis fans will never hear the end of it."

"What's Caray got against you, anyway, Meat?"

I stirred the martini while I brooded about it. "To hell with Tomato-Face. He's one of those emotional radio guys. All from the heart, y'know? I guess he thinks I'm letting the Cardinals down, and he's taking it as a personal insult."

"Well, you ought to spit tobacco juice on his shoe, or something. It's awful the way he blames you for everything that's going wrong. Other pitchers make mistakes and he's got a million alibis. No excuses where you're concerned, though. No, sir!"

"Let's not get off my pet subject, now," I said, handing her a water glass full of martinis. "I've got just enough of a mad on to cover Enright; and that's no small task considering he's the size of a small elephant." Dipping a potato chip into the sour cream and onion dip, I chewed on my dilemma.

"I shouldn't let these baseball writers bother me. There are some opinion-makers in baseball for whom I have a great deal of respect. One of them told me in Phoenix one day that baseball writers aren't really interested in what the public thinks. They write to please each other. They get together during the season to drink booze, free-load wherever and whenever they can, and listen to each other's opinions about baseball. Then they go to their typewriters and write whatever they forgot to say in the bull sessions. It wasn't put exactly that way but the suggestion that it is ridiculous to get mad at baseball writers was obviously intelligent advice."

"Well, that's true," she said, "but Enright is the kind of guy that gets one player on his list and that's the only guy he gives those special blasts of his. He must have considered it a personal triumph when he got the Cubs to trade you last year."

I laughed, although she had spoken a near-truth probably. "T-Bone Phillips told me in the outfield the other night that Enright is after *him*, now. In his column just last week Enright had T-Bone traded already."

"One of these days some ballplayer is going to be just mad enough to pop him one," she said.

Baseball writers as a rule are by no means abnormal. Some people even claim that they are human. Unfortunately, when the baseball writer becomes a fan, he loses most of his objectivity about the game. Writers on the afternoon papers, especially, are required to pull a rabbit out of the hat for each edition. The story of the game is usually stale news by the time the afternoon papers hit the street. To what extremes those writers can go, then, for a story!

Some baseball writers write with a stiletto dipped in their own venomous bile. San Francisco writers describe the baseball scene with all of the precision of three-year-old children finger-painting on the playroom wall. Philadelphia writers have the reputation of being sneaky, most of them. A player hardly dares open his mouth in Philadelphia even to yawn; a sports column will print the episode the next day and hint that some players may be smoking the wrong kind of cigarettes.

New York writers, by and large, were the fairest critics I ever saw in baseball. Unfortunately, National League teams don't go there any more. Dick Young was the greatest reporter I've seen. He printed many intimate, true stories about ballplayers. It seemed as though he had an invisible cloak that permitted him access to private locker room conversations. Some players said he was really a termite and crawled between the walls. But then, Young had his pet projects, too, and ballplayers resent being scapegoats, symbols, and story-material rather than normal men with a little extra athletic talent. Some people even claim that ballplayers are human.

May 14 — St. Louis

THERE is a fine line between constructive criticism and second-guessing. In a major league bullpen this fine line is trampled upon, erased, and laughed at, daily. Criticism in the bullpen is eminently unfair, or it just doesn't carry the proper sting. Managers who wish to observe the improper methods of second-guessing should tape-record a midseason bullpen session. Managers who once were pitchers usually are careful about how they criticize their ballplayers. "That second-guessing son-of-a-bitch" is an easily attached label. It should be avoided by all leaders.

"If Cincinnati thinks they're gonna beat the Braves out of the pennant, they're batty," I said. Milwaukee had just scored five runs to go ahead of us 7-3 in the sixth inning. I tossed a small stone at a peanut shell lying in the gravel that lined the bullpen area. An empty peanut shell when struck at the proper angle by a small stone will jump into the outfield grass. The pitcher or bullpen catcher who can do this earns a free beer after the game.

"How can you say that, Boom-Boom," said Green. "You only saw Cincinnati one game, and we don't play them again till July."

"You call me Boom-Boom one more time, big man, and I'll take my glove and go home."

Katt said, "You better get loose, Jim. Solly will probably use a hitter this inning."

"I been throwing all night," I said. "I'm ready. What the hell's he using another pitcher for, anyway? We couldn't score eight runs if they spotted us four."

Hemus wasted a hitter and I sneaked out to the mound. Charley Jones spotted me, though, and announced that I was the new pitcher. I flinched at the echoing boos.

"Never mind, buddy," I said to myself. "Where's the plate? You can get 'em. Mathews hitting, eh? We know how to pitch him, don't we? Tempt him with a sinker." He took it for a ball. "We'll give him a slide ball on his hands. . . . He took it again, eh? Lay one in there, buddy boy. Make it a strike. Harry Caray says you can't walk the first batter in an inning or he always scores."

Mathews drove the ball three-quarters of the way up the light tower above the pavilion. The ball rattled around in the tower and dropped onto the grandstand roof for a king-sized home run.

"That wasn't a very good pitch, buddy boy. Remember that. He hits the fast ball with two and nothing count on him over the fence. Next time we'll curve him, right?"

Any more tape-measure drives off me and there might not be a next time. Hank Aaron misinterpreted the red in my eye for wild anger. He took a slider right down the middle for a strike. "Maybe he's still looking for a knock-down, buddy boy. Hang another slide ball in there." I did, and he must have been. The Book *demands* a brush-back in this situation. I rubbed the ball between my hands, thinking, "What if I threw him a nice low change-up now?

"Don't be ridiculous, buddy boy! If he hits it, Pollet'll chase you clear back to Rochester!"

So I did, and Aaron took it for strike three. Aaron glanced at me as he stepped over the plate to return to the Braves' bench. He shook his head as though he had been unfairly victimized. As he passed Covington in the batter's circle Aaron said something. Covington grinned, patted Aaron on the pants, stepped to the plate, spit on his hands, and popped another change-up into the air at shortstop. A first-pitch change-of-pace? Nobody throws that!

Some days, it's better to do things backward.

As we began our half of the ninth the score was 8-4. George Crowe batted for me and I ran up to the clubhouse in order to beat the crowd into the shower. Punching a hole into a Budweiser can, I carried the beer with me so that I'd have something to do while soaking my arm. When I turned off the water and toweled myself dry, the radio was still blaring. The fans sounded like they were from Philly, roaring with unexpected pleasure.

"What's happening?" I asked Crowe, who had just walked into the clubhouse.

"Trowbridge is walking the ball park. They were takin' him out when I left."

Joe Garagiola's voice came from the radio. "Fred Haney must be chewing his nails off. There's nothing a manager hates worse than a pitcher who can't get the ball over the plate. . . . Now he's bringing in McMahon, his ace relief pitcher. This guy won't walk anybody. In the last couple years McMahon's become one of the best in the league. 'Cause he can get the ball over the plate with something on it. Haney looks a little mad out there . . . and Trowbridge isn't too happy with himself either. Well, at least McMahon'll make the Cardinals hit the ball."

McMahon made Cunningham hit a single, then he walked Blasingame and Cimoli to force in two runs. Out came Haney, out went McMahon, and in came Lew Burdette.

"I don't dare say it again, maybe," said Garagiola, "but one thing's sure according to statistics. Burdette won't walk anybody in. Just look at his record."

Burdette walked the first man he faced, to force home our seventh run. We trailed by one, with only one out, and Musial the hitter. "Now," said Harry Caray, "if Brosnan had just been able to hold them for two innings we'd be all tied up."

"That miserable second-guessin'. . ." I blurted out loud. "Eight runs they score and I give up the big one."

Musial grounded into a double play and sent everybody home unhappy.

136

May 16—St. Louis

"ROCK-AND-ROLL rattles my nerves, Stash," I said. I flipped the reject switch on the record player. Musial and I were the only players left in the Cardinal lounge, an air-conditioned room in the Cardinal clubhouse that is devoted to rest and relaxation before ball games. Musial looked up from the lounge chair on which he'd been lying. "Put something with some rhythm on there, James. I gotta practice," he said. He picked up two drumsticks and rattled the floorboards.

"You been benched today?" I asked. "Here's a Shearing record. You like jazz, Stan?"

"Sure. Any kind of music. What's the difference? Listen to this, now." He beat the drumsticks against the side of the record player, ruining whatever Shearing was trying to say on the piano.

"You're not playing today though, are you, Stash?"

Musial tossed the sticks on top of the record pile and said, "Nah, I'm resting today. After playing last night I'm still a little stiff. Better to rest a day. Then I'll be ready tomorrow. Let's go sit on the bench. You can tell me all about the world situation. What's new in the stock market?"

I never can figure out when Musial is trying to needle me. That's the mark of a good agitator. Stan never had much opportunity to enjoy the pleasures of the bench-warmer. Playing every day he had to take more needling than he had time to give. Loud laughter on the bench frequently means that some regular has just been cut up; in a diplomatic way, of course. Musial occasionally evinced a rare talent for agitation. If he only was able to sit on the bench now and then!

The game had already started when we reached the field. The bench in the Cardinal dugout is ninety feet long. The manager and his staff sat at the south end, near the plate. I usually sat at the far north end for the first two or three innings. On day games when the sun was bright I stayed on the bench as long as possible. Musial declined a chew, accepted a stick of gum, and said, "You pitchers got it made."

"How do you like watching the game from in here, Stanley?" I asked.

He frowned, bit his lip, and said, "That's where I want to watch these games from someday." He pointed to the press box atop the grandstand roof. Or maybe he meant the owner's private box.

"You just save your salary for another week or two, Stan, and you can buy yourself a ball club."

Musial's expression darkened slightly. "You're always agitating me about money. You don't resent the fact that I made my share out of baseball, do you, Jim?"

He had me there. I couldn't say "No" without telling a lie. I couldn't say "Yes" without fearing he'd think it was the truth. I didn't resent the fact of his share any more than I did Rockefeller's share, or James Thurber's share, or any other guy who had so much more talent than I. (Perhaps I had just a little bit of resentment to balance the unequal distribution.)

"Hell no, Stash," I said. "Why should I resent the fact that you just made more money in the time it took you to take one breath than I'll make all day?"

He laughed at my laughing at myself. "Let's talk about pitching. You pitchers got it made. Work one day out of four. Sit around the rest of the time. Maybe I shoulda stuck to pitching."

"Don't tell your wife you're going back on the mound. She'll have a heart attack. Roberts didn't look too sharp last night, did he?" I asked.

"He wasn't throwing as hard as he did in Philly last week. But I understand one of his relatives died the other day," Musial said.

"That probably took something out of him," I agreed. "People don't realize all the things that affect pitchers, y'know? Even managers don't stop to figure it out sometimes.

138

Take this Gordon over at Cleveland. He was quoted the other day as saying, 'Pitchers aren't human beings; they're freaks. One day they look good, or maybe one inning. Then they change for no good reason.' He said that nobody knows how to handle pitchers. He just prays!"

Musial nodded his head. "Gordon's right. You guys make pitching harder than it really is. All you gotta do is find out what a batter can't hit and pitch him there. You got any problems in the future you call time and ask me. I know how to pitch everybody in this league."

Such arrogance could only come from a first baseman.

May 20—St. Louis

SUDDENLY the sun has started to shine on us every day. The humid weather in St. Louis can put the damper on 'most any outdoor enthusiasm. But when a ballplayer is winning, even his sweat smells good.

The cigars in Hemus's mouth are bigger and blacker. He smokes them more slowly, obviously enjoying them for a change. His notebook has been blank for days; the pen with which he noted mistakes is dry. Keane and Pollet are smiling at least once a day. Walker has temporarily lost his ambition. Finally, the runs are coming.

Yesterday we scored eight runs on twelve hits; last Saturday we scored eight runs on twelve hits; the night before we got twelve hits and eight runs. Sunday and Monday it rained. No runs. No hits. Just rain. The habit should be forming in the hitter's mind. Why not brainwash the starting lineup so that they all would be depressed if they didn't make twelve hits and score eight runs per game?

"I said all along we'd start hitting, didn't I?" said Hemus. (What he said was, "You guys ought to be hitting better than you are." When did the "you" become "we," O wise and beloved leader?)

In the bullpen the unemployment sign has been hung out. What starting pitcher can't go nine knowing he'll get eight runs to work with? Pitching needs a positive, confident attitude; and when you know how to pitch, you completely dominate the situation. Nothing is more likely to give a pitcher a positive, confident attitude than eight big ones on his side of the scoreboard. Nothing, that is, except an independent income.

Bullpen conversation turned from agitation and second-guessing to bird-dogging and other games. Some pitchers like the bullpen because of the contacts they can make. A certain type of fan will sit daily in the first row behind the bullpen bench. There she can be seen with a ballplayer without her reputation being hurt. Some other fans sit six to eight rows farther back. These fans would rather be heard than seen by ballplayers. Major league bird-dogging is played under the same rules as street-corner scouting or drugstore cowboying. Only the results are different, to satisfy the ego. Or is it the id?

The old shell game regained its popularity, also. Mizell scared us by wobbling through the first inning. We had chosen sides in the pen, two men to a team, the first team to stone the peanut shell into the grass to be declared winner. The "stones" are actually small enough to be called half-pebbles. Only one-fourth the size of a small marble and considerably lighter, they come sixty to the handful. Green and I had scooped up a load when Mizell let a run score. Pollet, on the bench sixty yards away, wagged for our attention. He curled one finger on each side of his nose, miming a pair of glasses.

"Which one of us does he want?" Nunn asked me.

"I don't care. You want to work?" I said.

"Both of you better get up then," said Katt.

We both got up to throw, but Skinner hit into a double play before I could tell how my arm felt. Some nights I notice within the first ten pitches that I have left my best stuff back at the hotel. Laying off one whole week hadn't helped much.

"Let's get on with the game," said Green.

I picked up a handful of stones and aimed one at the peanut shell, knocking it a good two inches further. "Right out of bed," I said. "They ain't got a chance tonight, Greenie."

Bill Smith was paired with Alex Kellner. Kellner is known as the "King" because of his unerring accuracy with the thrown stone. He popped their shell with his first three tosses.

"The King's hot," cried Smith. "Look at him go."

Their peanut shell lodged behind a small rock, however, giving us a momentary advantage. "Gotta go to work now," Kellner said.

Meanwhile, out on the mound, Bob Friend of the Pirates was having his troubles. Three squibs, a bunt, a bad hop, and a long fly ball gave us four runs in the second. Friend had soured his pitching reputation by losing six straight games to start Pittsburgh's season. If this was the way he lost them he must be near tears. Sure enough. Cimoli blooped a single to right field and Murtaugh, the Pirate manager, came out of the dugout to remove Friend.

"Look at 'im go!" said Nunn. Friend hadn't waited for the relief pitcher to reach the mound. Tossing the ball at Murtaugh, he ran for the clubhouse.

"Jeez," said Green, "I think he's cryin'!"

"The poor bastard!" I said. I tossed the remainder of my stones away and fixed a new chew. There must be a better way to make a living.

May 22—St. Louis

ONE of the seemingly endless attractions of baseball that fans invent is the short workday, the easy hours. One of the most common gripes of baseball players is the irregular, sometimes intolerable, hours they keep. Somehow the word isn't getting through to someone.

141

After a dreary, soggy losing game on Thursday night we took to the air in order to be in Chicago in time for the two o'clock game today, Friday. Our happy-to-be-associated-with-a-major-league-ball-club pilot detoured around Hudson's Bay to avoid a rain squall and landed us at Midway Airport at three A.M. An hour's ride on a slow bus to the Knickerbocker Hotel left us with time enough for two decisions: go to sleep for five hours and feel logy during the game; or stay up the rest of the morning and feel lousy during the game. Some players, of course, have trained judiciously for the latter alternative. You sometimes can't tell the well-rested from the extra-relaxed . . . without a sobriety test.

Hemus, with uncanny and rare foresight, had sent the starting pitcher to Chicago the day before so that he'd have a good night's sleep. Theoretically, the pitcher needs his rest more than any other player because he works harder during the game. On the other hand, some pitchers are so upset after an unaccustomed good night's sleep that they are mentally incapable of doing their best.

I called my wife and told her to bring the kids to the game and we'd have dinner on the way back to Morton Grove.

"It's supposed to rain," she said, pessimistically canceling a dinner date before she accepted it.

"Come early," I countered. "We'll have lunch."

The clouds faked a storm once, then regrouped just north of the ball park to see if the umpires would ignore the threat. Nothing daunts some umpires. We started the game at two o'clock. The rain started at two-fifteen, a teasing drizzle that irritated the umpire but not hard enough for a postponement of play. Burkhart, the home-plate umpire, spent half his time looking at the sky, a fourth of his time watching pitches, and the rest of the time apparently thinking, a dangerous habit for umpires. Just call 'em as you think you see 'em, boys!

At the end of the sixth, Burkhart took his cap off to rub his head and two large errant raindrops spattered his skull. He halted play, ordered the nylon cover to be placed on the field and went to his dressing room for a cup of coffee. As soon as the field was covered the rain stopped, completely. Old Jupe laughed to see such sport, and my wife came storming down the aisle to the bullpen. "These kids are going to catch their death of pneumonia, Meat. I'll wait for you in the car. We're parked in the Cubs' parking lot."

"Pray for one downpour," I said.

"Let's go home, Daddy," said Jamie.

"Bring me a baseball," said Tim.

"Why don't you start loosening up, Jim?" said Pollet. "This long rest may have stiffened Blaylock's arm up."

The game continued. The drizzle returned in the eighth. We led 1-0 as the ninth began. Thomson singled and Jackson bunted. Blaylock tried to force Thomson at second and threw the ball into the dirt. Everyone was safe but Blaylock and me. Hemus took Blaylock out and told me to "Get offa here quick, now, and throw that runner out at third."

Hemus figured that the next batter would bunt, but he didn't. He struck out. Averill batted for Elston, the pitcher. "I'm not going to let this guy get a hit, now," I said to myself. "That might make Elsie the winner. Horrible thought."

Averill is a high-ball, inside hitter. We threw him a slider away for a strike, another one for a ball, then played trumps —a sinker down and inside. He banged it into the ground to my right and I said to myself, "Double play!" The ball bounced away from Boyer, rolled past Grammas, and trickled into left field. The runner on second ran home to tie the score. "Jesus," I thought, "when the hell am I gonna get a break?"

Goryl hit the first pitch on the ground to my right. This time it worked.

Another hour passed. Rain dripped lightly but steadily. The wind blew vigorously from the northeast, gladdening my heart. Banks hit a drive into left center that I kissed good-by, but the wind held it against the vines for B. G. Smith to catch. The rest of the Cubs pretended I was Christy Mathewson and retired in order.

As the fourteenth inning started I was the first hitter. "Now he'll take me out," I thought.

"No, I won't," thought Hemus.

Bill Henry was the Cub pitcher. He looked tired. Al Dark was the Cub third baseman. He looked tired, too. As a hitter I'm a pretty tired-looking specimen. The analytical solution was for me to bunt. I did. Henry let it roll toward Dark who let it roll to the bag. The 412 fans left in the stands booed this strategical byplay. I stood on first, looking for the bunt sign.

Blasingame laid down a beautiful bunt and I slogged a path toward second. The ball beat me but I dove head first, anyway. What grand fun it is to run bases! Just like when I was a kid.

Cimoli then hit a long fly ball into the gloomy haze of right field. Thomson played the ball as if he were afraid it might explode on contact. Keane jumped joyously at third, waving Blazer home with a run. Cimoli later scored on a fly ball.

Only three outs to go and I had my first win of the year. It sometimes is hard to get that cherry. I could almost hear my wife faint in the parking lot. She gets nervous. Long was the first hitter for the Cubs. I walked him on four pitches and Harry Caray fainted in the press box. "Never walk that first batter. He'll always score!"

Thomson swung at a bad pitch to help me out. I wasted a slider away, then came inside with a sinker. He hit it perfectly, right to shortstop, for a double play. One lone fan booed Thomson. Dark looked at three straight strikes. Frequently I'll throw Dark four or five sliders in a row. But why fool around with that wind blowing in? He's still looking for something besides a fast ball.

"Meat, we've been sitting here for hours!" my wife said when I finally found the car.

"Be glad I'm not superstitious. I'd make you sit in the car every game I pitched."

She growled at Timmy, who was throwing the ball at the car window. "We'll get half a dozen phone calls tonight wanting to know why you can't beat anybody but the Cubs." She laughed. "Isn't it funny. Why can't you, Meat?"

Any old club in a storm, I always say.

May 25—St. Louis

To the pitcher his Earned Run Average is a precious statistic. It represents a certain, measurable, accountable value. The E.R.A. is frequently marketable; it commands a price from the club owner. Its value, in dollars, is often distorted during the traditional bargaining between general manager and pitcher.

"You led the league in E.R.A., yes, but you won fourteen and lost fifteen. You weren't even a .500 pitcher! How can a manager win a pennant with pitchers who can't win half of their games?" Or:

"You won twenty games, yes, but look at your E.R.A.— 3.75! That's a lot of runs to overcome. Good thing our side scored so much when you were pitching." Or:

"You led the league in E.R.A., and won twenty games, but the wind blew in every time you pitched; and your defense played spectacularly behind you. Besides, you didn't strike out twice as many batters as you walked, and you know how important that is." (It is not nearly as basic as wins and losses or E.R.A., but the G.M. has to have some argument. Branch Rickey's pitching ratio of strike-outs and walks is a current fad.)

The Earned Run Average is often hidden, semantically, during salary discussion, but in pitchers' minds its sparkle is undimmed. It can be said that twenty wins stem from a combination of good hitting, good fielding, good pitching, and good luck. The pitcher controls only two of those factors, and sometimes his defense fails him by not playing where he told it to. Twice as many strike-outs as walks represents a

Power Ratio that too often indicates that the pitcher has one superior pitch (his strike-out pitch). A good pitcher may not have superior stuff yet know how to pitch. His pitching ability is best reflected in his Earned Run Average. From experience professionals come to realize that a good pitcher will have a good E.R.A.; conversely, a pitcher whose E.R.A. is consistently under 3.50 gains a reputation of being a pretty good pitcher.

The number of games won by a good pitcher is somewhat incidental. It depends upon whether or not his team can score more runs than the opposition while he is still the pitcher. This, in turn, is dependent not only upon whether or not he is a good pitcher, but upon whether or not he is a good hitter. Traditional managerial strategy often dictates the use of a pinch-hitter for a pitcher, even if the pitcher is doing well. Again, a good pitcher will be replaced if he gets in trouble in a late inning if the relief pitcher is a good pitcher. The theory obviously is that a fresh good pitcher is better than a tired good pitcher. However, the good relief pitchers are humanly capable of giving up runs, also. They might make the starting pitcher's good game worthless as far as records go.

As for the relief pitcher, his chances to win games are too often dependent upon managerial whim or the smile of Fortune to merit consideration. His great value is his ability to save games, but his desire to preserve a good pitching performance for someone else may be stymied by his own tired arm. A relief pitcher may be used daily, especially if he is going good. The "save" is most vulnerable to a defensive failure or Fortune's frown, since the pitcher can afford to give up no runs during the time he is in the game. A run scored off a good relief pitcher is invariably the tying or winning run of the game. His E.R.A., alone, can be called the general basis of the relief pitcher's reputation.

The Earned Run Average details the number of runs attributable to the pitcher. During any nine innings the good pitcher bears the responsibility for the opposition scoring just three runs. Consistent success at this job is the hallmark of a good pitcher. Errors by his teammates, lack of runs scored while he's the pitcher, losses chalked against his record—none of these should dull his reputation in the professional observer's eyes.

In addition to his E.R.A. and his salary, the good pitcher prizes the challenge he receives when he goes to the mound. After he has had a bad day against a certain club, the good pitcher wants the chance to show what he has learned, and how he can apply his new knowledge. Knowing today why he was shelled yesterday is the good pitcher's most important asset. Confidence in himself is his reward; winning is the icing on the cake.

The confident, winning pitcher is king of the hill. To him just breathing is a pleasure, eating is not just a habit. Smiling is easier, pitching is fun.

May 27—San Francisco

"LAST night I was in bed at eleven o'clock," I said to Green. We sat behind the bullpen, beneath the grandstand of Seals Stadium in San Francisco. "I was listening to the Giant-Dodger game. The Giants' announcer said, 'That's the kind of break that happens to some pitchers. Like poor Harvey Haddix tonight.' Then, Fowler comes in to relieve for L.A., throws a grand-slammer to Wagner, and the dumb announcer forgets to say what happened to poor Harvey Haddix. I had to get up and go out to get a paper."

"That's as good an excuse as any," said Green. "Nobody goes to bed to stay at eleven o'clock in California."

"Why not? It's just as good in California beds as anywhere else, isn't it?" I frowned at him for interrupting my train of thought. "Anyway, Haddix *almost* pitches a perfect game for twelve innings, and this sports editor out here wants to give him a seat in the Hall of Fame. What ever happened to the old saying, 'Almost but no cigar'?"

"He must have pitched a hell of a game, though, Broz," said Kellner. "Can you imagine it, walking out toward that mound in the seventh and eighth, and seeing that scoreboard staring at you."

"Yeah. I'm not trying to take anything away from Haddix. What I'm driving at is what Haddix said after the game. Sure he pitched a great ball game. That's credit enough for an old pro. Why do the Faithless Scribes have to make something else out of it? Why don't they just describe how he did it, and leave it go at that? Once in a lifetime a guy pitches a game like that. Let him cry in private.

"Anyway, the A.P. quotes him, 'Before the game I didn't feel good. I've been fighting off a cold and I figured to do my best.' Well, that's what any pitcher is liable to say. Then, after Haddix almost pitches a perfect game and loses, he says, 'It was just another loss but it hurt a little more.' Now, that sounds like a real good pitcher. That's an old pro talking. He's tired out completely, he did his best, and it wasn't good enough. So it's just another ball game."

"Burdette must have pitched a pretty good game, too," said Green. "Bet they didn't even mention his name."

"Lew was just being stubborn, not letting the Pirates have a run. Wonder how he felt after the game?" Kellner said.

"How would you feel?" I asked. "I remember one year I was in 'B' ball at Waterloo, and a nineteen-year-old kid had a no-hitter with one out in the ninth against us. Our manager, I forget his name, let me hit for myself. This kid's winning the game 6-0, and we hadn't scored six runs in a whole week, so I just waved at three pitches and sat down. Not that I might have gotten a hit, anyway, but why not let the kid have a moment of glory? Our next hitter bunted down third and beat it out for the only hit we got. I thought that was real bush, myself."

"The game's never over till the last man's out, Broz," said Kellner. His tone of voice indicated a measure of concern for my having taken a dive.

148

"We lost a hundred games that year," I said. "Whenever the other team got three runs, that was all she wrote. I thought the kid deserved a break, that's all. I wonder what ever happened to him?"

"He's probably still trying," said Green. "What's his name? Maybe I played against him."

"I don't remember," I said. "That was a season I tried to forget."

A bristle-chinned vendor unstrapped his tray of miniature Willie Mays bats and National League team pennants. "Let me sit down, boys," he said. "Any of you guys want a coffee?"

I shook my head. "What inning is it?" I said.

"Last of the fifth," said Green, who had gone out to the bullpen bench to bum a cigarette.

"Let's hurry up and get this over with," I said. "The Club Hangover is swinging."

May 30—Los Angeles

As I unpacked my duffel bag in the Los Angeles Coliseum locker room I could find only one pair of baseball shoes. Ordinarily that's all I wear, and hardly ever do I miss the second pair. Twice during each season I'll rip the leather on my right shoe and require a replacement. This year the rip came early; the bullpen mound at San Francisco is composed of old lava. It slices shoe leather like a razor slits skin. Fortunately I hadn't yielded to the temptation to throw the torn shoe through the Frisco locker room window after the game. I would have looked ridiculous, even in Los Angeles, pitching in my sanitary hose.

"How the hell could I forget them?" I mumbled to myself. Boyer, who shared my locker, glanced at me as I spilled shirts, uniform, jock straps, and books onto the cement floor.

"What's the trouble, James?" he asked. "Forget your stuff?"

I could feel the blush on my cheeks, but restrained my temper. You can never tell when Boyer is needling you. So I hadn't been doing too well; I still had good stuff!

"Everything's gonna be all right, dad. What size shoe do you wear?" I asked him.

"Small, James, too small," he said. Boyer pointed at the slitted-toe shoe in my left hand. "What's wrong with that one? You guys in the bullpen oughta all wear slippers like that. Smoke your pipe during the game. Know what I mean?"

"How can I go on the field with my pitching shoe torn up?" I moaned. "Jocko sees this and he'll throw me out of the game."

Jocko Conlan is the oldest, wisest, and sharpest of National League umpires. He knows his decisions are perfectly correct; it is useless to argue with him. His regal demeanor when calling a play or giving advice to young players may justifiably be compared to that of God Almighty. And why not?

"Kid," he said to me one day in 1954, "the next time you come up to the plate I want you to have on a new pair of shoes. Those are a disgrace."

My shoes were only three seasons old at the time and had been patched with the best cowhide. "Conlan's a snob," I concluded. The next day the Wilson Sporting Goods Company suggested to me that it's easier to pitch in the big leagues wearing baseball shoes with Ne-O-Lite soles. I was willing to try anything at the time, and when Wilson offered me two pair of shoes a season in exchange for my signature, I grabbed the man's pen. "Watch Jocko's eyes pop, now," I said, gloating.

Jocko didn't see me again for two years. The Cubs sent me to Texas ostensibly to save me from being killed on the Wrigley Field mound. "Every time Brosnan sticks his head out of the dugout somebody hits a line drive at it," said one of the Cub coaches.

Conlan and the National League's hitters welcomed me back in 1956. Jocko eyed me up and down, noted the shined shoes, the properly rolled pants (two inches below the knee), sniffed to see if my sweatshirt was reasonably fresh, and said, "Brosnan, you're all right. Work hard now, and you'll be a good pitcher. You got the stuff."

Each spring he repeats this same speech. One of these days, maybe . . .

I didn't run with the pitchers before the game. "If Pollet asks me why not," I decided, "I'll show him my shoe." The outfield grass in the Coliseum is thick, and usually wet at dusk when pitchers run. What if I caught pneumonia in my pitching toe? Might mean the pennant.

Cheerfully I scrunched into the far corner of the dugout as the game began. Green plumped himself down beside me, belched, and groaned, "Why don't he play me, tonight, with Podres pitching? I always hit lefties real good, right?"

"Gene, buddy, you can play on my team any old night," I consoled him. "Don't ask me how Mighty Mouse thinks. Why don't you call Devine and ask him to play you or trade you? That's getting to be a popular saying nowadays."

Green suddenly grabbed his glove and dashed outside to the bullpen. In the Coliseum, where all ball games are haphazardly conducted, the visitors' bullpen is ten and half feet north of the dugout. A similar arrangement exists in another semi-pro ball park at Millington, Maryland. Only the players have been changed, to bring higher ticket prices at the gate.

Green spent most of the game in the bullpen. The Dodgers threatened to score in every inning. Broglio, who relieved Cheney in the second for us, fought the Dodgers gamely with his big curve ball until the eighth. Broglio fought the Dodgers, who scored just three times; Broglio fought Smith, the catcher, who smothered most of Ernie's best blows (a spinning curve ball that caroms off the plate against a catcher's shoulder carries a wicked punch); Broglio fought dramatically with Shag Crawford, the umpire. Crawford won every round.

Broglio, though still a rookie, has mastered the art of agitating the umpire. The mobile features of his lightly bearded Italian face assume an expression of heartbroken sorrow when an umpire misses a pitch. Ernie can also sneer mightily, if the umpire misses a second pitch; or he'll smile, sardonically, as if to inform the fans that the umpire is, unfortunately, incompetent, but what can you do?

One of the most graceful, almost ballet-like, gestures that pitchers use to irritate the umpire's pride requires, ordinarily, years of practice. Broglio must have worked on it during the off-season. One second after a miscall is made, Ernie pirouettes to his right (if he were a southpaw he'd turn to the left), his outstretched arms swooping skyward, his bleeding (from sweat) palms upturned in fervent plea to the gods. Rigoletto, in his aria of frustrated torment, is a gay and jolly troubadour by comparison.

As the innings go by and his curve ball breaks bigger and better, Broglio plays an encore of embittered mimicry. Resting his palms wearily upon his kness, he rocks back and forth. Head down, staring at the ground, he growls. It looks like he's talking to the Devil, himself. *Satanic* is an easily mastered, though impolite, language.

Swearing has a useful psychological function. Man can cry no longer after his childhood ends; groaning is discouraged as unvirile. As a nervous stimulant in a crisis swearing is unequaled. For reasons of prudish public relations the only acceptable method of swearing in the National League involves Silent Screaming. Audible cuss words are subject to fine; the words, and the equivalent fine in dollars, are publicly displayed in the locker rooms for the ballplayers' studious regard. Some expressions are worth more than others, both monetarily and psychologically.

Broglio's wide mouth and thick nether lip produce a bubbling-caldron effect from Silent Screaming. The observant umpire, or other interested parties, may notice the howling of dogs in the distance. Silent Screaming, by masters, often reaches a high pitch.

Shag Crawford, the umpire in our game with the Dodgers, had a typical set-to with Broglio. The big curve ball is difficult for an umpire to judge. The best umpires admit it. Some astigmatic physicists have declared that there is no such thing as a curve ball. Some umpires waver between science and sanity when it comes time to call a curve ball a strike. From the angle of the dugout it often appears that a reasonably attentive umpire could hardly have missed the pitch.

"Get those bottle caps out of your eyes, Crawford, you homer!" said the Dugout.

Crawford tore off his mask, and ran toward our dugout. Broglio had needled him for an hour, agitated him, and finally caused his ears to twitch. (The dull, phlegmatic umpire simply turns red at the neck. Crawford quivers when the needle jabs home.)

"You! Get outa here!" Crawford yelled. "Crowe! You hear me, get outa here!"

"Who, me?" said Crowe. George had just walked to the water fountain, and hadn't opened his mouth except to drink. The noise of the final straw falling on Crawford's patience had come from near the water fountain. Somebody had to go.

"Shag! It wasn't Crowe, Shag. It was me, Shag!" said half a dozen Cardinals. Crowe jumped out of the dugout and ran after Crawford. "How can you throw me out? I didn't say a thing! What's wrong with you, anyway?"

Some umpires have trouble with the big curve ball. I can see why Crawford may have missed a pitch or two. But Crowe is six feet four inches tall and weighs 230 pounds.

June 3——Pittsburgh

"What's an introvert, Prof?"

Cunningham and I stood in the outfield at Forbes Field, in Pittsburgh, as the Cardinal batting practice began.

"An introvert, Joey, is a guy who stands in right field during batting practice, saying nothing to anyone, and catching only those baseballs hit right at him that might be dangerous."

"You're an introvert, then, huh?" Cunningham said. "You might be surprised but I'm interested in things like that. You read a lot of books. Where can I learn more about introverts and extroverts? I want to know what I am."

"If I don't get to pitch pretty soon," I said, "you can learn something from me. I'm going to become an extrovert and blow my top."

"Yeah," Joe said, "you haven't pitched since that time you won in Chi. It's funny."

"Hilarious," I agreed. "Where you playing, today, Joe? Did he tell you?"

"As of right now, this minute, I'm starting in right field. But there's an hour left before game time, so don't mark me down in your score card yet."

"It's about time he let you play every day, Joe."

Cunningham shook his head. "I don't know about this right field, though. Tell me, Prof, you think I'm improving out here?"

"Stand around here with me and you'll improve yourself right back onto the bench," I said.

"You're kinda bitter, aren't ya, Jim? In Japan, you were full of laughs all the time. Everybody was beginning to think you were really a nice guy, after all."

I smiled a bitter smile. "That's when I was going good, Joe."

"You weren't pitching though, remember."

"In Japan, Joey, you didn't have to pitch to go good."

"Whaddya tryin' to say, Professor?" He laughed and ran back to the dugout to take his hitting practice.

Pollet sneaked up on me as I dozed. "James, wake up. You're startin' the second game in Philadelphia on Sunday."

What a way to be jolted from a lazy reverie!

"Did you say 'startin' Sunday,' Howard?" I asked. "What's going on?"

154

"Don't you want to start?" Pollet asked.

I shrugged my shoulders. My nerves had been conditioned all spring for the tensions of a relief pitcher. "Sure, why not?" I said.

But this is so sudden, Solly. There must be something fishy going on. Not having pitched in a week, I should be strong, though. I'll go ask Bauman if he's got any of those nine-inning pills. Imagine! Starting a game!

June 7—Philadelphia

RIDING on the train back from New York to Philly I figured it out. Hemus had decided to trade me. Philadelphia needed a relief pitcher; and I was a relief pitcher. To avoid the chance that I might not get into a game at Philly Hemus decided to start me. After June 15 there could be no trades between teams. June 15 was only one week away; just time enough to set up a showcase. There was no other sensible reason. I had pitched poorly against Philly three times within the last six weeks. But we had lost ten games already on the road trip; another would be hardly noticed. If I pitched well, Philly might give up somebody of value. Hemus had played for Philly in 1958 and must know the players he wanted on his club. Hemus didn't like me. I didn't like Hemus. I didn't like Philadelphia either. It's too far from New York. Why couldn't he have started me against San Francisco? That's a good town.

By the time I reached Connie Mack Stadium I had talked myself into a depressing cynicism. Warming up before the game I didn't feel right. Just hot under the collar.

Ashburn led off for Philly. "I'll curve him," I thought. Ashburn looked at four curve balls and walked.

Bouchee hit second. "I'll jam him with sliders," I thought. Bouchee popped up.

Freese hit third. "I got to keep the ball down," I thought. Freese hit a high slider into the upper deck of the left field stands. The Philly fans started to laugh, again. (Those miserable fans.)

Philley hit fourth. "I'll be careful with him," I thought. "Last time I overpowered him with fast balls. Wind's blowing out to right. I'll make him hit to left." Philley pulled a sinker ball into right field for a single. I could see action in the bullpen down the right field line.

Harry Anderson hit fifth. I had played semi-pro ball with Harry when I was in the Army. "He can't hit the ball up and in," I thought. Anderson ripped a slider up and away from him off the scoreboard for a triple. Hemus ran to the dugout phone.

Sawatski was sixth. "Keep the ball up on him," I thought. I felt helpless. My directions weren't getting through to my arm. Sawatski lined a 3-2 pitch into right field. "At least I didn't walk him," I thought.

"Just like batting practice!" yelled a miserable fan.

George Anderson hit seventh. "Here, Sparky," I said to myself. "Hit it." George Anderson lined a single to center. Out of the dugout came Hemus.

How do you like that for a start?

June 8—St. Louis

BY THE time I woke up in the George Washington Hotel, in St. Louis, my family had arrived from Chicago for the home stand. Two weeks together in the summer! Another Brosnan first. "You're just going to have to talk Hemus into letting you drive me back on the twenty-second, Meat," she said. We unpacked the car, the bags, the condiment boxes, and the booze carton. "I just can't make that drive alone with two kids in this heat. I'm exhausted."

"Maybe we won't be making this trip any more after this week," I said. "After that catastrophe yesterday in Philly I've got a hunch I may not be wanted in St. Louis."

156

"Or anywhere else, for that matter," she said sympathetically. "What in the world happened to you?"

"Here, Daddy," said Tim, "let's play ball." He threw a small black handball at me.

"Why in God's name don't you give this kid a book or something? Play ball! That's all he thinks about." I rolled the ball under the couch to discourage him.

"What did Pollet say?" she asked.

"Old Two-and-Two?" I laughed. "He talked about everything but pitching during the second game. I was out in the bullpen. Man, have they made changes out there."

"Who'd they send out?"

"Gene Green, for one. And Nunn and Bill Smith. And Essegian. You don't know him, do you?"

"No," she said. "When did all this happen? I don't get a thing in that Chicago *Tribune*. Just the White Sox. Who cares about the White Sox?"

"Devine met us in Pittsburgh last week," I said. "The ax started to fall the next day. The trading deadline is Sunday. I'm positive Hemus started me 'cause I'm up for sale."

"Oh, God, Meat," she moaned. "Where could they send you that would be better for me than here? I couldn't commute to any other city in the league. Do you think the Cubs might take you back? That's the only club in the league you can beat."

"That's the only reason they'd take me, too," I said. "I'd love to go to Frisco."

"You get traded to San Francisco and we've had it!" she cried.

"You never know," I said. "Let's go out to Musial's for dinner tonight, okay? You don't want to cook on your first day in town."

"What's the headwaiter's name here?" I whispered to her as we walked into Stan & Biggie's restaurant.

"I don't know," she said. "You're supposed to remember things like that."

"I never can, though," I said. "Walls used to get all over me when I was rooming with him because I didn't pay attention to the right names. Of course, Lee was a greeter in a night club himself once, you know. I guess if you do recognize these guys they give you a better table."

We were ushered into the back room, away from the crowd. Jamie and Tim asked for a cocktail, also. Tears flowed. A near-by customer groaned.

"How lucky!" Anne Stewart said. "We get practically a private room, almost in the kitchen. What a celebrity you are!"

"Don't be sarcastic. Complain to Musial when he comes in." I ordered two lobsters, and a steak for the kids. "Stan says the only decent thing they serve here is lobster, or rare beef."

"They've got the best lobster you ever tasted and you know it," she said.

"You haven't been to San Francisco yet, dear girl."

"Get off that, will you, Meat," she said. She raised her martini and smiled. "Here's to your E.R.A., honey. It must be gorgeous by now."

"You mean my lifetime, season, or starting-pitcher E.R.A.? I asked. "I figured it out on the plane last night. As a starting pitcher this season I have an Earned Run Average of 108.00! Another Cardinal first." I drained the martini and gave the olive to Jamie. "Did you know that last year at this time I was leading the league in E.R.A.? I read it in the *Sporting News* Sunday before the game."

"Why do you call Pollet 'Old Two-and-Two,' Meat?"

The waitress tied a bib over my chest. I drool a lot when I eat lobster. Timmy snickered at me for having to wear a bib. "Pollet has a theory about pitching that he's exceedingly stubborn about," I said. "Whenever a pitcher gets a count of two balls and two strikes on a batter he should throw a fast ball. Says Pollet. It doesn't seem to make any difference whether or not the pitcher *has* a fast ball or not. That's the pitch he has to throw, or answer to Howard. But I don't know.

158

"A couple of years ago I got knocked out of a game in Tulsa, so I sat in the grandstand with Ray Hayworth, the Cubs' scout, and Bill Meyer, the old Pittsburgh manager. Meyer had Pollet on his club once. We were watching the game and talking about pitchers. Who knew how to pitch, and like that. I mentioned Pollet and said I thought he was the smartest pitcher I had ever known. Within ten minutes Meyer had shattered my high opinion of Pollet. He accused Howie of being more stubborn than smart in his pitching. He said that Pollet would find one thing working for him and he'd base his ideas about pitching on that one thing.

"Now you know every pitcher is different from every other pitcher. What works for one won't work for another. Not necessarily, anyway. I don't think that Two-and-Two Theory is worth the breath to deny it. Hal Smith is getting a mental block about it. Every time a pitcher throws something besides a fast ball on a two-two count, and gives up a hit, Pollet tells Smitty, 'I told you so.' If the batter *doesn't* get a hit, Pollet still insists the fast ball would have done better."

"Eat your lobster, Meat," she said. "Before it gets cold."

Musial arrived in time to say hello and buy us an after-dinner drink. While he signed his autograph on a dozen menus for his baseball-fan customers, he confessed that business was so good that he was going to buy another bank. "That'll give us three banks with combined assets of a hundred million dollars. It's easier to do business that way."

"Now there's a celebrity," Anne Stewart sighed as we drove in overstuffed silence back to the George Washington Hotel. The room clerk called to me as we crossed the lobby to the elevator. "Solly Hemus was here just a while ago, Mr. Brosnan. He left this letter."

My blood bubbled suddenly. "That's it," I thought. "He's gone and done it." I took the sealed envelope, stuck it in my back pocket, and opened the elevator door. Anne Stewart blinked at me and said, "Please read it, Meat."

"Upstairs," I said. Bad news is best put off. Where could I be going? Philadelphia? Pittsburgh? Rochester?

I walked into the kitchen of the apartment, picked out a paring knife, put it back down on the cabinet, and ripped the envelope open with my finger. Quickly I scanned the note.

"It's from Devine," I said. . . . "We're going to Cincinnati."

"Oh, no!" she cried. Tears mingled with her moans. "Oh, God, Meat, not that. I'll never be able to drive from Chicago to Cincinnati!"

I put one arm around her shoulders, holding the letter in my other hand. "It could be worse. You can always take the train down." Mentally I reviewed old *Sporting News* statistics, upsetting my orderly consolations of her wounded spirits. What position were the Reds in? How had they been doing lately? Who's pitching over there? What's the manager's name? We had played Cincinnati just one game all year so far.

"What?" I said, vaguely having heard her ask a question.

"I said," she said, "who did they trade you for?"

"Jeffcoat," I said. "Straight swap, I guess."

"Jeffcoat!" she cried. "Couldn't they get more for you than that? Oh, honey, they just wanted to get rid of you."

"Bing wants me to call him, it says here. And Hemus, too. What should I call *him*?"

"I don't think it's a bit funny at all," she said. "Cincinnati! That's the most miserable place in the summer. My sinus will kill me down there."

("At least you've decided to go," I thought. "Will you want to go when they finally send me back to the minors next year, or in '61, or '65?") I sat back on the couch, half-breathing as I waited for indignation to flush good red blood to my head. Nothing happened. I took a deep breath, then exhaled slowly. It's true. The second time you're sold you don't feel a thing.

June 10—St. Louis

THE phone started ringing at eight-thirty in the morning. Between talking long-distance, packing all the bags and boxes and bottles again, and convincing the kids that Cincinnati had a nice zoo, too, I tired myself even before we hit the road back to Chicago. The Reds were playing the Cubs for the next three days.

"Yes," I said into the phone, "that's one good part of the deal. I can drive my family to Chicago. It's a tough trip for a woman alone with two kids. . . . No, I wasn't surprised. . . . I felt that I might be traded for sometime. . . . Sure, I think the Reds have a better ball club than St. Louis. It's a break for me. . . . No, I don't mind pitching in Cincinnati. I was born there but I haven't lived there since I started to play ball. . . . Thank you, same to you . . . Good-by."

"Who was that one?" Anne Stewart asked.

"Sports editor of the Cincinnati *Post*, I think. Or maybe he's just a reporter. Joe Quinn. He said he used to watch me fifteen years ago when I played American Legion ball. Can it be that long ago?"

"You spend any more time on that phone and we'll never get to Chicago today," she warned me. "You're supposed to see Devine when you get your stuff at the ball park. That clubhouse man, what's his name, called while you were packing the car."

"Nuts to him," I said. "I haven't got time to see Devine now. I'll talk to him when we come in Friday. The Reds come here from Chicago, y'know. I gotta pay the clubhouse dues, too. How much money did you leave in the bank? I owe him fifty bucks anyway. Then there's this hotel bill. And money for the road trip to the West Coast. Maybe I'll have to see Bing and ask him for a loan!"

The phone rang. She said, "Cincinnati, again. Gabe Paul. Who's he?"

Gabe Paul, the general manager of the Reds, wished me well, welcomed me aboard, and demanded to know why I wasn't in Chicago for the two o'clock game with the Cubs. His assurances that he was happy to have me on his club were tempered with several phrases of displeasure. Where was my enthusiasm? Wasn't I as happy as he was? Why hadn't I hopped the first plane to Wrigley Field? His speech was succinct, his voice crisply modulated, his telephone manner formidable. "This guy can really talk," I thought. There's nothing I love more than a good conversation. My ability to make a first impression depends upon verbal expression. "If you'd just keep your big mouth shut," says my wife. But I must express myself in my own way, for better or worse.

Paul and I sparred for a few minutes; he parried my belated request for permission to report a day late. I answered his question about enthusiasm with an unnecessary blurb about the great opportunity it was to be associated with him. He feigned modesty, and urged me to grab opportunity when it came my way. "Don't vacillate," he said.

Good God in the foothills! A general manager who uses the word "vacillate." That's enough to give anybody enthusiasm. We hustled out of town.

June 11—Chicago

THE high-pitched, almost girlish, laughter of Yosh Kawano, the Cubs' clubhouse man, greeted me when I arrived at Wrigley Field. I parked my car in the Cub parking lot (to the disgust of the police sergeant who takes his "clout" from fans who wish to park near the ball park. My station wagon takes up space for one and half cars, at a buck per car). I tipped Eddie a large hello, and headed for the Waveland Street entrance

162

and the long walk beneath the stands to the visiting club's dressing rooms. Kawano, rushing from the Cub clubhouse on one of his mysterious and urgent errands, spied me as I entered the gate, carrying a dusty Cardinal duffel bag.

"Finally got rid of Hemus, didn't you, Jim?" he said, as I clapped a hand on his shoulder. In my years with the Cubs Yosh Kawano and Al Scheuneman, the Cub trainer, were my closest friends on the club. Together, Yosh and Al could usually figure out most of my ballplayer's problems. Had I needed advice or consolation about my relations with Solly Hemus I'd have gotten them from Kawano and Scheuneman. But, of course, having matured as a ballplayer, I did not need advice. I just got rid of Solly. And how mature can you get?

"Yosh, is everything all right?" I asked, as I usually do. "You tell Doc that I'll be up to see him tomorrow before the game. What time does Grumpy leave the clubhouse?"

"Scheffing won't mind your coming into the clubhouse," he said. "You're welcome any time up there. You oughta know that, Jim. Doc and I'll protect you." Yosh laughed at such a likelihood.

"Yosh," I said, "I gotta run. You and Doc are coming out to supper, aren't you?"

"As soon as you invite us," he said. "Good luck over there. Wish you were over here."

"Me, too," I lied. What the hell, I hadn't had time to become unhappy with the Reds, yet!

The Reds were half-dressed by the time I walked into the clubhouse. The half-dress uniform of the Cincinnati club is the same as that of every other club I ever played with. Except the Reds wear solid red stockings over their sanitary hose. The visiting clubhouse man stood at the door as I climbed the stairs.

"Joe," I said, "I'm back already. Where did you put me?"

"You're in Jeffcoat's locker," he said. "Next to Frank Thomas."

Clubhouse men try to put each player in the same locker

every time he comes into town during the season. Since there are seven different men to each locker off and on during the year, the task of keeping the arrangement straight is painstaking, even for a clubhouse man. But why not make a man feel at home on the road? Provide comfort, earn a bigger tip.

The gloom of night prevails in the visitors' clubhouse at Wrigley Field, even with all the lights on. If I couldn't find my name (or Jeffcoat's) above a locker I could always look for Thomas instead. I didn't have to.

"Oh no," he said. "There's goes ten points off my batting average."

"Hello, Frank," I said, as he held out his hand. "You're really having a lousy year, aren't you?"

"Whaddya mean," he said.

"Well, we hadn't played you but once this season over at St. Louis. I know damn well you were counting on eight hits off me. What do you think you'd have hit last year if I hadn't pitched against you?"

"About what I'm hitting now, I guess." He smiled.

"That's nothing to laugh about, Thomas," said Frank Robinson, who shoved a huge hand at me.

Of all the reasons why I was glad to be traded to Cincinnati, being on the same team with Frank Thomas was most satisfying. In the three and a half years that I had been pitching against Thomas I hadn't gotten him out enough to remember. He had personally beaten me in three games, and had one streak of nine straight base hits, six of them for extra bases. Though he was now having a bad year at the plate so far, all he probably needed was to see me wind up on the mound and it would all come back to him.

I set my bag down on the chair and walked around the room to say hello, good to see you, glad to be here, etc. My tour of the clubhouse wound up at the manager's cubbyhole. Mayo Smith looked up from the lineup card he had filled out in triplicate. "Jimmy," he said, "glad you're here. Now, I want to talk to you in a few minutes. When did you pitch last? Never mind. You're ready to go now, aren't you? Right. Get dressed, then, and we'll have a little chat."

In Jeffcoat's locker I found a pile of red sweatshirts, a uniform, a dirty cap, and a wool-and-nylon windbreaker, all the property of the Cincinnati ball club. The shirts were too big for me, the cap too small, and the sleeveless uniform awkwardly ill-fitting. No sleeve on the uniform shirt means more freedom for the arms, I suppose. It didn't feel right to me.

Just after we started batting practice rain fell, chasing fans under the stands and ballplayers into the dugout. Mayo Smith cornered me there. "I have a proposition for you," he said. "What would you rather do, start or relieve? Now, I like to think of you as a relief pitcher. What I saw of you over at Philadelphia last year makes me think so. You seem to get tired about the seventh inning when you start a game. Right?"

I started to say, "Who doesn't?" One of the indelible blots on my pitching career has been my inability to go nine innings. Since only 20 per cent of all starting pitchers in the majors *do* go nine innings, I feel less ashamed than I should be, perhaps. Smith, who had managed Hemus at Philadelphia in 1958, had seen me lose a two-run lead twice in the late innings. In both games I had breezed for seven, then blown my victory.

"Yes, sir," I said, "whatever you think I can do for you I'll try my best. I feel that I can pitch in the majors, both as a starter and a reliever. I've done both, and had fair success most of the time. But, whatever you say."

"Well, now," he said, "which would you rather do?"

"It makes no difference to me," I said.

"I want you to be happy out there, doing what you think you'd like to do," he said.

"It's up to you," I said. The rain fell, the humidity rose, and I wondered if we'd ever get to the point. Mayo had already stated his opinion—I couldn't start. The only thing I had left to be happy with was relief.

"Here's my reason for talking to you like this," he said. "I'm desperate for a good relief pitcher, somebody who can come in and stop them for an inning or two. We score runs. I've got no complaint about that. But did you know that seventeen times this year we've had a lead in the eighth and ninth innings, and fourteen times the pitchers have blown it?"

I shook my head. "That's baseball," I thought, facetiously.

"If we had won just half those games," Smith went on, "we'd be right up there with the Braves right now instead of in sixth place. I need a relief pitcher and I think you can be the man. Now, what do you say?"

"Like I said before, Mayo, you're the boss. I get just as much kick out of saving games as I do out of winning them. I know I can pitch better than I have so far this season. I never did get myself straightened out over at St. Louis."

"You're a better pitcher than that, we know," he assured me.

June 12 — Chicago

"Just what kind of pitcher are you, do you think?"

Clyde King, the Reds' pitching coach, has a reputation for erudition. An anomaly among pitching coaches, he wants to know WHY instead of WHO, WHAT instead of WHEN. His analysis of a pitcher's style is subjective rather than objective. He had startled me with his approach.

"I really don't know what to say," I said. "What kind of pitcher do these guys say I am?"

"You're answering my question with a question," he chided me. "We won't get anywhere that way. Now, I haven't seen you pitch, so I don't know what kind of pitcher you are, myself. I've talked to the hitters on this club. They say you've got a lot of good stuff, but you're inconsistent with it. One time you'll throw a real good fast ball; the next fast ball might be straight, nothing on it. What would *you* say is your best pitch?"

166

"The one I rely on?" I asked. He nodded his head. "Well, I'd have to say I throw my slider when I'm in a jam."

"Don't you think those hitters know that by now?" he said. His attitude was that of a pedantic teacher who already knew the answers and asked questions to see if *I* knew them. Which is all right with me, as long as he had the answers to *my* questions, too. "What's wrong with your fast ball?" he asked.

I fingered the baseball he had handed me as we sat down in the bullpen. "There's nothing wrong with either one of my fast balls, I guess. I just prefer to use them to set up a hitter for the slider or change or curve, whichever is working best for me."

He gave me a quizzical look. "You have two fast balls, you say? Which is the better of the two?"

I shrugged my shoulders. Neither one of them appealed to me at times. Once in a while they both moved pretty well. "I prefer to use the one that sails away from a right-handed batter. It's better to pitch away, if possible. But that gives me three pitches that move the same way—the curve, the slider, and the sailer. And that's not too good."

"Yes," he said, "and—"

"But," I interrupted, "my sailer hasn't been moving this year. I have to let it go at a certain angle—about three-quarters instead of overhand. My other fast ball has to come directly overhand, and I've been getting the two mixed up. When I come in between, neither of them works much."

"Let's get a catcher. I want to look at what you're talking about." He called Pete Whisenant out from the bench. "Mayo might want to use you for an inning today. But a little throwing now won't hurt you."

King stood behind me as I warmed up. Discounting my last short term in a Cardinal uniform, I hadn't pitched in ten days. My arm felt strong, almost heavy, and the ball moved well. For ten minutes I threw as King directed me, mixing my two fast balls with curves and change-ups. ("We know you can throw the slider," he said.) Whisenant, another former roommate of mine (on the Cubs in 1956), shouted exuberant commands. "Give it to me right here, now. Put a little something on it. Atta boy, big man. Wow, has this guy got great stuff, Clyde. You oughta win twenty, you big stiff!"

King called a halt, took the ball, and led me back to the bench. "Pete," he asked Whisenant, "if you were hitting against Brosnan what would you look for?"

"Bross?" he said. "Well, he'd get me out on his slider a couple times, maybe, but eventually he'd hang one and I'd cream it. Bross thinks too much. And he doesn't give the hitter credit for doing some thinking, too."

"What the hell do you think I'm thinking about on the mound, Whiz?" I protested. "I'm thinking: what are you guys thinking? You oughta give me credit for respecting you, too."

"Jim," said King, "I really think you should forget about that 'sailer,' as you call it, and concentrate on your other fast ball. It rides in to a right-hander pretty well and much more consistently. Another thing. Move over on the mound. Pitch from the right-hand corner of the rubber. Bend your back leg as you start your motion home. That'll make your arm and back follow through better and keep you from being high with all your pitches. And, please, start to throw that fast ball more often. You got a better fast ball than I thought you had. You got a better one than you think you have, too."

King's advice was specific, personal, and easy to understand. I should have realized, myself, that my trouble with high pitches had stemmed from a lazy back leg. (In order to keep his pitches consistently low, a pitcher as tall as I am has to dip his back knee in order to lower the line of the projected trajectory of his pitch. Especially when he throws the slider and fast ball as often during the game as I do.)

"But if these guys think my slider's my best pitch, and the catchers at St. Louis and Chicago think so, too, why should I argue with them and throw fast balls?" I wasn't going to give up my simple style of pitching without an argument.

"Don't be simple, Bross," said Whisenant.

"You just try those things, Jim," said King. "You want to improve yourself, don't you? Wouldn't you like to make it easier on yourself out there?"

One thing all pitchers share in common is a desire to make the job easier. At last I had heard some specific directions that had come from direct observations. If King and I weren't on the right track, we were at least headed somewhere.

"Bross," said Whisenant, "you just listen to me and Clyde, and everything's gonna be all right."

"Did you hear where Grissom quit?" I asked.

"Yes, sir. That's too bad," said King. "He had a very sore back, I understand."

Grissom's decision to retire had come just ten days after he'd returned to the active list. He had made two torturous trips to the mound in that time and had been treated as painfully as he must have felt. The vision of Uncle Marv shambling determinedly to the mound like a great St. Bernard bringing relief to a floundering pitcher would haunt us no more. He'd always been on the other side until this year, so I could hardly remember his pitching with pleasure. Admiration, perhaps; respect, certainly. Yet, Grissom's presence lingers in my memory. His was a pleasant, patient personality. He made me feel like someday I might learn to be a pitcher. Marv had class. He was a true Old Pro.

June 13—St. Louis

WE HAD driven from St. Louis to Chicago in a Chevrolet station wagon. Like my wife said, it was too long a trip for comfort. The plane ride from Chicago to St. Louis three days later was too short; I hardly had time to collect my thoughts. Full of advice and newborn ambition I was still a victim of a certain indignant regret. A rash of doubt irritated my ego. Why did Devine trade me? What was the real reason? I determined to see Devine and ask him.

At four o'clock I boarded the bus to Busch Stadium. The Cardinal front office was full of scouts and bonus babies. Devine left me to cool my heels while he talked with Hemus upstairs. I had just about lost my desire to talk with him when his secretary came into the anteroom, humming to herself.

"Oh, Jim!" she said, blushing. "I forgot to tell Bing you were here. Why don't you go on up? He's getting ready to go to dinner, but I know he'll want to talk to you."

"Thanks, Helen," I said, and climbed the stairs. Hemus and his cigar rose from a chair as I looked into Devine's office.

"Come in, Jim," said Devine. "What can I do for you? I'll see you later, Solly."

"Hello, big man," said Hemus. "How are you?"

I waited till Hemus had gone before opening my mouth. "First of all, I want to pick up my check, Bing, if I can. Instead of waiting till the fifteenth. I wonder if you could have it made out for me while we're in town. I have a chance to pick up some stocks and I need the money."

"I believe your check is in the clubhouse, Jim. I'll check on it for you, though. Anything else?"

I hesitated. My chair was comfortable. We were alone. The office help had gone home. Devine seemed to be as friendly as ever. No hard feelings, Bing? I threw off caution and jumped in.

"One question, Bing. If you'll give a frank answer, I'll be grateful. Why did you get rid of me?"

"It seemed like the best thing to do," he said. He spoke swiftly, running his words together as though his thoughts were a bit tangled but would come out all right if they were whisked into sound as rapidly as possible. "You weren't doing as well as we expected. We thought the change would be good for you and for us, of course. The feeling was that you weren't helping us and weren't getting any better although we knew you could do better. We tried to get the best we could for you and we think Jeffcoat will help us. But I still wish you luck at Cincinnati, and if you straighten out over there and do as well as you should nobody will be happier than I will. I don't share the idea that I should wish you bad luck and hope you have a bad year just because I traded you. On the contrary, no one is happier than I am when Sam Jones wins ten games already this year for San Francisco, and Moon is doing well at L.A. Of course, we're happy with White and Cimoli or I might not feel so good. Are you going to start against us this weekend, incidentally?"

I said that I didn't know. "Mayo hasn't given out any information about Sunday, though. He says he's going to use me in relief." I sat up straight and leaned over on his desk. "Do you feel that I let you down, Bing?"

"Well, we all think you're a better pitcher than you've shown so far, and of course you looked awfully good this spring so we were counting on you. But after many years in this game I try to find a reason for such, uh, failures as we've had with you and I think maybe we just weren't able to find yours. Solly has said that he just didn't seem to be able to get the work out of you."

Ah ha! It takes a quick ear to catch a specific statement. "Did Solly ask you to trade me, then?"

"We all work together on things like trades. It was a decision that we all agreed upon. It is my responsibility to answer for the success or failure of the ball club. My job is in jeopardy when you and the ball club in general aren't doing as well as can be expected. Naturally I want to win more than anything else and if personal relationships interfere with winning then I must do my best to straighten things out. In your case I believe that we've made a move that will help everybody concerned. I hope so. I hope you have a good season at Cincinnati. As good a season as Jeffcoat has over here."

He sounded as if he'd said as much as he was going to say. I rose and shook his hand.

"Thank you, Bing. I've enjoyed our relationship, anyway. Good luck to you."

My check was in my locker along with two bills from the Cardinals and a fan letter from Florissant, Missouri, that said Devine was a louse, Hemus was a bum, and I was still all right. I had not finished dressing in uniform when the meeting started. Smith called me over to his locker and said, "We have played this team only once all year so far. Is there anything that any of these guys are doing that I ought to know about?"

I looked at the score-card lineup. "Blasingame has had a lot of success hitting to left field, but I think you can still jam him and curve him. Keep the ball down, I'd say. He and Cimoli love to hit-and-run. Cimoli's been hitting mostly to right. He's hit that screen a lot this season. It's just the right distance for him, I guess. He hates to be knocked down, I know, and he complains about being jammed a lot. I guess that's the best way to pitch him. He's a long way from the plate, but it's hard to get a ball by him on the outside corner, unless he's been set up pretty well."

"How about Bill White?" asked Smith. "He never looked like a .300 hitter when he was at New York."

"Bill's a pretty smart boy. He was supposed to be a low-ball power hitter, and everybody pitched him up high at the start of the season. Then he went to punching the ball, and now I'd say he's a better high-ball hitter. At least he's a good one. He's been hot, recently, I know. He's got quick hands. You can't change up on him much. The rest of these guys you know. Oliver's playing left field, I see. I didn't see enough of him this spring to say how he hits, and they brought him up just before I was traded so I don't remember too much about him. He strikes out a lot, I know. Probably has trouble with breaking stuff. He's got a lot of power."

"What's wrong with Musial?" he asked.

"I thought last year that Stan started to have trouble getting around on the ball. He's not as quick with his wrists as he used to be. But don't make a mistake! When he's feeling all right he's still a sweet hitter."

Musial stood at the batting cage with Cunningham as we

trooped onto the field after the meeting. I slapped a hand on Stan's shoulder.

"You think we'll get fined for fraternizing if Secory sees us talking here, Stash?"

"Why, James, where you been?" he said. "I've been looking all over to find somebody to talk to during the game."

"Why don't you buy Hemus's contract and ship him out, Stan? Then you could play whenever you wanted."

Cunningham poked me with his bat. "Secory's waving at you, Prof. Let's not get us fined now. Stan and I can't afford it. Right, Stanley?"

Musial tossed the heavy bat aside and walked into the cage to hit. His first three swings sent balls into the right field screen. What a sweet swing!

The night air turned warm, the mosquitoes buzzed busily, and the score stood at 1-1 as we took the field in the tenth. My new roomie, Tom Acker, was the pitcher. White singled, Boyer beat out a ground ball, and Acker wild-pitched them to second and third. Cunningham took two high pitches for balls, and Mayo called time to take Acker out and bring me in. The fans, yelling for the kill, greeted me with more-than-gracious applause. Harry Caray booed, probably, but some fanatics are incorrigibly ill-spirited. It is not unusual for a ballplayer to be unpopular one day, only to change uniforms and be welcomed a week later. Fans reserve their loudest criticism for the home team.

Dotterer, the Reds' catcher, and Smith both asked me how I was going to pitch to George Crowe, who was obviously going to pinch-hit for Flood.

"I'll have to jam him, and hope he pops it up," I said. "He takes the first pitch a lot. We'll give him one good fast ball for a strike and then throw him breaking stuff on his hands."

They both nodded. I walked Cunningham purposely to load the bases, poured the fast ball into Crowe for a called strike, then threw the slider. Crowe popped it up, but into right field. Bell came in three steps, caught the ball, and threw to the plate as White raced home from third. I cut in front of White to back up the plate. The throw was true. Dotterer reached for the ball as White slid for the plate. Suddenly the ball took a little, last-minute hop. Dotterer, one eye on the ball, the other on White's leg, didn't time the hop of the ball and it bounced off the edge of his glove into my bare hand as I stood a few feet behind the plate. It might have been a close play.

"You made the right pitch," said Mayo in the clubhouse. "Do you think you can start on Sunday?"

"Why not?"

June 15—St. Louis

ONE of the first decisions a pitcher must make when he knows he's to pitch the second game of a Sunday double-header is what time to eat breakfast. Some managers allow the second-game starter to report to the park after the first game has started. He then eats normally, four hours before his game is most likely to begin. However, rain or extra innings may prolong the start of the second game. If the pitcher eats four hours before the first game he may feel starved by the time the second game begins. Mayo declined to permit me a late arrival. "You can rest at the park just as well as at the hotel," he said.

"When will I eat, then?" I said, dismayed. It's just an old superstition, of course, but starting pitchers love to be given special handling.

My second decision of the day involved whether or not I should chew tobacco during batting practice and during the first game. I was too nervous not to. My spitting area had just turned brown when Harry Caray came down the steps into the dugout. "Here's my wife's chance," I thought. He said, "Hi ya, Jimmy boy." I aimed at his shoes, subconsciously wishing him ill. But my head turned at the last second and the tobacco splashed on the dugout steps. "I'll just ignore him," I decided. "Two-faced old . . ."

Caray sat next to Mayo Smith, wheedling opinions from him. "And what do you think of Solly taking himself off the active list? He says he can think better if he doesn't worry about keeping in shape," said Caray.

Ah, so! Hemus not going to play, eh. Not going to take a chance. Well, it's just coincidence that I'm starting today. He *knows* I wouldn't throw at him, even if I got a chance. I wouldn't think of giving him a low slider right on the knee. Nah!

We lost the first game to make it three losses in a row. As King handed me the warm-up ball for the second game, he said, "We have to have this game. Go as far as you can, now, and we'll bring you help if you need it."

I needed it in the first inning. After Ricketts, a Cardinal rookie pitcher, had walked home one run in our half of the first I told myself, "Just hold them, now. We're gonna bust loose and score ten runs." I walked Blasingame to start the inning, and walked Musial five hitters later to force in the tying run. Smith came out to talk to me.

"Just settle down, now," he said. "Clyde says for you to bend your knee. Everything's high. Now, I know you can get out of this. You got good stuff."

Hal Smith bounced a slider back to me and we were out of the inning, but I couldn't help brooding on the bench. "Nothing's going where it should. I *know* how to pitch these guys but I can't seem to do it."

The innings and hours rocked by, bumpily. I was in trouble every inning. Most of the time I pitched from a stretch, knowing that the hit-and-run or steal was on, and hoping Dotterer could throw somebody out. If I didn't make a bad pitch, I made a wild pitch and walked the batter. When I did make a bad pitch with runners in scoring position, however, the batter lined into a double play. I gave up trying to pitch and tried to throw my best stuff every time, hoping it came close to the strike zone.

By the end of the seventh inning I had thrown 150 pitches and the third finger of my right hand was bleeding from a punctured blister. The temptation to beg off pitching any more tormented me. Deservedly, over the years of my career, I had gotten the reputation of a late-inning Blister-Finger. At the end of six innings, my pitching hand inevitably developed a blister, I lost my stuff, and had to be relieved. "Blisters" was my nickname on any opponent's bench in the Pacific Coast League, 1955. Although I won seventeen games that year I needed a lot of help, and my reputation as a pitcher was slightly soiled. In the spring of '58 I finally decided, "I'm never going to be taken out of a game because of a blister again. It just isn't going to bother me any more." It's amazing what self-hypnosis can do.

Frustration ate at my pride as I sat on the Busch Stadium bench. I *had* to ignore the irritation of my bleeding finger. "It hurts when I throw breaking stuff but I can't control that anyway. So, forget it," I told Smith. Mayo, nevertheless, signaled to the bullpen to warm somebody up, and we promptly scored two runs to take a 3-1 lead.

As I trudged out to the mound in the eighth inning I had an additional frustration plaguing my conscience. "Goddamn it, I don't want to blow this, now. For Christ's sake, let me have an easy inning." Boyer lined a double off the left field wall and out came Smith waving for help. Pena came in and retired the side. I ran across the field, through the Cardinal dugout, up the stairs, into our clubhouse. As the ninth began I was at the mirror shaving and praying that Pena could hold them one more inning. He did. The radio sighed, tearfully. "Well, we won one game, anyway," cried Harry Caray. "We shoulda won that second one, too. Ricketts pitched a fine game in his first start for the Cards. It's too bad. The winner for Cincinnati was that fellow we traded. He needed help, though, in the eighth. But he still gets credit for the win."

"Shut that bum off," I said, happily.

June 18—En Route to San Francisco

"WHAT are you figuring out, Broz? Your batting average?"

I looked up from the writing table that had been inserted into my plane seat. The roar of the DC-7 motors outside my left ear was stupefying. Willard Schmidt stood in the aisle, stretching and shaking himself to relieve the stiffness of our day-long flight. Willard pointed to the paper on my table.

"No, no, Will," I said, "this is just one of my more morbid pastimes. I've been working out how much I'm worth dead. If all four motors of this plane stop, the nose turns over, and we land head-first in the Grand Canyon down there I'd be worth five times as much as I will if we land safe in Frisco."

"Yeah," he nodded. "But what good would it do ya?"

"Don't be so matter-of-fact, Willard. With all the insurance the ball club takes out on you, and double-indemnity clauses, doesn't it give you a feeling of affluence to make this trip to the Coast?"

"Feeling of what?" he asked. "Could you break that down into smaller words. I'm working a crossword puzzle."

"No, I can't, Will," I said. "When I'm talking about millions I gotta use hundred-dollar words."

"Save a couple bills for tips, there, man," said Frank Robinson. He walked by us, yelling to Pinson in the plane's galley. "Two milks and a coffee!"

Robinson returned with a tray of food, swept my money-fantasy papers onto the floor, and said, "Here ya go, man. Suck it up."

"You and Pinson always serve the food on these plane trips, Frank?" I asked.

"That's right. We feature quick courteous service from our sparkling clean kitchens. You got any complaints?"

177

"Where's the beer? The Cardinals always had a couple of cases aboard for these long flights."

"The beer was all gone five minutes after we left the ground. We got some serious drinkers on this club, man."

"You got any champagne? Or, like that?"

"Next stop for that jazz," he said.

The next stop was the International Airport in San Francisco. Hiding my chagrin at losing all that insurance money again, I rushed into the lobby, and headed for the telephone booth. We were scheduled for three games with the Giants, two of them day games. That gave us two free nights. Arrangements had to be made to free-load two dinners. That is not difficult on the West Coast. One of the principal economic motivations in California is reciprocal free-loading. "You get me two tickets for the ball game and I'll buy you a drink, feed you a meal, get you a date, etc." Five phone calls later I was set for two suppers and a lunch.

"Who are you with now?" asked the Free-loaders.

"I'm with you, dad, of course," I said. "Let's have dinner at your place and I'll bring you up to date."

It's easy.

Newcombe won the first game of the series, 2-1, under the lights. We lost the second game, under the sun. Ever since I'd joined the club, we'd played .500 ball on the road. The Book says that a ball club that breaks even away from home should be a pennant contender. The Book is a rich fund of bad logic. Why aim to break even? Why be half-ambitious? Win 'em all, or lose 'em all. Be great champs or big bums.

"That big bum can't get anybody out. Why don't your manager get him outa there?" yelled a free-loading fan behind the bullpen. In the sixth inning of the third game of the series we trailed 6-3.

Nuxhall stood helplessly on the mound, muttering to himself as Giant base hits fell safely all over the ball park. Of the thirteen Giant hits, nine had been bloops, squibs, or

Texas League singles. The wind, blowing in erratic gusts, had dropped two pop fly balls into right field instead of in Robinson's first-base glove. Temple, the second baseman, had booted three ground balls to add to Nuxhall's frustration.

"Tomorrow's paper will say Nuxhall was *blasted* for thirteen hits. Watch and see," I said.

"Joe's had this kind of luck all year long. I never saw anything like it," said Lawrence.

"What are you doing down here, Brooks?" I asked him. "You're a starting pitcher, aren't you?"

"On this club, who knows?" said Lawrence. "Mayo hasn't made up his mind, yet. But then, the season's only half over. We oughta get straightened out during the All-Star break."

"Don't be bitter, Brooksie," I said. "Maybe Mayo won't even be around. I heard today that rumors are flying. Some gamblers got Smith fired already."

"What hotel are you staying at, Bross?" asked Whisenant. "We never see you around."

"Gotta make the rounds, Peter. Club Hangover, the Blackhawk, Fack's."

"I didn't know you like jazz, Brosnan," said Lawrence. "What do you dig? Basie? Progressive? Dixieland?"

"I try to make every scene, man," I said. "You dig Brubeck?"

Lawrence nodded. "How about Thelonious Monk? And Oscar Peterson?"

"Crazy," I agreed. "Mulligan. Chet Baker, Kai Winding."

"Yeah," he said. "Miles Davis. Charlie Parker."

"Hold it, man. We're talking two different languages, Brooks," I said. "Do you listen only to Negro musicians?" This was the first time I'd talked seriously to Lawrence. Best to find out if he was stuffy about being a Negro. Some of them are. Why they feel they have to be better than us I don't know.

Lawrence studied me carefully, his lips pursed, his eyes

179

slightly closed. Then he grinned. "You can't agitate me, Brosnan. We're talking jazz, right: You like Brubeck; I say Monk. But I dig Brubeck, too."

"I dig music, myself," I said. "Don't make much difference to me what color the player. You can't color the music."

"Now you *are* trying to give me an argument," he said.

I tossed my chewed-out cud of tobacco into the outfield. "We'll have to make it at the Blackhawk some night next trip. Diz will be in town."

"Good," he said. "Let's do that."

June 21—Los Angeles

The Dodger sportswriters greeted us with fearful adjectives. "Redleg Sluggers Threaten Our Pitching." In the ten days I'd been with the Redlegs our "sluggers" hadn't threatened anyone but the batting practice pitchers. We had scored fewer runs than the Cardinals during that time. Frank Thomas *did* hit his 187th batting practice home run, setting a new club record, but that didn't help much during the games.

Having discussed the Dodger hitters on Friday, Mayo said he'd like to say a few words.

"Men, we look dead." He walked back and forth letting his analysis sink in. "You know what I mean?" No one said a word. "We're not hitting. We're not fielding. We're not running the bases. We just look dead. You know what I mean?

"I don't know what to do, really. I hate to take your money. I just don't like to do that. But something's got to be done. I want to say this. I want to see every pop fly, every ground ball, run out from now on. Just as fast as you can go down that line. You know what I mean? Even if you haven't got a chance, hustle. Otherwise, it's going to cost you. Now, let's go out there and beat somebody for a change."

(Just once I want to hear a manager say, "Quit hitting pop-ups and easy ground balls. If you're gonna hit the ball in the air, hit it out of the park. If you have to hit a ground ball, knock an infielder over with it." A little positive thinking. Insist that the ballplayers make some money, not suggest ways to lose it.)

Mayo stopped me as I started toward the outfield to shag balls during batting practice. "How's that finger coming?" he asked.

"It looks a lot better. Still tender, though. I'll have to build up a callous again or I'll get a blister every time I pitch. You want me to throw batting practice?"

"No," he said, "I might have to use you in the bullpen. I don't want to, though, if you think it will bother that finger."

"Are you going to use me in relief from now on, then, or not?" I asked him.

"I don't know, yet. I have to find somebody who can go nine innings. But you better not throw today."

Lawrence started for us and gave up five runs in the first inning. That was plenty for the Dodgers.

The next night Drysdale pitched for L.A., and that was plenty good enough. Our hitters, still mulling over Mayo's advice, scored two runs in each game as a token effort. The hitters moaned about our lousy pitching; the bullpen talked, wistfully, about hitting.

"The trouble with these guys," said Whisenant, "is you can't teach 'em anything."

"You can't teach a man hitting," said King. "You can teach him how to think hitting—what a pitcher is doing to get him out. But he's either got the ability or he hasn't."

"You take Thomas, now," I said. "Wally Moses has worked with him ever since I've been here. And Wally knows as much as you can know about the mechanics of hitting. But he can't bat for Thomas. He can't keep that fear out of

Thomas's head that the pitcher is going to jam him so bad that his thumb will get hurt again. That's Frank's trouble. He's scared to swing the bat."

"Frank's always been a wild swinger," said Schmidt. "Wally was a different type hitter. He controlled the bat till the time the ball hit it."

"Nobody can see the ball hit the bat. It's physiologically impossible," I said. "But that's neither here nor there. Thomas can learn to control the bat. He'll be a better hitter when he does. Dave Philley used to be a wild swinger when he was first up in the majors. In the last couple years he's been a lot better hitter. He beats my brains out anyway. And he says as he got older he got smarter and figured pitchers better, but mainly he cut down on his swing and added thirty points to his average. Now he waits on the pitch longer and doesn't get fooled as often."

"How you gonna wait on a guy like Drysdale?" asked Johnny Powers. "You can just barely see his fast ball under these lousy lights."

Drysdale brushed Robinson back with a pitch.

"He oughta get fined, the big bastard. Knocking a guy down when he's got a four-run lead. Did he ever have to pay that fifty-buck fine?"

"Nah! They were just trying to make an example out of him to satisfy some old woman who writes for the *Sporting News*."

(Drysdale, upon being fined fifty dollars for allegedly hitting a batter deliberately, was quoted as saying: "I've got one way to pitch righties—tight. If it costs me five thousand dollars I'm gonna pitch that way. What am I supposed to do, lay it down the pipe? How can an umpire tell whether or not a pitcher is trying to hit somebody or not?" Brilliantly logical! Who's trying to hit the batter? The idea is to make him hit the dirt and stay loose from then on, not put him on first base!)

"Did you hear what Robinson said to Pinson after Vada

hit the home run the other day? Pinson ran round the bases so fast you'd have thought he was trying to beat out a bunt," I said. "Robby shakes Vada's hand when he gets to the bench and says, 'Little man, you just better stick to singles and leave the long ones to us cats who know how to act 'em out.'"

"That Vada can sure go," said Whisenant.

"I wish one of 'em would start getting on base so he *could* go," said Schmidt.

By four o'clock the next afternoon every man in the lineup was moving. Fifteen runners scored for our side; the sun was hot but our hitters were hotter. Only the telecasting crew was nervous. The game was televised back to Cincinnati. The monitoring truck sat in the runway leading to the clubhouse. As I ran back to get another pack of tobacco I stopped to take a peek at the four different views of the game.

"Finally we got a 'laugher,' Frank," I said.

"Yeah, but if we don't get this game over in ten minutes it's going to cost another nine hundred bucks. Tell Newk to just lay the ball in there and let 'em hit it."

The divergent angles of the camera were fascinating. I thought of my wife's complaint: "Why does the TV camera always catch ballplayers picking their nose, or scratching their behind? It's not very pretty."

I watched till the last Dodger was retired. It didn't look a bit undignified.

June 24 — Cincinnati

BACK home again in Cincinnati.

"How many tickets do you want?" I said into the phone. . . . "That's a lotta box seats. . . . I guess I can get 'em. The way we been going I don't think we're gonna pack Crosley Field. . . . Mom coming with you tonight? . . . She's never seen me pitch at a major league ball park, has she? . . .

Well, tell her to get there early. You sometimes can't see the starting pitcher if you're ten minutes late."

The threat of rain ended when I started to warm up. Through the grandstand I could see blue sky on the horizon. The thunderclouds rolled away and the wind that had been blowing hard from the southwest (the worst direction) died down. I noticed the flag flapping limply against the pole in left center, and I breathed a sigh of relief. First good omen of the day. My blister finger popped open even before I completed my warm-up throwing.

"You think you can make it?" asked Smith.

"Why not?" I said. "I'll give it a try. It bothers my breaking stuff mostly. I'll lay off the curve and use my slider."

As "The Star-Spangled Banner" boomed from the Crosley Field organ I said to myself, "Big boy, your job tonight is to concentrate. Have an idea on every pitch and make every pitch count."

Tony Taylor hit first for the Cubs. "He's been hitting pretty well lately," I said to myself. "Keep the sinker down and in. Make him hit something into the ground. He uppercuts the ball slightly." Taylor reached for a slider away from him and lofted the ball over shortstop for a single. Great start!

"You little Cuban Hot Dog," I said to myself as I looked at Taylor standing on first. "Dark's gonna hit-and-run probably. He hits the ball in on him better to right field than the ball away. Make him hit the slider." Dark swung at a belt-high slider on the outside of the plate, and popped it up. "Pretty good stuff on that pitch."

Walls came to the plate. "My old roomie! Last time at St. Louis he hit a good slider right on the nose. He must be looking for it. I'll make him hit the sinker." Walls wouldn't bite on two inside fast balls and I eventually walked him. With Banks up, and only one out I was already in trouble.

"Wonder if Mother is here, yet," I thought. "I can't take a chance throwing Banks a breaking ball away and down.

184

That's a good double-play pitch but if I make a slight mistake I'm behind three runs." I shook off Bailey's signal for the curve; shook again on the slider; and again on the slider when he returned to that sign. He obviously didn't want the old hummer. Why not? It ain't hummin' tonight? I stepped back off the mound to rub some ideas into the ball. Bailey must like my slide ball. Maybe it's better than it feels when it leaves my fingers. (Most of the pitcher's control on breaking balls lies in his fingers. I had a bad finger. I must have poor breaking stuff. Q.E.D. Well, Bailey probably never heard of Q.E.D., so why not give him what he wants?)

Banks went for the slider, up and away from him. Not a classic pitch, but he was late with his bat and popped it up. Two high sliders and two pop-ups. I had either a good slider or a lot of luck.

Long was next. "Try to jam him with a fast ball or a slider," I said to myself. Long hit the slider on a line to left field. "Don't fall down, Lynch," I said as I ran to back up home plate. Lynch didn't move till the ball landed in his glove.

"That's your bad inning, Jimmy," said Mayo. "Keep that back leg bent now. Your fast ball's alive."

I'd only thrown one. The slider must look like a fast ball from the dugout. That's good. That's the way the slider should look. "Doc," I said to the trainer. "Let's go to work. This finger's bleeding. You got any collodion we can put on it?"

Anderson fished through his satchel and pulled out a bottle. "This'll do the trick, my boy. Just let old Doc take care of your finger. You take care of the batters. You can't use a Band-Aid, I guess, huh?"

"No, Doc," I said "Not only is it illegal but I lose my grip on the baseball."

"Okay, swell. Let's try this stuff, then. Put a coat over the sore. There. Now, see if that sticks on there when you throw. Stings a little, doesn't it? That just proves you're alive, my boy."

Lynch, Robinson, Bell, and Bailey scored within a dozen pitches and by the time I returned to the mound I felt like a new man. Nothing like a four-run lead to give a pitcher courage. "They'll have to drag me off this mound before the sixth inning, now," I said to myself.

Thomson hit sixth for the Cubs. "Why waste a slider? Jam him with the sinker right away. That's what I'll throw him eventually anyway." He hit it to Kasko at shortstop for one out.

Moryn. "Keep the ball in on him, and fast. No slow stuff." Moose swung and missed three high sliders. Damn! That's a pretty good pitch tonight.

Sam Taylor. "Same as Moryn. Nothing out over the plate." Sammy fanned on the same three pitches. Eight quick throws in four fast minutes and I felt like a pitcher again.

Twice more I went through the Cub lineup. Walls hit a 3-2 fast ball ("Don't walk him," I said. "Make him hit it to get on.") for a single to center. In the next inning Thomson reached for a slider that I meant to waste and hit it past me on the ground into center. Noren ("How do I pitch him?") hit a line drive over short for a single. ("Better keep it in on him next time.") But for the most part my arm worked like a well-oiled machine. The batter came to the plate. My experience classified him. My mind told my arm what to do. And it did it. It seldom happens precisely that way.

With a shutout in reach as I started the ninth, I told Anderson to pour on the collodion. He had covered the finger each inning but it soon wore off. Blood-marks dotted the baseball after each sinker pitch. But as a psychological prop the collodion kept me together for nine innings.

Walls took a slider for strike three to begin the ninth. Banks, as he stood at the plate, crouched a little deeper in the box. I had jammed him the last two times up. "I better go away with the slide ball this time," I decided. I didn't get the slider far enough away and Banks whipped the fat part of his bat against it. "Uh-oh!" I thought. "There she goes." The ball took off for the center field fence, but the wind caught it and blew it toward right field. Pinson chased it, running like a greyhound after the rabbit. "Good Lord! what a catch!"

Long took two straight strikes. "Why not experiment a little?" I thought. "Think I'll throw him a change-of-pace. Defy the Book." Long grunted as he saw the expected fast ball change speed. He swung at the ball anyway and bounced it to Robinson who tagged first and stuck the ball into his back pocket.

"Oh, no, Robby," I said. "That one's mine."

June 28—Cincinnati

Life in the Cincinnati clubhouse in midsummer is lived in the raw. Pregame uniform is jock strap and shower clogs. The thought of putting on a flannel uniform over woolen socks and undershirt starts the sweat rolling.

"How many electric fans you got in here, Chesty?" I asked the clubhouse man.

"Not enough," he said. "It's too hot already, isn't it? I don't envy you guys goin' onto that field today."

"I'm not going, myself," I said. "It may get to be a hundred on the mound like it did yesterday and I'm staying right in that air-conditioned dugout."

Willard Schmidt walked into the clubhouse, with his sport shirt already unbuttoned. "Pitchers hitting today, Jim?"

"No, Willard," I said. "You know pitchers never hit on Sunday."

"Good," he said. "It's too hot to swing a bat."

"You got an air-conditioned house, Will?" I asked.

"No. Why?"

"How do you sleep at night in this heat?"

"On my back," he said. "Don't get personal. You got your family living in a hotel?"

"Yeah," I said, "but I don't know whether it's good to have an air-conditioned room to sleep in or not. This heat knocks you over when you come outside."

"Better to have a frigid wife to keep the bed cold," he said. "I don't like 'em."

The trainer's room filled rapidly. The trainer keeps a large jug of salt pills next to the vitamin tablet bottle and players reach for a handful whether they intend to sweat or not. Big Don Newcombe lay on the table, Doc Anderson kneading Newk's mountainous torso, rubbing oil into his big arm. Frank Robinson sat on the other massage table staring at his bandaged wrist.

"Everything all right, Robby?" I asked.

He rose from the table, gave me a dirty look because I'm a pitcher, and walked out of the room.

"Guess he can't play, huh, Doc?" I said.

"Guess not," said Anderson. "What kind of guy is that Anderson over at Chicago? The pitcher?"

"He's a nice kid," I said. "I don't think he was throwing at Robby. Consciously, that is. But when a guy is hitting pitchers the way Robinson was hitting the Cubs, you gotta expect him to be knocked down. He must have had ten for fifteen off the Cubs in the last six games."

"Well, Anderson got him good, I'll say that for him," said Schmidt.

"Robby was probably hanging in there looking for Anderson's curve ball," I said. "You know, two years ago when I was with the Cubs Anderson didn't even have a curve. He sure has improved."

"Hey," said someone in the other room, "Doc, tell the Whale to get off the table so us regulars can rest a little bit."

Newcombe grunted, unpoetically.

As we started out of the clubhouse to the field, Schmidt said to me, "How about coming down to the bullpen, Brosnan? Your wound still bothering you?"

"This terrible heat might cause it to start bleeding again,

Willard," I said. "No, it's all right. I think I could go a couple
. . . hitters."

I walked under the grandstand to the ramp leading onto the
field, bumping into Broglio at the gate.

"Everything all right, Ern?" I asked. "How much weight
did you lose yesterday?"

Broglio grinned, then groaned, "God, musta been ten,
twelve pounds anyway. I didn't think I was going to make
it."

"You just wanted an excuse to shave your beard, is all," I
said, punching him in the arm as he walked out into the sun.
Broglio had vowed, just before I left the Cardinals, not to
shave till he won a ball game. He had lost his first five games.
Since then he'd won two in a row. You never know what
will work for some pitchers.

By the end of the first inning I wished I was in the bullpen, just to get away from the suffering. The Cardinals
scored seven runs in the first inning on four hits and three
errors. Mayo moaned audibly, biting his lips, mussing his
silver-streaked hair till he no longer looked like a successful,
retired Florida rancher, but more like a man in the last
throes of bankruptcy. "What are you gonna do?" he mumbled half to himself.

If he didn't know, neither did any of us. The Cardinals
spent thirty minutes batting in the first inning. It looked like
we might not get home till eight o'clock. Dipping a sponge
into ammonia-treated water, the grumbling hitters squeezed
some life onto the backs of their necks and battled back. They
got as close as 8-6 in the fifth, then pooped out.

After an ill-tasting lunch of crackers and cheese, ice cream
and grape soda, we went back out for another try. The
Cardinals, by winning the first game, had moved ahead of us
into sixth place. (Here I had thought I was moving up in the
league when I was traded.)

"Jim," said Clyde King, "you come down with us to the
bullpen. Mayo says we have to win this game. He's going

to use both you and Purkey in the late innings if he has to."

("If he hadn't botched up his pitching staff all year using starters in relief he might not be in such a position," I thought. Ballplayers ought to know where they stand.)

"Why did Burkhart throw Thomas out in the ninth?" asked King.

"Frank had to get in the last word. He thought the pitch hit him, and Burkhart didn't. It looked from the dugout like it was all settled, then Thomas stepped back out of the batter's box and said something else. You know the Donkey. He never knows when to stop," I said.

The Cards scored nine runs before we could get one in the second game, and the fans, full of beer and indignation, booed each move that Mayo made.

"They're gonna run him outa town just like they did Tebbetts," said Purkey.

As the sun sank behind the grandstand in the seventh, we scored. Ricketts, the Cardinal pitcher, retired two men but had to leave the game when a line drive bounced off his knee. Jeffcoat relieved, gave up three straight hits, and left the mound wtihout getting a man out. McDaniel relieved Jeffcoat, and gave up two more hits, the second a double by Newcombe. Pendleton tried to score from first, but the heat, fatigue, and the ball caught up with him at the plate to retire the side. Eight runs!

"Now, that's the way this club should look," I said. The incredible excitement of a succession of line drives can stir the most cynical baseball fan. "It's hard to believe, isn't it? Eight line drives!"

"Yes," said King. "If only this club could score those runs before the other team. We get a lot of runs but they don't seem to make the job any easier on our pitchers. If the pitching's good, the hitting's off. And vice-versa."

"Jeffcoat's mad at you, Bross," said Whisenant. "You're making the trade look bad."

190

"If I'd only known *he* was going to look so bad!" I said, facetiously. "Poor guy. Caray will rip *him*, now."

Eight runs was one run short. That's the way it stayed.

July 5—Philadelphia

WILLIE JONES joined us in Philadelphia. I associated Jones with trouble; on two May nights he had started rallies for the Phils while I was pitching for St. Louis. Apparently the Phil management didn't consider that of much value, for they traded Willie to Cleveland. The Indians used him for a week, then looked around for a buyer. The way he hits me, I'd buy him any time, just to keep him out of my hair. He shook hands with me regretfully; another pitcher he could no longer hit.

The Philadelphia fans who had booed Jones with all the mighty fervor of an outraged mob (typical of Philadelphia fans) greeted him in a Cincinnati uniform as if he were the Prodigal Son. They gave him a standing ovation which reduced him to tears at the plate. Even the Phillies' ballplayers, embarrassed by their own unprofessional sentiment, applauded Jones from the steps of their dugout. What makes a ballplayer look better in an opponent's uniform?

Even without Jones in their lineup the Philly batters treated me as badly as their fans. I started the game, and in the third inning Freese hit a grand-slam home run to knock me out of the box. I never did recover from the blow; I still think about it. Freese just isn't that good a hitter, and it just wasn't that bad a pitch. The rest of our club, however, recovered enough to win the second game of the twi-night doubleheader, and also the Friday night game. These two wins kept Philadelphia from climbing over us into seventh. With the first half of the season coming to a close our momentary escape from the cellar was greeted like a reprieve . . . for the club if not for the manager. Mayo Smith said to a sports-writer before the double-header, "Last year I was in the first division, closer to first place than I am now. And I still got fired. So what are you gonna do?"

Clutching a two-game winning streak to our hearts we headed west to Pittsburgh, regarding the Fourth of July hope-fully. Not only did we have virtually an off-day (to play only one game on a holiday reduces work to leisure), but we seemed to have a better-than-average chance to win a third straight game. Bob Friend was scheduled to pitch for the Pirates. In past years this prospect was a chilling one; the pitcher scheduled to work opposite Friend would say, pessi-mistically, "Why in hell do I have to draw the best in the league every time!" The season 1959, however, had deflated Friend's reputation. He looked like just another pitcher, proficient but beatable. "He's not quite as fast as he was," said the hitters, "and he's not getting his breaking stuff over when he has to. He's always been around the plate with his pitches but he gives you more to hit now."

Our hitters got ten hits and a couple of walks but could squeeze just three runs out of the traffic. The Pirates scored four times, the last run coming after the third out had been apparently called. Bailey tagged Groat sliding home with an inside-the-park home run. Bailey then dropped the ball, which rolled an inch and a half toward the Pirate dugout before Bailey could snatch it up again. Umpire Delmore in a dramatic gesture signaled Groat out and failed to see the fumble. The second base umpire, however, detected the error from his position 182 feet away in center field. His piercing vision, unerringly centered on the play though three ballplayers and a dust cloud hindered his duty, is a tribute to the aggressive-ness and hog-headedness of some National League umpires. Protest by Smith, Nuxhall (the pitcher), and Bailey, though colorful and worth while recording, was unavailing.

So, what are you gonna do?

Acker pitched four shutout innings after Groat was called

safe. He bought the early edition of the Sunday paper to read about the game.

"Rooms," I said to him, "you're making your salary drive a little early, aren't you? That's about four good games in a row."

"Don't worry about me, mother," he said. "I see where you're starting the second game tomorrow."

"Who says?" I asked.

"The paper's got you scheduled. You and Purkey."

"Somebody oughta tell me, don't you think?"

Jeez, here I had three starts in three months. Now I get two more in three days.

"Who's working for them?" I asked.

"Guess you'll get Kline," he said.

"That figures," I moaned. Leaving Acker to watch the Saturday night Westerns on TV I went across the street to Danny's.

"You are pitching tomorrow, Jimmy?" Danny asked. "Then I will come to see you. But first I will fix you a meal so that you will be strong and pitch a good game. Maybe I still want the Pirates to win but it should be a good game. I will go to the kitchen and pick the roast beef myself for you."

Like fatting up the calf for slaughter. Danny didn't even smile.

During the first game on Sunday rain fell in thunderous large drops, but it quickly stopped. The Pirate ground crew had trouble starting their new motor-driven infield cover. By the time the tarpaulin reached the outfield grass the rain had ceased. Then the motor wouldn't work and the ground crew couldn't get the field uncovered. While the fans hooted impatiently the players on our bench relaxed, and I scanned the western sky to see if more rain was coming to cancel my game.

"Joe Brown paid forty thousand dollars for that damn

thing," said Purkey, "and the first time they try it, it falls apart."

"Another bonus beauty flops," I said. "General managers have nothing but bad luck when they spend money in big chunks like that. That's why they're stingy when it comes time to talk contract."

Using a crowbar, the crew foreman finally jammed the cover back into its hole, and we proceeded to lose the game 7-5. Drizzle fell briefly as I warmed up for the second game. "Piss or get off the pot," I said to the clouds. The game started.

In the second inning I had the bases loaded with two out, and Kline was the next Pirate hitter. Kline is not a good hitter, even for a pitcher. "For Christ's sake, don't walk him!" is the usual pregame strategy. A lousy hitter, however, presents a special psychological problem for me. "What do I throw him?" I don't dare just lay the ball in there for him to hit it, but I don't dare to start working on him, either. What if I walked him?

Bailey asked for the slider and I threw it. Kline lunged at it and hit a ground ball to my left. On a normal infield Robinson would have charged in from first base to field the ball. The Forbes Field turf, however, has the consistency of a hardwood floor. Kline's grounder moved right along toward right field. "Come on, Temple, where in hell are you?" I prayed. Temple never got to the ball, which rolled into right field to drive home two runs.

Virdon hit next. "This guy hits me like he owns me," I said to myself. "That's why he's got such a big smile when he says hello. I better load one up. He's never seen me throw one, yet." The pitch didn't move much but Virdon popped it up to right, anyway.

The bases remained practically untrodden for the next six innings. Having hit against Kline twice I didn't think he had too much stuff, and *he* had a hit off *me* so I couldn't have been too impressive. Mayo greeted me as I came to the dugout after the seventh.

"Let's let Whitey hit for you, Jim. Nice game."

"Yeah," I mumbled. "Great." Lockman grounded out for me and I ran over to the clubhouse, feeling a bit depressed. Is it better to get shelled as I did in Philly, or frustrated in a 2-0 game? Sometimes I think it's better to be bombed. You know where you stand . . . or stood. The black mark on your record is no smaller when you pitch well enough to win but still get beat.

"Brosnan, who usually doesn't pitch too well against the Pirates," said the Pirate radio broadcaster, "pitched well enough to win this game."

"Go to hell," I said. "You got any beer, Tommy?"

The first rule I'd heard about when I joined the Reds was "No Beer in the Clubhouse." But clubhouse men usually can find some when absolutely necessary.

"It's Sunday, Broz," the clubhouse man said. Pennsylvania has blue laws, too.

"Yeah, I know. You got any beer?"

"How many you want? Couple of your guys ordered some for the bus trip to the airport."

"They aren't hitting today anyway. To hell with 'em. Can you let me have six? I'll drink a couple now, and take the rest with me. I've got a three-hour wait for my plane to Chicago."

"Goin' home during the All-Star game, huh?" he said.

I took my shower, standing near the doorway, trying to distinguish between the noise of the water and the noise of the crowd in the stands. Maybe we could tie it up. Only two runs to get if they don't get any more off Pena.

"Three days off. I'm not even going to watch the All-Star game," I said to myself. "Damn game."

As I dressed, Tommy handed me a bag of beer and a can opener.

"Man on first, Bell the batter," said the radio. "Come on,

Ronnie, get old Ding-Dong out of there. . . . Here's the pitch. . . . Oh, my, that one's gone. Upper deck. She's all tied up."

I tossed my shoe up in the air. That's the way. Gussie! Pulls me right off the hook. I punched a hole in the beer can. "Now that tastes good, like a beer should," I said.

July 8—Morton Grove

THE phone rang at seven-thirty. We were still in bed. I reached up for the receiver.

"Who in the world would dare call us this early?" my wife said.

"What do you say, Donald? Is everything all right?" I said into the phone. "It's Don Studt," I whispered to my wife. . . . "Nice of you to call so early, Don. What's new? . . . . What d'ya mean 'who's gonna be the new manager?' . . . . Sure I like Mayo. Why not? He's treated me fine. Lets me pitch when I want to, never gets on anybody. Just like Solly Hemus. You know what I mean? . . . Phooey! I didn't care whether Hemus lost his job or not. What do I care if he starves. . . . Yeah, I'm leaving in about an hour for Cincy. We got a workout at eleven o'clock. . . . What the hell, if I make it, I make it. . . . No, I didn't watch the All-Star game. We all went to Brookfield zoo, instead. . . . Don't make bad jokes. We went on a picnic. . . . You should try it. Fresh air, sunshine, it'll kill you. . . . So the Cardinals are ahead of us, so what? . . . I'm happy, I'm happy. I'd rather be with Cincinnati than any other club in the league. . . . No, I haven't read the paper. I'm still in bed. . . . With my wife, yeah . . . Oh, just as good as ever. What's in the paper? . . . . Oh. . . . Great. . . . What I mean is GREAT! I like him. . . . Yeah. . . . Thanks for calling, Don. Say hello to Gwen. . . . See ya. . . . Let's get together next time the Reds are in town. . . .'By.

196

"That was Donald E. Studt. We've got a new manager," I said.

"Who?" she said.

"Hutch," I said.

"Oh, God, there goes your starting job!"

July 9—Cincinnati

WE DROVE to the airport on the northwest side of Chicago so that I could catch the helicopter to the south side airport to catch the plane to Cincinnati.

"Now what excuse are you going to give Hutchinson for your not being at the workout yesterday?" my wife asked.

"I'll tell him I missed the helicopter, the girl gave me the wrong time. What's wrong with the truth?"

"Nothing, usually. You should try it more often."

The plane ride was too quick for me to finish *The Wapshot Chronicle*. When I get involved in a book my mind doesn't operate properly till I read my way back to reality. I told the cab driver in Cincinnati to take me to Crosley Field, and settled back into my book.

"Did ja hear about the new manager the Reds got?" asked the cab driver, rudely.

"Umph!" I said, holding my book closer to my eyes.

"Hutchinson. He was in the cellar out on the Coast, so they hired him. They never shoulda got rid of Jimmie Dykes. You know? I been watching this Gabe Paul. He's always hirin' managers who got fired someplace else. Hutchinson. He gets fired at Detroit. Then he gets fired at St. Louis. So Gabe Paul hires him. What for? He better go out and get some pitchers. That's what those bums need."

"I understand Hutchinson's a pretty good manager," I said. "The Cardinal players liked him last year, they say."

"Yeah, I guess maybe so," said the cab driver. "Like Lou Smith writes in the *Enquirer*, all his players respect Hutch.

They call him the Big Bear, or something like that. He was a pitcher, wasn't he?"

"So I understand," I said. I put my book into my coat pocket and closed my eyes. Get a fan started and it's impossible to shut him off without a switch.

"Hope Hutchinson can do something with those bums he's got pitching for him. I been listening to the Reds' games for ten years and I've seen 'em make more dumb moves," he said. "Why, look at the dumb plays these guys made already this year. They'd a won twenty more games if Jimmie Dykes was the manager. Or even Birdie Tebbetts."

"How many times have you been at the ball park this year so far?" I asked him.

"I haven't been able to get out there yet, 'cause I drive at night a lot. But I listen to most every game. That Waite Hoyt sure calls a good game. Newcombe's pitchin' tonight. He's about the only pitcher the Reds got, y'know. Should be a good game."

The cab pulled up at the main gate of the ball park. "Take me around to the other gate, down by the clubhouse," I said.

"You're a little early. They don't open the gates till six," he said. He drove through the parking lot to the press gate, jumped out to take my bags from the trunk, and noticed the United Airlines name tag on my suitcase. "You ain't Jim Brosnan, are you? The Reds' pitcher?"

I nodded.

"Well, glad to meet you, Jim!" he said, and held out his hand.

I gave him two bucks, picked up the bags, and walked up to the clubhouse.

There was no one in the manager's room as I walked by to my locker. Willard Schmidt greeted me. "Nice of you to join us, Brosnan. Have a nice vacation?"

"Get off my back, Willard," I said. "I was unavoidably detained in Chicago. Did you have a nice workout? Hot, I guess, huh?"

"Some of us pitchers threw for twenty minutes. Not everybody was there, of course."

"Forget it. You can use the work," I said.

"Well, I'll tell you," he said. "I got a call early yesterday morning. 'Be in the office at nine-thirty.' Gabe wants to see me. It was just a meeting to introduce Hutch, but I thought I'd had it."

"Don't be silly, Willard. They're not gonna get rid of you. What would Hutch do for laughs?"

The clubhouse man warned each player not to go out of the clubhouse till after the meeting. "Hutch wants to talk to you," he said. I hid in the latrine till the chair-scraping and hushed conversation indicated that the meeting was about to start. I couldn't make up my mind whether or not to apologize to Hutchinson for having missed the workout. Hutch seems to be embarrassed by apologies. If you do wrong, you should figure out why, vow never to do it again, and forget it. That seemed to be his philosophy. The most he'd do is fine me, anyway. Still I waited till the last moment, then had to take a chair at the table right in front of him. He stood, waiting for attention. I sat down, riffled the envelopes containing player passes that lay on the table, and looked up to see Hutchinson staring at me with half a smile on his face. He winked at me and murmured, "Hi, Jim." (What the hell, why do I worry!)

"I met most of you fellows yesterday," said Hutchinson, "Most of you I knew already. Most of you know me." He paused and looked around the room. "I like to win. That's the only way to play this game. To win. We're all like that. From now on I'm running this ball club. If you have any problems come to me. I'll handle them or I'll get somebody to do it for me. On paper this club looks better than the standings indicate so far. I don't know why . . . yet. Some people say you've been playing a little too conservative, that you don't bump heads enough on the field. All I got to say to that is if somebody bumps your head the only thing to do is bump back.

Now I'm not going to say to you pitchers that you should knock somebody down just because they're takin' a shot at you. I can't say that and I won't say that." He paused, emphatically, timing his words perfectly. Half-turning his head, he grinned, and said, "But I don't care if you brush a hitter back once in a while. Just to let 'em know you're out there."

He picked up a score card. "Newk, you want to go over these hitters? I just want to add one thing. I'm glad to be up here with you. We're going to start winning. We might as well start tonight."

July 11 — Cincinnati

OUR first home stand under Hutch was scheduled for just five days. My wife stayed in Morton Grove rather than commute to Cincinnati for such a short time. I moved into the Brosnan family mansion on Price Hill. Free-loading on one's family is so much more satisfying to one's conscience. In fact, I got a better room than I'd had as a mere member of the family.

"Your wife says you won't be starting any more because Hutch is manager. Is that right?" asked my brother Mike. Unaccountably he had risen from bed before noon and had shown up in time for breakfast.

"What you doing up so early?" I asked. "And when did Anne Stewart say that?"

"I've got a game this afternoon," he said. Mike pitched American Legion ball. "And she mentioned it the last time she was down here. That's when the papers were talking about who would be the new manager. Doesn't she like Hutchinson?"

"She wouldn't dare not like him!" I said. "And so far she's wrong. I'm starting this afternoon against Antonelli."

"I hope I do better than you will," he said, laughing like a brother.

"Well, you go play your itty-bitty game and let me worry about the Giants," I said. "I would draw Antonelli, though. Even in the Army I never beat him. He was at Fort Myer when I was at Fort Meade and we hooked up a couple times. He used to strike out eighteen of our guys a game."

"Even you?" he said, in phony amazement.

"Your trying to get on me, kid," I said. "Don't play with fire."

"Would you rather be a starter if Hutch would let you?" he asked.

"I don't know," I said, thinking about it. "I'd say he's better than most managers in handling starting pitchers. He lets his starter go a long way. If you're rested and ready and he says you're his best for the day, you have to prove it to him that you're not. Which is good for a pitcher's morale in the long run."

"The way the Reds score runs, a starting pitcher has a chance to win a lot of games, doesn't he?" said Mike.

"Well, we score runs just like any other team in the second division," I said. "You read too many sportswriters. They think they can prove our pitching staff is lousy because the Reds score more runs than anybody else. That's the most misleading statistic in baseball."

"Why?" he asked.

"Most of the time a potentially high-scoring team will run up a potful of runs in one or two games, then may score once or twice a game for a week. The pitchers depend on the hitters to bail them out; the opponent's pitchers think they have to bear down extra hard; managers tend to play for the big inning too often rather than take a run any way they can get it; and everybody gets hitter-conscious instead of correlating hitting, pitching, running, and defense. You follow me?"

"No," he said.

"Well, you better stick to your own brand of baseball, and stop trying to run mine. Okay?"

"I'm not trying to run anything," he protested. "I get my

opinions from the papers. Lou Smith always writes, 'Competent Observers Say Such and Such Is True.' I have to assume he's right, don't I?"

"I don't know whether you're trying to be sarcastic or not," I said. "By 'Competent Observer' Lou Smith means himself, and the 'Competent' means he's not legally insane."

"You're just bitter 'cause he never mentions your name," said Mike.

"He quoted me twice, just after I was traded," I said. "What I was supposed to have said I never would have said even if he had asked me which he hadn't since I'd never even met the man yet."

"Okay, okay," Mike said. "If Hutch lets his starters go so long, how come he used you so much in relief last year at St. Louis?"

"First of all, I was going good. Secondly, St. Louis is a hellhole in the summer and a pitcher can't be expected to go nine innings without getting pretty tired. Why not bring a fresh pitcher in if he's going good? Then, there are plenty of other reasons that all managers nowadays operate with."

"Like what?" he asked.

I ticked them off on my fingers. "The lively ball, bigger players, and better bats. They make every hitter a potential Babe Ruth. . . . You can't afford to make any mistakes on the mound so the tension gets to you, especially in low-score games. The tension gets to you *and* the manager. Also, the ball parks are all small in this league except for Milwaukee and Pittsburgh so that adds more pressure on the pitcher. The umpires don't make it any easier on us, either. They've shrunk the plate and the strike zone so much. There are just two umpires in the league who consistently give you a strike on the outside corner. And where the strike zone used to be from the shoulders to the knees, it's now from below the letters to above the knees. Some of those bubble-heads interpret that rule to mean the strike zone is between the lowest button of the shirt to the top button of the pants crotch. So the pitcher has to come in with the ball if his first two pitches just miss and—Boom! . . . the ball goes out of the ball park and you go out of the game."

Mike nodded his head. "They're using relief pitchers this year it seems even when they don't have to."

"The relief pitcher used to be second-rate; now he's usually as good as anybody on the staff," I said. "Some managers tend to panic when the starter gives up a hit in the late innings. So they drag in a fresh man. Then, too, the percentage of right-handed pitcher against right-handed hitter and lefty against lefty is used blindly. It's supposed to be a percentage move. A lot of guys think percentage always means one hundred, I guess. It's all a part of personal panic and overmanaging. The trouble with it is the manager seldom lets his players in on the reasons why he does some of those things, and the player ends up thinking instead of doing."

"You think too much yourself, Lou Smith says," said Mike.

"Go lose yourself a ball game," I said. "I gotta go to the park."

Antonelli had pitched two consecutive shutouts, and he started out on another. For six innings we made just two hits, and no runs. The Giants' Spencer hit a ball past my left shoe for a single to start the fourth. I should have caught it. Brandt bunted him over. Landrith took two balls and a strike. "I'll throw one fast ball past him," I thought, "and strike him out with a curve." He hit the fast ball through my legs to drive in a run. Bressoud hit the next pitch against the center field wall. It landed just six inches above Pinson's glove although I gave it all the body English I could to bring it back far enough for the catch. Antonelli bounced my best curve ball over my head and Landrith scored as Kasko threw Antonelli out at first. One foot lower and I catch the ball on the bounce. . . . No-run scores.

Bressoud hit a double in the fifth on another slider. In the seventh I tried to jam him with a fast ball and he hit it over the left-field wall. The wind blowing out to left didn't hurt the drive any. It landed just behind the fence. Davenport doubled and Kirkland singled for the fourth run before Hutch started to warm up another pitcher. I was ready to collapse from the heat and fatigue, but I hadn't walked a batter so Hutch must have thought I was just being dramatic about the sweat that soaked my uniform. Even my cap was wet. The temperature on the field was ninety-nine degrees and I'd thrown 125 pitches. Mays and Cepeda were the next hitters, and I could feel my strength ebbing. But Willie struck out on a 3-2 curve and Cepeda took three strikes while looking for an inside fast ball that he could hit out of the park. I staggered off the mound figuring that I was through for the day. Hutch said, "Let's see you go one more." I swallowed two more salt pills, the sweat having virtually stopped. There was no more in me. I made it through the eighth, somehow, but we lost the game. I lost thirteen pounds, also, for a completely wasted day.

"How could you get Mays and Cepeda out and let Bressoud beat you?" asked Mike when I got home.

"Go stuff your head, kid. How would you have pitched him?"

"Bressoud's hitting .214 and you let him get two doubles and a home run," said my other brother, Pat, when he arrived for dinner.

"Good God in the foothills! Let's forget it."

"You should never have lost that game," said my dad. "How can you let a guy like Bressoud beat you?"

"If I wasn't so damn tired," I said, "I'd leave home."

July 14 — St. Louis

THE smile of Fred Hutchinson is a treasured one. His ballplayers vie hopefully for it. By playing well and winning they earn it. (Hutchinson snorts at plain luck.) Miserly with his laughter at all times, Hutchinson is miserable in defeat. The depth of his frown is in direct proportion to the length of his losing streak. His grappling with frustration is a tableau of tormented humanity.

Hutch had little to smile about in his first week as our manager. We lost three games to the Giants. At least we scored some runs. The Seattle ball club which Hutch had left in the Coast League cellar had averaged three runs per game for him. That's not much to work with. Like an expert mechanic presented with a better-quality motor he viewed our club with bright eyes, if not a happy smile. What power! Listen to that Robinson swing the bat! Look at that ball go!

The Dodgers followed the Giants into Crosley Field and Hutchinson met them with a cold and hungry stare. We won both games from Los Angeles and Hutchinson led us into St. Louis with just the bare hint of a grim smile on his face. Bob Broeg, the wise young sports editor of the *Post-Dispatch*, joined us in our Busch Stadium locker room, gathered six ex-Cardinals around the ex-St. Louis manager for a photograph, and welcomed us all. The caption that appeared beneath the picture the next day—"Ex-Redbirds Now Redlegs"—echoed smiles of personal statisfaction. The faces of Schmidt and Whisenant, of Kasko and Lockman, and even of Hutchinson, could hardly have looked any more optimistic. And I saw myself smiling in St. Louis for only the third time this year.

Carrying a copy of the *Post-Dispatch* with me I walked down Maryland Avenue to the cafeteria to eat, to read about Hutchinson's successful attempt to smile, and to cut out the picture for my wife's scrapbook. Clyde King had preceded me to the cafeteria and he motioned for me to sit with him.

"I didn't know any other ballplayers ever ate here," he confessed. "Let me see the paper while you eat."

"It's all about Robinson. Have you ever seen anything like the way he's been hitting? It scares you," I said.

"He's been hot for three weeks," said King. "I believe he's hit over .500 during that time. Almost unbelievable."

"How would you pitch to him, Clyde? You don't dare try

to pitch him away. If he ever hit the ball through the box it would kill you. That ball he hit against the left field wall last night was a line drive all the way."

King smiled. "I'm glad I don't have to worry about it any more. I'd have had to pitch him away; that's the way I pitched."

"You happy being a coach?" I asked. "Do you think it helped you to manage for a couple of years?"

King toyed with his salad. "I'd rather manage. There's more responsibility, but there's much more satisfaction. As a coach you can do only so much on your own."

"Did you always want to manage, even as a player?"

"No, I can't say that. A man that I respect a great deal told me that I should do it. And whatever he said always had a deep influence on me."

"That was Rickey, I gather," I said.

"Mr. Rickey," he said, frowning slightly at my lack of respect, "is a very persuasive man."

I spilled horse-radish over my corned beef. "Would you have liked to manage this club?" Before he could answer I continued. "Would you have run it like Mayo did?"

He blinked his eyes as I chomped down on the horse-radish-covered beef. "Dad gum it, Brosnan, you can't expect me to answer things like that. Next thing you'll be asking me if I like Hutch or not."

"You don't have to like him if you don't want to, Clyde," I said.

"Nobody said I didn't, now," he protested.

I wiped my mouth and poured hot water over the tea bag in my cup. "You're a pretty good psychologist, Clyde. Do you think a ballplayer has to like his manager and his teammates to be effective?"

"Ballplayers and managers don't have to like each other necessarily," he said, "but they should respect each other. You didn't care much for Solly Hemus, did you?"

"Hemus didn't like me," I protested. "So I didn't like him.

206

But I've been thinking. With the Cardinals, I was beginning to lose confidence in my pitching ability, and over here I've proved that I can do just as good a job as ever. So my guilt feelings about Hemus must have had a direct effect on my pitching."

"How do you know he didn't like you?" asked King. "What did Hemus do? Or say?"

"I can't think right offhand of any particular thing," I said. "But I never could shake that feeling of hostility. Then I'd say to myself, 'You're over twenty-one. Why can't you take off and forget it all?' Of course, a ballplayer just can't change jobs like that. So I got mad at the whole goddamn world."

King flinched at my profanity. His prudishness about language had been subject to frequent needling in the bullpen. I tried to change the subject from my personal confession.

"Clyde, this is probably an impudent question, and it certainly isn't pertinent, but don't you ever use any cuss words?"

"It's not necessary. . . ."

"Why?" I said. "It certainly belongs in a ballplayer's language. I hardly notice it any more, myself; and I was taught to consider cussing a *sin*. Why, the other day I took my family to the zoo in Cincinnati. We had to park a long way from the animal houses. My little boy started to drag about halfway up the hill and he said, 'Daddy, where's the damn zoo?' I had already answered him before I realized what he said. A woman behind us gathered her three kids around her as if they were going to catch a disease. Ridiculous!"

"You oughta be ashamed of yourself, Jim," he said.

"It was just a word. Why should I be ashamed of a word?" I said. "Can you tell me a better way to get rid of anger? Until I learned to release my frustration I used to make a spectacle of myself on the mound. Didn't you ever get mad when you were pitching?"

"The worst thing a pitcher can do is to get mad, at himself or at anything else. It ruins his concentration."

"You must be superhuman, Clyde. Or I just am half grown-up. I say cuss it out and forget it. You have to get rid of it somehow. The tough part of it is learning how to cuss yourself. After I learned how to call myself the same things I called umpires and lousy infielders and bad breaks, why, then it was easier to concentrate on my job."

"Let's talk about Solly Hemus," he suggested.

"That's a bad word, Clyde!"

July 16—St. Louis

BROGLIO and I were the scheduled pitchers for the Thursday night game. When I came up through the Cardinal dugout with a well-oiled arm, Ernie grabbed my arm and asked if everything was all right. I told him he'd look good in a beard. We weren't about to lose another game all season. He asked me if I'd like to trade pitches—he'd throw me a fast ball to hit if I'd give *him* one up in his eyes. I asked for a high slider and we agreed on arrangements. First pitch the first time up for each of us. Such friendly arrangements between opposing pitchers are only good so long as each thinks the friendly gesture won't interfere with winning the game.

By the time I got to hit we had a three-run lead and all I got from Broglio were good curve balls. Which I never could hit; it should be illegal to throw them to pitchers. By the time Broglio hit I was struggling to retire the side before my lead vanished. Since he'd thrown me good curve balls I decided to reciprocate—the double-crossing Dago. Only I didn't have a good curve. Broglio lined a *hanging* curve into left field and Hutchinson growled loud enough to scare bears in the St. Louis Zoo. One thing a pitcher should never do is let the opposing pitcher get a base hit to drive in a run.

Already I had walked four men in four innings. This is one more than I usually walk in nine innings, and three more than Hutchinson would like his pitchers to walk in thirty days.

Hutchinson as a pitcher depended upon pin-point control of his pitches. That is, he could throw a curve ball that broke eight inches at the proper moment to upset the batter's timing into a six-inch-square area of the strike zone 90 per cent of the time. The modern strike zone is barely the size of *Time* magazine. Hutchinson failed to appreciate his achievements largely because they were so necessary to his livelihood. How could anything so basic be difficult?

"For Christ's sake, bend your back a little bit," he said to me after Broglio's base hit. "You know you can't pitch high and get away with it." We still had a one-run lead and I vowed to mend my pitching manners. Cunningham and White drilled two low fast balls into center field to start the fifth. I might have caught both balls had I anticipated them. But such good pitches shouldn't have been hit at all, much less so hard.

"Boyer will bunt, probably," I thought. "I'll waste a slider outside just to find out." Bailey took off his mask and walked out toward me. "Forget it, Gar, I know what to do," I thought. But he wasn't even looking at me. Suddenly, Hutchinson loomed up in the left-hand corner of my vision. "Make Pena get the ball over the plate," Hutch said. He held out his hand for the ball which I had just rubbed up till it felt comfortable.

"What for?" I said, stupidly stupefied.

When Hutchinson makes up his mind to take a pitcher out of a game there's no argument worth while making. I could debate with myself, though. "Jeez, I haven't even settled down yet and I still have a one-run lead. In my last two starts I didn't get any runs at all for fifteen innings and I stayed in the game. What's the story?"

No one in the shower room could tell me. No one in the stands knew. The bus driver who took us to the airport and the pilot who flew us to Chicago could not have cared less. We had won the game, anyway, and celebration was in order. My roomie told me to go to sleep when we arrived in Chicago. We had six hours to rest before the next game.

My wife sympathized with me when I called in the morning. "You just better tell Hutch that you want to start and you deserve to start and why did he take you out so quickly and why did he let Newcombe stay in for eleven innings two nights before that and—" But I cut her off in time to catch the bus to the ball park.

"Don't you think you took me out a little quick?" I asked.

Hutchinson greeted my hesitant query with a raised eyebrow and an amused twitch of the left corner of his mouth. "You don't think you were pitching good ball up till then, do you?" he countered. "*I* didn't."

"Maybe not," I conceded. "But it seems to me that you don't trust me as a starter. Isn't it true that you think of me primarily as a relief pitcher? Is this Hook you're bringing up from Seattle going to take my starting job?"

"Let me just say this," he said. "You've got good stuff and you're a pretty good pitcher. I may use you in the bullpen now because I know you can do that job for me. Not every pitcher can. Newcombe couldn't, for instance, and these two kids can't. I have to use Hook and O'Toole because they're going to develop only if they get a chance to do a lot of work. They're going to start in rotation and pitch in turn if they get shelled eight times in a row. As for you, don't worry about it. You'll get plenty of work."

He patted me on the back, pushing me toward center field, where I shagged the fly balls that crashed into the wind barrier from Lake Michigan. Although it was a warm summer day, the wind came from the northeast. As a general rule wind blows from warmer to cooler surfaces and should have been blowing out—away from the plate. In the spring, Lake Michigan is warmer than Wrigley Field and pitchers delight in the beauties of the vine-covered walls. Not too many home runs are hit into the wind. In the summer the lake draws the southwest gales that blow pop fly balls into and over the vines. Chicago Cub batters seldom complain about the heat. Why bite the helping hand of Nature?

Don Studt drove me home after the game, which we lost 1-0. "What are the baseballs for?" he asked, pointing at the two autographed balls in my lap.

"Anne Stewart wants to give them to some kid who has to undergo a hundred operations in order to walk. He's a baseball fan, I guess. She tells me that I should give away my share of autographed baseballs to kids like that rather then just anybody who might ask for them. She doesn't realize, I think, that an autographed ball often pleases the nubile female on the road. I sell my balls to the single players, naturally."

"Naturally," he agreed, and asked for names and numbers.

"You met Phil Clark, didn't you, Donald?" I asked him. He nodded.

"Well, the Cardinals traded him out of their organization the other day. Another close friend of mine that they got rid of. I feel like I was a contaminating influence over there. Next thing you know they'll be trading Cunningham."

"You going to be happy in the bullpen?" asked Studt.

"Why not? Hutch says I will be."

July 19—Chicago

THE bullpen welcomed me with cutting remarks and well-sharpened needles, which they inserted into my wisecracks. Above anything else, a sense of humor is necessary for life in the bullpen. Once admitted and accepted in camaraderie, a relief pitcher may even suggest a serious topic for conversation. Like baseball.

"You know what this Hook said yesterday?" I asked. "He told me that in the Coast League they're saying that it's easier to pitch in the big leagues than in the minors. That's what somebody at Seattle told him. I'll be damned if he's not proving it, too."

Hook pitched against the Cubs as if they were not quite up

to Pacific Coast League caliber. Not only did he get them out with ease and dispatch but he looked as if he knew what he was doing on each pitch. Many young pitchers *act* as if they know what they're doing—it's the television influence on youth—but seldom does their pretense meet with the approval of the cynical veterans on the club.

"He's got a *good* fast ball, a live fast ball," said King.

"How fast is a good fast ball?" I asked.

"Just fast enough, Bross," said Whisenant. "It's not the speed of the ball alone but the pitcher's motion, and the spin on the ball, and how much the ball moves. . . . Lotta things involved in a good fast ball."

"Did you know that the biggest curve you can throw is seventeen inches?" I said.

"Who says?" asked Schmidt.

"Some professor in Washington. He runs the Bureau of Standards, I think."

"Who'd he pitch for?"

"He was an outfielder in college," I said.

"That figures."

"I believe I'd rather have a good slider than a good curve," I said. "Good hitters complain about the slider more than any other pitch. Most of the good hitters in *this* league do—Musial, Mays, Whisenant. That right, Whiz?"

"Bross, take away sliders and curve balls and I'd be the best hitter in this ol' league," said Whisenant. "And if you made every pitcher throw left-handed they'd never get me out. Whoops!"

"Then you could play 'Boo on You' with Rogers Hornsby and Frankie Frisch. To hear them talk, they never would make an out if they played today. Old-time ballplayers! Years ago they must have had five guys in the league who hit .400 and a hundred and ninety-five who hit .214! They had to have. When the old-timers get through talking about how much better the hitters used to be, they talk about how much better the pitchers were thirty years ago. Any major leaguer who played at least twenty-five years ago was, automatically, better than anybody who plays now. He had more guts, more desire, and chewed more tobacco. And despite that (or because of it) he drew fewer fans to watch him play, made less money, and almost lost his memory completely."

"Brosnan," said Schmidt, "we're going to enjoy having you down here with us, I can see that. All we have to do is get you talking and we can all go to sleep."

After the game Don Studt called to tell us that rain was forecast for Sunday so why didn't we drive out for a steak. He had just removed the meat from the freezer when we arrived.

"Don't worry. I promised you food. You'll get some," he said.

He suggested that we have one small drink. Don spells "drink" with a "u" not an "i." After several toasts to Solly Hemus for making the party possible we got down to some serious suburban recreation. The competition is keen, but baseball conditions the body. Ah! Life in the Open Mind!

Hourly forecasts from the weather bureau invariably predicted rain for the next day. "It'll start pouring any minute now," they said. This soon sounded like "Double-Header Canceled." We celebrated our day off prematurely.

"As long as it's going to rain, why don't you stay to eat?" said Don . . . or Gwen. It was almost midnight.

"What's cookin'?" I mumbled to him . . . or her.

"Steak," they said. "We promised."

My wife prayed all the way home in the car. I prayed the rest of the night. It was too late to sleep. We prayed for rain and it came thundering down with the dawn. Rain is good for the flowers, and it makes grass turn green. Rain on the bare head will cool the brain and shrink the head back to normal. It rained all day.

What the hell, when you start going good, the breaks come your way. (You have to watch out for that tonic water, though.)

213

July 22—Milwaukee

SOME days just add to the confusion. They're full of questions that can't be answered.

Which way is it to County Stadium?

I had taken a detour on my drive from Chicago for the first game of our series with the Braves. I wound up in a West Milwaukee suburb. Since the Braves had lost seven games in a row the fans denied their very whereabouts. It took me an hour longer to find the park.

Did Jim Hearn cry when he heard that he lost another game yesterday?

Hearn had been released by the Phillies in May. He was the pitcher of record, however, in a suspended game with the Pirates. The game was completed on July 21 and Hearn was debited with the defeat, although he was in Georgia when the game ended. Wonder if all those days in between are credited on his pension record?

Where are you going to manage next year, Clyde?

King's gradual disenchantment with coaching led to rumors that he was after a job as manager. He refused to commit himself. Agitation commenced. When conversation lagged, someone would ask King where he was going.

"Which one of us are you gonna take with you, Clyde?" was a variation that annoyed him.

"I'm not taking Brosnan or Schmidt, I know that," he said. "You two guys are the worst agitators I ever saw in baseball."

"You mean the best, Coach," said Schmidt. "Take us with you to the Continental League, Clyde. Rickey's promised you a job as manager over there, hasn't he?"

King denied it as the phone rang. Hutch asked for Lawrence to warm up as we went into the ninth leading the Braves 4-3. O'Toole was our pitcher and he needed three outs for his first complete game in the majors. He walked the first man to face him.

"Don't second-guess now, Clyde. Wouldn't you take Rocky out of there now before he loses the game?"

"Dad gum it, Brosnan, I can't tell you that!"

"How do we know if you'd be a good manager or not," said Schmidt, "if we don't test you under game conditions?"

Spahn batted for himself. He tried to bunt three times, fouled out, and broke his bat in disgust.

"Looks like Spahnie's luck has run out. He's won more games just like this in the last inning than any pitcher in the league."

Avila, who had just been purchased from the American League, came to the plate.

"How do you pitch him, Clyde?" I asked.

"Hutch knows him. He was in the other league with him, I think."

Hutchinson came out of the dugout to talk to O'Toole, clapped him on the back, and walked back to the bench. O'Toole threw Avila a high fast ball and he hit it over the left field fence.

How do you pitch Avila?

July 24 — Cincinnati

FRANK THOMAS handed me a large package as I walked into the clubhouse.

"Here you are. All you tobacco-chewin' free-loaders come and get it," he said. "My free tobacco just arrived."

"Frank," I said, "do you think it's fair for you to accept this stuff? You don't chew it. All you do is endorse it in advertisements. Don't you ever feel like you're misleading millions of tobacco-chewing kids? They read that their hero, Frank Thomas, chews tobacco and they think it's all right for them, too. You're sickening the youth of the nation, Thomas."

"*You* chew it don't you. Why?" he asked. " 'Cause you like the price, that's why. It's free."

I put a package in my locker and went to the trainer's room for two antacid pills. Even the mention of chewing tobacco gives me heartburn in late summer. Must be the heat. But do I stop chewing during a game? No, sir! Can't kick the nasty habit. (Double-headers damn near kill me.)

"How come we didn't change the signs when Hutch took over?" asked Acker in the bullpen.

"What for?" said Schmidt. "There ain't ten guys in the league that are interested in 'em. Nobody on our club is."

"Stealing signs is the most overrated idea in baseball," I said. "The only sign worth knowing is the other team's hit-and-run. And even that is useless 60 per cent of the time or more. How many clubs have even as many as three hitters who ever hit-and-run?"

King agreed. "Take some pitchers. They give away their pitches by something they do before throwing a pitch. They use different grips for different pitches. Some cock their wrists before they throw a curve ball. Another guy will hold the ball loose for fast balls, tight for breaking stuff. But the coaches are the only ones that can see the pitcher doing those things. And half your batters won't take the sign from the coaches because they don't trust them."

"The coach has to let the batter know what's coming somehow," said Lawrence. "All the pitcher has to do is listen to the coach. As soon as he learns the coach's signal to the hitter he throws a fast ball instead of curve. And maybe comes in tight with it. From then on no batter will trust the coach."

"The Yankees never bother with stealing signs and they win more pennants than anybody else. Crosetti got the reputation of being a great sign stealer just because the Yankees won so many games when he coached third base. So he comes out in the paper with the statement that he never stole a sign in his life!"

216

"Just a bunch of hogwash," I said. "Gives the coaches something to do besides count baseballs and pick their noses. You can't steal a pennant. You gotta score runs."

"Wish we'd score one," said King.

Hook had a shutout as we hit in the eighth. But we hadn't scored a run, either. Hook was scheduled to be the third hitter in the inning.

"You don't think he'll use a hitter for Hook, do you, Clyde?" asked Whisenant.

"You wouldn't, would you, Clyde?" asked Schmidt.

"Clyde's gonna wait till after the inning's over," I said. "Then he'll tell us, Willard."

Kasko preceded Hook, however, and hit a fly ball down the left field line. The ball headed directly over the bullpen where we sat, leaning in toward the line, wishing the ball fair. The wind, blowing toward right field, curved the ball toward the foul pole. Whisenant flapped a towel toward the field, yelling "Fair ball!" Three of us, standing along the line, waved our arms to indicate that the ball was going to hit the pole. The ball hit the wall, an inch foul, and caromed off the foul pole into the seats behind the bullpen.

"Too bad," I thought. "Just missed."

"Wait a minute, Bross," said Whisenant. "He called it a home run."

"He must be out of his mind. At best it could only be a double."

"He musta thought it hit the screen above the fence. It was pretty close."

"We'll take it," said Schmidt.

"Why not?" I said. "Do you think we should tell the umpire, Clyde?"

King laughed and stepped into the dugout for a drink of water. The phone rang. King answered it, and told me to loosen up.

Hook started the ninth by walking Freese. I started to throw hard in the bullpen as Hutchinson ran out to the mound, but he let Hook stay in the game. The next two hitters struck out. Sawatski batted for the Philly pitcher. Again Hutch went to the mound to talk to Hook.

"Don't let him hit a fast ball," I thought, assuming that Hutch was saying the same thing on the mound.

Hook couldn't get his curve ball over, though, and finally came in with the "hummer." Sawatski drove it into the bleachers for two runs. Koppe doubled, and Hutchinson waved me into the game.

"That goddamn Sawatski couldn't hit a change-up with a paddle," he muttered, as I reached the mound. "I just get through telling him, 'Don't throw your fast ball.' Couldn't hit a change-up if you told him it was coming." Hutchinson was still grumbling to himself when we reached the clubhouse.

July 27 — Cincinnati

MAJOR League Rule 16.2 says: "While the game is in progress no player shall converse with fans in the stands nor sign autographs."

One sign that the Cincinnati fans had regained a positive attitude toward us was the increasing number of requests for autographs. A losing team draws indifference rather than the veneration to be expected from baseball fans. The adult fan shrinks at contact with a consistent loser. Only the kids are faithful seekers of autographs. They, of course, use the autographs as symbols, and trade them in lively player markets just like real club owners. (One Newcombe was worth ten Brosnans in the late July trading.)

The boxes of baseballs to be autographed increased from two to three each day on the clubhouse table. Reggie Otero, the coach in charge of seeing that the ballplayers didn't give away more baseballs than the front office, questioned, in his colorful Cuban English, every request for a ball to be auto-graphed. Fans, adult as well as pre-teen-age, flocked to the parking lot where the ballplayers exited from the clubhouse. It took Frank Thomas, an inveterate signer of autographs, an hour some nights just to get to his car after the game.

The Cardinals, who were having trouble beating anybody else, came back to play us four more games. In less than five weeks we had played twelve games with St. Louis. They won six of the first eight. When Hutch took over he said we could beat them any day of the week.

Mizell started the first game for the Cardinals. In a foot-stomping rage he walked the first three men to face him. From the bullpen Mizell's pitches looked close to being strikes, but the bullpen is 328 feet from the plate. From the Cardinal dugout, ninety feet away from the plate, Hemus swore that Mizell's pitches were close enough to be called strikes. Swearing, of course is impolite; swearing at umpires is forbidden. All Hemus got for his squawks was the thumb from Stan Landes, the umpire. Hemus rushed out to the plate, squeaking additional protests, pushing his nose up to Landes's chest, like a mouse berating an elephant.

"Hemus is going to lead the league for the first time in his career," I said. "I bet he's been thrown out of more games this year than all the other managers put together."

"You're keeping up with Solly, aren't you, Brosnan?" said Schmidt. "I was under the impression that you didn't care for him too much."

"What in the world ever gave you that idea, Willard?" I said.

The Cardinals didn't recover their poise for two games. That's the way it goes in baseball. The first two innings are the worst in the game; psychologically. A team thinks it gets a bad call against it and is affected the rest of the game. Some people say the solution is to have the umpires warm up before the game just like the players do. Others contend that um-pires, when heated up, are inclined to be fractious and miss calls in a suspicious manner. He who gets an umpire hot gets burned.

Hemus did a slow burn twenty-four hours later, also, as Broglio and McDaniel lost a four-run lead to enable us to tie the score in the seventh. Quietly, I sneaked onto the mound to pitch the eighth. The Cardinals threatened with two outs, and George Crowe, the best pinch-hitter in the league, glared at me confidently while I reviewed my last attempts to retire him. This time he didn't get around on the high, tight slide ball and I made it to the bench. Hutchinson wisely used a pinch-hitter for me as we scored two runs in our half of the eighth and Lawrence wrapped up the game by retiring three men in a row. I sat motionless during the ninth, watching Lawrence save my win. It's tougher, it seems, to wait them out. You sweat almost as much sitting down as you would pitching for yourself.

By winning we came to within a game of sixth place. The Pirates lost, also, and the Cubs. We could see no real obstacle to the first division. Even fourth place has a little prestige— about two hundred dollars a man from the World Series kitty.

August 1—Cincinnati

JOANNE and Lee Walls joined us for dinner after the Friday night game with Chicago. There are only two restaurants worth attending after a night game in Cincinnati so it wasn't surprising to find ourselves in the wrong place for a gala night out. Two martinis, however, brought a smile to my wife's face; and Joanne took off her glasses, an act that announces she doesn't care if she *can't* see anything. It's fun time.

"What did Scheffing have to say after the game?" I asked Walls.

"What did Hutch have to say after Altman hit the home run?" he countered, laughing.

We had won the game 5-4. Johnny Powers, batting for me with two out in the ninth, hit a home run to win. Earlier I had gone into the game to save Newcombe's two-run lead. With two out in the ninth I served up a hanging curve ball to Altman and he hit it into the right field bleachers to tie the score.

"That was the first game Hutch put me in to save this year," I said, shaking my head. "What a dumb pitch. I should have stuck with the slider."

"How about Elston, then?" said Walls. "He knows better than to throw Powers a fast ball. He says it was a good pitch, right on the outside corner, but Scheffing really ate his ass out. Elston called him a second-guessing s.o.b., which he is, but they finally cooled it."

"I just love to see Elsie get beat," I said.

"He's pitched real good ball for us, though, Broz," said Walls. "He may be a Hot Dog but I don't know where Scheffing would be without him."

"Hutch nearly rammed a hole through the air-conditioning duct with his fist when I threw that high curve," I said. "It was a stupid pitch, anyway. I never should have thrown it. I'll be in the doghouse for a month."

"How many wins is that for you, now?" he asked.

"Five. Two in five days and I pitched a total of three innings. Breaks are going my way, dad," I said. "I'm over .500 now. Five and four."

Walls smiled, happy for me like an ex-roomie should be.

"We're going to knock you guys right out of fourth place this weekend," I said to him. "Believe me, we're hot."

The sun was hot, too, Saturday in the bullpen. We curled a hose on top of the bullpen roof, turned the water on, and lay across the bench throughout the game, sweating in comfort. The Crosley Field bullpens are built like battlefield bunkers. They're well equipped, with a water fountain, a telephone, and a long bench against the back wall. But you can't see the ball game if you sit down. Of course, if you decide to lie down no one can see in, either, to criticize your lack of attention.

The Cubs scored two in the first but we scored seven in the third. Purkey, the pitcher, hit a grand-slam home run to cap the rally. We almost moved, we were so excited.

"Your roomie just hit one out with the bases drunk, Willard," said King.

"He always did say he was a good hitter. I'll never hear the end of this, though."

"Why don't you go lay on the grass outside, Willard," I said, "and I'll fan you with a towel like you'd just fainted?"

"No, no, that's too far to go in this heat. You might wave that towel around a while and stir up this air."

"It's a pretty heavy towel," I noted.

"Let it lay, then," he said. "Let us know how we make out, will ya, Clyde?"

We won.

August 4—Cincinnati

ON MY way to the Cincinnati airport for our four-day trip to California I stopped to pick up Willard Schmidt. He and Clyde King both lived along my route to the airport.

"We've got plenty of time, Jim," Willard said as he dumped his suitcase into the back seat. "We don't have to pick up Clyde after all. He's going to Rochester as their new manager."

"Well. He got what he wanted, then, didn't he?" I said. "What happened to Cot Deal at Rochester? Did he quit?"

"The paper said he resigned. Rochester's in last place. He's coming here to take Clyde's place, incidentally."

"Glad to hear it. Cot's a nice guy, isn't he?"

"Naturally. He's from Oklahoma, too," said Schmidt.

"Is it true, Willard, that you're a successful cattle rancher during the off-season? I read that in the Reds' yearbook."

222

He grunted. "I don't know where they come up with stuff like that. I'd *like* to be a successful cattle rancher during the off-season. In fact, I'd just like to be a successful anything right now."

"There, there. You're all right in my book, honey. You don't look so good this morning, though. Have a tough off-day?"

He rubbed his hand over his eyes. "Kids'll drive you crazy. I've got to go on the road to get my rest."

"Nobody rests in California. Maybe Doc will give you some Dexamyl to get you through the week."

Ellis "Cot" Deal met us in Los Angeles.

"I hope you still got a sore arm, Cot," I greeted him. "Clyde ran us so much he couldn't comb his hair his arm was so tired."

"My arm is in good shape, James. How are you?"

"Everything's going to be all right," I said. "How did you get your arm to come around?"

"I've got some exercises I do with an iron ball. I'll have to show them to you. Your arm sore?"

"Hell, no," I said. "I only pitch once a week or so. What was all the shooting about in Cuba? I hear you nearly got killed."

He shook his head and whistled. "I tell you, I never felt so lucky in my life. You read about it, of course. I'd been thrown out of the game against Havana and Frank Verdi took over for me coaching at third base, see. These Cuban soldiers were shooting off their rifles in the stands! And a stray bullet knocked Verdi over and hit the Havana third baseman. Well, that was enough for us. We packed up and came back to the States. But, think of it. I could have been standing at third instead of Verdi, and I'm an inch or two taller than Frank. The bullet went through his cap and bounced off the helmet liner he wears inside it. Had I been there the bullet probably would have gone through my ear."

"I believe your hair's turned gray there around your temples," I said. "Glad you're still with us. How's Green doing?"

"Gene was a little disappointed when he came down from the Cardinals, and he stayed red-assed for about a week. But pretty soon he came around and started hitting real well for us. How did Solly look while you were over there?"

"Solly and I didn't see eye-to-eye on much of anything, you know. I probably couldn't criticize him objectively if I tried. But I will, anyway. Hemus tried hard, I'll say that for him. Maybe he tried too hard. He tends to overmanage and he gets panicky for no good reason at all. You'll see. We play 'em a couple more times this year."

"The hardest lesson a first-year manager has to learn," said Deal, "is not to overmanage. You can't help yourself, some-times. The panic gets to you."

"Yeah, but that goes for any manager. The good ones seem to control themselves. You know Hutch, of course. He's got a fist of iron . . . I mean a *will* of iron."

Deal laughed at the slip of my tongue.

"Would you rather manage than coach, Cot?" I asked.

"I'm happy to be here," he said, smiling.

"Great. We're happy to have you. And I'll never ask you again."

August 7—San Francisco

MIDSUMMER weather in San Francisco is comparatively cool. Instead of hibernating all day in an air-conditioned hotel room, ballplayers can be spotted walking down Market Street or up Maiden Lane (a favorite trail). With our last night game of the season in the Seals Stadium fog still hours away, I decided to get up early enough for lunch. My address book suggested a phone call. I dialed the office of *Time* magazine and asked for Bob Boyle.

"Hello, Robert," I said. "Shall we have lunch?"

224

"No," he said, and my heart stopped. What was this? Would I have to pay for my own lunch? "Jane wants you to come to dinner tomorrow night, and I want you to do me a favor," he said.

"Since your wife's cooking compares favorably with the best San Francisco cuisine, I'll be happy to do you a favor. *Was ist's?*"

"I want to take a poll of your ball club on who they think will win the pennant—Milwaukee, L.A., or the Giants. If *I* ask them they'll probably pick a team, all right, but if you ask them they might give you reasons why. Will you do it for me?" he asked.

"Consider it done," I said. "I'll bring the results to dinner. What did you think of Antonelli's blast? What exactly did he say?"

"Same old crap about how tough it is to pitch with the wind blowing out. I've got a clipping quoting him," said Boyle. "Actually he attacked the writers for printing his words almost as strongly as he blasted the ball park. He's getting a crybaby reputation."

"Among these sob-sister sportswriters out here that should be in perfect taste," I commented. "Were the two home runs that the Dodgers hit really cheap? Antonelli called them lousy fly balls, didn't he?"

"I wasn't there. Apparently they landed just beyond the fence, and the wind was blowing pretty hard. But Drysdale pitched in the same wind and he didn't give up any home runs."

"He's a different type of pitcher, Bob. My sympathies are with John," I said. "Antonelli will get a pretty good riding from our bench tonight, I guess."

The wind blew hard enough to help Whisenant hit five straight pitches into the left field bleachers during batting practice, a feat that I duly noted before asking him, "Okay, Muscles, who's going to take it all, the Braves, the Dodgers, or the Giants?"

In my quick tour of the outfield during batting practice I found that the bullpen crew as well as starting pitchers favored the Dodgers. "They got the pitching. And they got the best defense." Our rinky-dinks, who hit for ten minutes, then helped the pitchers shag for the regulars, favored the Braves, on their superior hitting. When I completed my poll of the regulars in the clubhouse, I still found little enthusiasm for the Giants. The veterans of our club favored the Braves slightly. Of course, they had quite positive opinions as veterans are so inclined. Over all, the Dodgers won the poll. "If all three teams go into the last week locked up, the Dodgers' pitching will do it," was the consensus.

Antonelli won his game Friday night, 3-2. The wind, which dies down after dusk, had little effect on the game. It picked up velocity in the morning, however, and blew briskly all Saturday afternoon. We scored two in the first inning but Hook walked three Giants in a row to start their half and Hutch called for Pena, who got out of the inning with a tie ball game. We picked up seven more runs in the next three innings. Pena gave up a homer in the third, and another to start the fifth. When he loaded the bases Hutch waved me in. As I took my first warm-up throw I nearly fell back off the mound. A gust of wind had caught me off-balance. Antonelli laughed loudly on the Giant bench.

Each inning as I walked toward the mound I heard myself say, "How can you pitch in this park on a day like today? It's ridiculous. You can just throw and pray. And I ain't got a thing today." My prayers held up well except for two pitches —Alou hit a ball halfway up the left field bleachers, and Kirkland hit a home run over the back wall of the right field bleachers to give me the league leadership in long-ball throwing. The most encouraging advice I could get from my own teammates during my performance came from Frank Thomas at third base. "Just hang in there, Brosnan. We'll get 'em somehow."

The Giant fans moaned angrily whenever I managed to

retire the side. How could any pitcher who threw two such long balls get anybody out? In the ninth, with two men on, they howled for my scalp. Hutchinson sat back in our dugout apparently oblivious to the expected carnage. I was too tired or terrified to think my way out of trouble, so I threw exactly what Bailey called for, hoping he knew what to do. Brandt, pinch-hitting with two out, guessed wrong at a curve ball and Delmore called him out.

I staggered slowly over to our bench, mopped some sweat from my face, wrapped a towel around my neck, and waited for the official scorer's decision as to who got the win. Pena had retired fourteen men and given up two runs. I'd relieved him with the bases loaded, and gone on to retire thirteen men. Also, I'd given the fans a great thrill by dishing up two long home runs. Did I get a "save" or a win?

"Winning pitcher, Pena," came from the field microphone.

"That figures," I muttered. "The dirty, no-good, lousy . . .!"

I was still mumbling to myself when the cab pulled up at Boyle's apartment. He greeted me with a bottle of gin and a bottle of vermouth in his hands.

"Mix your own. You do it better than I do. Jane will have one, too," he said. "Did you hear over the radio? Solly Hemus just signed for another year."

I drank several extra martinis.

August 13 — Cincinnati

Our chances of overtaking Pittsburgh and finishing in the first division were no less difficult than the pennant chances of the three top contenders. We had to win all six remaining games we had with the Pirates. Since it was absolutely necessary we saw no reason why we wouldn't do it. The schedule presented a greater problem. We had to play (said the revamped National League schedule) nine games in six days, five of them on the August 14-16 weekend, and the other four with Milwaukee.

Gabe Paul recalled Bobby Henrich, a shortstop, from Savannah, Georgia, and Henrich reported in time to warm up pitchers in the bullpen during the Milwaukee series.

"Why in hell didn't Gabe bring up a pitcher, Cot?" I asked.

"He didn't consult me, Jim," Deal said soothingly. "Besides, Henrich's a seasoned traveler and Gabe knew he wouldn't panic when the notice came. Right, Bob?"

"I wish they'd pay me by the mile for this season," said Henrich. "I left L.A. in the spring to train in Florida, was optioned to Savannah, came back here in June when McMillan was hurt, was sent to Seattle when Mac got back in the lineup, went back down to Savannah from there, and now I'm back in Cincinnati because McMillan is hurt again. If I'd gone straight up in the air on March 1 I'd be at the moon by now."

Neither Purkey nor Acker showed up at the ball park. The news that both had the flu made everyone in the bullpen sick. "Who's going to comb my hair for me after this weekend?" I asked Deal.

"Don't worry about it. Incidentally, if Purkey can't pitch Thursday, you're nominated."

"Well, isn't that just too sweet," said Schmidt. "That means he won't be in the pen all week."

"Oh, no, it doesn't," said Deal. "Hutch says you guys will just have to double up."

"I've got a cramp in my arm already, Ellis," I said.

When the fifth inning started on Thursday night I also had an eight-run lead. Pinch-hitter Lee Maye led off for the Braves. I had never pitched to Maye before. "He'll be taking one strike anyway," I thought. "Then I'll try to jam him with the slider. It's working well for me." I laid the first pitch right over the heart of the plate.

Maye hit it into center field and I turned around to look at the Milwaukee bench. How could Haney let him hit the first pitch when he's eight runs behind? It just isn't done. Avila bunted, a move that I expected even less than Maye's first-pitch single. I waited for Bailey to come out from behind the plate and field the ball, and he waited for me to come off the mound. Avila got a base hit. Mathews took three sliders just inside, fouled two others off, and then walked as I missed with a curve just outside. Five good pitches in a row and I still couldn't get him out. The fans started to grumble and Hutchinson called the bullpen.

I knew I'd be out of there if I didn't get Aaron. He had already hit two sliders right on the nose in his first two times up. He was also hitting .385 or something like that. "I'd better waste one slider and gamble on him leaning into a 'hummer.' If I can jam him good on one pitch I'll be able to go back to the slider which is my best pitch." Aaron tommy-hawked the high inside fast ball and bounced it right back to me. Bailey took my throw to the plate and doubled Aaron at first. The entire grandstand breathed a sigh of relief. "Hutch has gotta let me stay in here now," I thought.

Covington fouled off four sliders just like Mathews had, and I tried to outthink him. "He can't be looking for a change, now. I'll slip it right by him." He hit it over the center field fence to make the score 8-3. "There goes my shutout," I thought.

The tensions of the inning plus the heat and humidity undermined whatever strength I had left after throwing eighty-seven pitches, many of them frustratingly good ones. In any given game a pitcher expects 80 per cent of his good pitches to result in outs. (In Crosley Field *bad* pitches are frequently called gopher balls in the next morning papers.) The Braves, however, were either taking my good pitches or fouling them off, neither action pleasing me. Some good pitches must be "set up," that is, certain sliders are no good unless the batter is guarding against the jamming fast ball or the low sinker. And a good breaking-ball hitter must be given a peek at a close slider or curve before he's susceptible to a hummer on the hands. One "good pitch" may involve two other pitches. I was tired.

Pinson homered in our fifth but I had to go back to the

mound all too quickly. Before the inning was over I could feel myself "pushing" the ball, and hoping for a mediocre swing. Torre popped up a high curve that he should have "creamed," and he cursed so loud he woke my brother Mike who was watching the game on television. Avila singled sharply on my next pitch, a crackling noise that brought Hutchinson to the mound. He said, "It's a hot night. I'm bringing in Pena."

I showered and poured a bottle of rubbing alcohol over me to stop the nervous sweating. Pena held the five-run lead through the seventh, by which time I was driving home to watch the end of the game on TV. With a cold beer in one hand and a burning cigar in the other I waited impatiently to celebrate my sixth win.

"Come on, Orlando, you bean bandit," I yelled at the TV screen, "get 'em out one more time."

Aaron, Adcock, and Logan singled to knock Pena out in the ninth. Nuxhall got Crandall but gave up a single to Lopata and a double to Pafko. Avila walked to load the bases and the score was 9-8. I spilled my beer, cursed the day I ever got into baseball, and shocked my mother, who said, "You ought to be ashamed of yourself. A grown man crying about baseball. It's only a game."

Lawrence relieved Nuxhall and went to 3-2 on Mathews while I urged him in a hoarse whisper, "Don't walk him, Brooksie. Don't let 'em tie it up. Make him hit the ball." Mathews popped up to make it seem just like a game instead of a moment of truth.

August 15—Philadelphia

HUTCHINSON reminded us before the first game of our five-game weekend series with Philadelphia that we had a good shot at the first division. A World Series between Cleveland and Los Angeles would mean $400-$500 per man. "That's worth putting out a little extra from now on," he said. "We can beat this club four out of five games. We're a little short on pitching but so are they. Let's go get some runs."

Hutch led with his ace, Newcombe, but the "Tiger" didn't have it. He was bombed out in the second, and when Acker, still groggy from the flu, had trouble retiring the side we trailed by eight runs.

"Looks like a long weekend, Broz," said Lawrence.

It was a long game, at least. With Pinson and Robinson getting five hits apiece we scored fifteen runs on twenty-three hits and Lawrence had a four-run lead as the Phils batted in the ninth. I was the only pitcher left in our bullpen.

"How do you feel, Jim?" asked Deal. "Just in case."

"Let's not talk about it. I guess I can pitch to one man if I have to. But don't ask me how I feel."

Lawrence couldn't get the side out. Four singles around one strike-out gave the Phils two runs. With men on first and second Hutch waved me in to pitch to Gene Freese. My record against Freese for the year was enough to chill any manager's heart. Hutch may not have known it. He said nothing to me except "There's one out." I took the ball from Lawrence and said, "I owe you one."

Freese fouled off a high slider as I gulped fresh air. "Gotta be more careful than that," I said "Brush him back now and go with another slider, down and away. Or at least down." Freese jumped at the slider and hit it on the ground to Kasko. "Don't take a bad hop, now. Please, ball." Kasko tossed it to Temple, whose throw to first beat Freese to the bag and we'd won it. Hutch met me with a strong grip and a little smile. "Nice going. How's your arm feel?"

"It aches. But no more than when I went out there."

Lawrence joined me at the trainer's table. "We're even," I said, as he held out his hand. "Don't shake it too hard. It may come off."

We won the second game and the Saturday game to put us seven games above .500 since Hutchinson became manager.

231

No other club in the league could make such a statement. *Sports Illustrated* magazine sent its ace baseball writer to Philadelphia to find out what happened to Cincinnati.

"I know you'll want to buy me a drink while I tell you, Roy. Let's go in the bar here in the lobby."

Roy Terrell, in his thorough, painstaking research on the question, had decided that I had more experience with Hutchinson's managing than anyone else on the Reds. "And Hutch is responsible, isn't he, for the club's improvement?"

"If you look at it from a managerial viewpoint, yes," I said. "From a player's viewpoint, partly yes and partly no. The material was always there, of course. Hutch can't make a thoroughbred out of a plow horse. He's done one thing. Straightened out the pitching staff. And I say that even though I can't raise my arm."

"He's used you both starting and relieving, hasn't he?"

"Yes," I said, "but only in an emergency do I start. I belong in the bullpen according to him, and I'm no longer questioning him. He makes his pitchers believe in his decisions. Probably the rest of the team thinks the same way. What the hell, you gotta think twice before arguing with him. They don't call him The Bear for nothing!"

"Everyone who ever played for him calls him a nice guy, though," said Terrell.

"Every man to his own definition. I wouldn't describe him as a 'nice guy' myself," I said. "Which doesn't mean I don't like him. I've known managers that I would call 'nice guys' but I didn't even respect them much less like them. Just being a nice guy doesn't entitle a man to respect. He may earn his *own* self-respect and have peace of mind but that just irritates the hell out of me. How can my leader have peace of mind when I don't?"

"We were talking about Hutchinson," said Terrell.

"Okay. Look at it this way. Most ballplayers respect Hutch. In fact, many of them admire him, which is even better than liking him. He seems to have a tremendous inner power that a player can sense. When Hutch gets a grip on things it doesn't seem probable that he's going to lose it. He seldom blows his top at a player, seldom panics in a game, usually lets the players work out of their own troubles if possible. When he straightened things out here we started to move."

"Do you think you'll catch the Pirates?" he asked.

"If we can get rained out Monday or Tuesday so we can get a little rest, I think so. Pena and Lawrence must be tired and I know my arm's ready to fall off right now. We've all been throwing in the bullpen every day now for over a week. With the two kids starting regularly the bullpen has been up and down half a dozen times during a game. It's not how many games you actually pitch in relief that gets you, y'know. It's all those times you heat up. You have to be ready to go in so you have to stretch that muscle every day and sometimes more than once a day. The arm seldom gets a proper rest. Then you start to baby it and you're really in trouble. A little rain would do us some good."

"How about Mayo Smith?" Terrell asked.

"I wasn't around long enough to be able to analyze him, Roy," I said. "One thing I will say. I thought he was a nice guy."

August 19 — Cincinnati

"Rigney may have lost the pennant last night, Cot," I said. "He insulted us by starting that kid. He obviously was saving Sanford for Milwaukee."

"Maybe that's all he had to pitch," said Deal.

"This is no time of the year to be giving away games. He didn't want to waste a regular starter against Newcombe. Tiger's beaten the Giants five time this year. But, what the hell, Rigney's got to get a good pitching job in this bandbox, and the kid might have better luck in Milwaukee with a big park to pitch in."

"He couldn't afford to lose a game to the Braves, though," said Schmidt. "And who says Sanford could beat us here? Rigney should have pitched Stu Miller."

"This club can't beat Miller," said Johnny Powers. "He just tosses up that junk he has and everybody falls flat on their face."

"I'd like to have his junk," I said. "He's got to be the best pitcher in baseball today. With his stuff he can't afford to make one mistake and hope he fools a hitter."

"You can catch his fast ball in your teeth," said Powers.

"Don't let him hear you say that, John," said Deal. "You're liable to catch one in your ear."

"It's positively cruel, I think, for people to refer to Stu Miller as a junkman, or a magician. . . . You'd think he was just hanging on in the majors instead of leading the league in E.R.A. Sportswriters and broadcasters make Miller out to be some sort of clown on the mound. And yet get some big strong kid who can throw a ball through a wall and has the brain of an idiot . . . *he's* a prospect for the Hall of Fame."

"You want to be Miller's agent, Broz?" laughed Deal.

"I'd make more money with him than with most of these hard-throwing kids with heads to match."

"The next time they have one of those field events for long-distance hitting and accuracy throws they ought to get a machine to measure fast balls," said Purkey. "I bet some outfielders can throw harder than good pitchers. And it doesn't mean a thing."

"Those field events are a joke," I said. "But that one the other night was a true farce. Did you see it, Willard? They had disk jockeys and politicians and sportswriters throwing a ball from home plate toward the center field fence. Lou Smith proved once again that he doesn't belong on the same field with professional baseball players. His throw rolled barely to second base. I've puked farther after reading some of Smith's columns in the paper."

"You're just mad, Broz, 'cause he hasn't had you on his TV

show," said Purkey. "You gotta be nice to those guys."

"Better loosen up, Jim," said Deal. "Hutch will probably use a hitter for Pena."

"Why, Cot? Pena hasn't given up a hit in five innings," Schmidt said.

"Why, Willard, I thought you'd been sleeping and here you've been watching all along. Go get warm, Brosnan."

Stretching my arm gingerly I heated up as Whisenant ran up to bat for Pena. The score stayed at 3-2 while I pitched the eighth. We scored seven runs in the last of the eighth, however, as the Dodgers used four pitchers to retire the side. All of a sudden, it seemed as though every time I walked on the mound runs started to cross the plate.

With an easy win in sight I walked out to the mound in the ninth, smiling. How could I lose this one?

"We'll wipe that smile off your face, you queer bastard!" came from the Dodger dugout.

"Queer!" What vulgar emotion.

Essegian hit my first pitch into center field for a single. Something's got to be done about managers who don't follow the Book when they're six runs behind. It says the hitter should take a strike. Why, the pitch to Essegian wasn't even over the plate and he gets a base hit!

Roseboro pinch-hit and I walked him. Hutch jumped off his chair in the dugout and the crowd moaned. "This is ridiculous," I thought. "I better bear down." But it was too late. When I reached back for a little extra it wasn't there. I panicked. My slider wouldn't break; I didn't dare change up; the fast ball moved all right but I couldn't control it.

Ron Fairly swung at a bad pitch and flied to left. Furillo hit for the pitcher. "Make him hit the ball on the ground and we got a double play. He's got a bad knee," is what I should have been thinking. Instead, I recalled a home run he hit off me on a tight fast ball, and a double to right center on a high fast ball on the outside corner. "And he's a better breaking-ball hitter with men on," kept flashing through my brain. Furillo took a low slider that Bailey picked out of the dirt. The crowd booed. It may have looked like I was scared to throw a strike. Furillo took a half-swing at the same pitch for a strike. I tried to jam him good to move him back from the plate but he hit a soft line drive just over Temple's head. Temple backpedaled, turned the wrong way, and timed his jump badly. The ball fell for a single, the bases were loaded, and Gilliam came up to hit. I always have trouble with Gilliam. He has a good eye for a strike and seldom bites after close pitches. Either I lay it in there for him or he doesn't swing.

He took a walk. My pitches weren't even close to the strike zone. The fans howled for my head. Six runs ahead and I walk a man home! Hutchinson stormed out of the dugout. I didn't wait for him to chew me out. Tossing the ball at him as we crossed paths I headed for the clubhouse. But he got to me with a contemptuous snarl, "That was the worst exhibition I ever saw!"

It was the first time he had ever questioned my ability and I reacted just as I knew I would. "Well, screw you, Hutchinson," I said to myself as I elbowed my way through the crowd to get to the clubhouse. "Here I pitch my goddamn arm off for you and look what I get." My arm started to ache in sympathy with my wounded pride.

The Cincinnati radio broadcaster said, as I entered the clubhouse, "Well, we're going to wait now and see what the official scorer does about declaring the winner of this game." Obviously Lawrence had retired the side on one pitch. "Brosnan is the pitcher of record, but Pena pitched outstanding ball, and he certainly deserves more credit for the win than does Brosnan."

Good God! I never even gave a thought to that. How can they do this to me?

"Here's the announcement," said the radio. . . . "Well, the scorer called Brosnan the winner. But, I don't know, the rules should be changed to cover situations like this. I certainly don't think justice was done in this case."

236

"Why, you no-good . . ." I muttered. "How about the Frisco game that I saved for Pena? What did you say then?"

I ran into the shower, rinsed off the sweat, wiped myself dry, and dressed rapidly as the clubhouse filled with somewhat subdued ballplayers. My miserable performance had taken some of the elation from a solid triumph.

"Hang in there, Roomie," said Acker.

You'd have thought I lost the game.

August 20—Cincinnati

THE newspapers noted that my win gave Cincinnati its first season series over the Dodgers since 1944. So it was an historic event. The bullpen hardly paid attention to it. Willard Schmidt, his smile lurking in the verbiage, said, " 'Competent Baseball Men' said in the paper this morning that you were lousy last night."

"May he be forced to read his own garbage for eternity," I said. "And he didn't say it, either. You're just trying to agitate me. Don't. My arm's sore."

"So is Pena's," said Deal. "If Purkey needs any help you're in there again tonight."

"How about Willard? He's Purkey's roomie," I complained. "I'm not kidding, Cot. My arm's hanging."

"Let's hope we don't need anybody," he said.

Purkey breezed through four innings. With two out in the fifth he struck out McDevitt, the Dodger pitcher. Bailey, however, dropped the ball and McDevitt beat the throw to first. Before Schmidt could get the side out, the Dodgers had scored seven runs. Such a little break (the ball rolled only fifteen feet away) didn't appear to be worth much but the Dodgers acted as if they deserved it. As if they were looking for it. Acker relieved Schmidt in the sixth and threw a high fast ball to Moon, which used to be a cardinal sin when Moon played for St. Louis. Moon hit the ball over the center field fence. Lockman then batted for Acker and I walked up to the bench with my barely warm arm. ("There's only so many pitches left," I had told Deal when he asked me if I'd thrown enough in the bullpen.)

McDevitt dusted Pinson off with a fast ball as I walked into the dugout. All season long Pinson had hit just about everything the Dodger pitchers could throw. But with a five-run lead and two men out the knockdown didn't set well with Hutchinson.

"He shouldn't have done that," said Hutch. "No reason for it. Maybe he should eat a little dirt, himself. No reason for that kind of thing."

McDevitt was scheduled to hit second in the Dodger eighth. "Maybe Zimmer will get on first and McDevitt will bunt, I hope," I hoped. But Zimmer struck out and I had no choice. "He's got to be looking for it," I said to myself. But he wasn't and the ball plunked him in the shoulder. "Christ, he didn't even move," I thought.

The Dodger bench roared its disapproval and I looked the other way. Gilliam bunted down the first base line, but I wasn't about to have him climbing my back and I let the ball roll. It stayed fair as the Dodger bench yelled "Chicken" in several profane languages. McDevitt, too, added a comment as he stood at second base.

"Hey, Four-Eyes!" he yelled. "You hear me, Rabbit Ears. Why don't you go read a book?"

I turned around, rubbing the ball between my hands. "Listen, you little punk, there's an old proverb, 'Book Say Pitcher Who Knock Down Batter Get Ball Stuck In Ear.' Just be glad my control is lousy."

The umpire at second base told me to get on with it and I struck out Neal. Moon then topped a ground ball toward first. Robinson fielded the ball and tossed it to me as I crossed the bag. The throw was behind me and I had to reach back for the ball as Moon clobbered me, knocking me over the bag.

238

I tripped backward, my head banging on the ground, my glasses sailing down the right field line. The ball stuck in the webbing of my glove and Moon was out. I didn't feel too good, myself, but I'd be damned if I was going to let anybody think so. Not only did I make it to the bench (limping slightly for applause) but I went back to the mound in the ninth.

My ankle swelled visibly and my wrist hurt from the fall, but my arm ached too much for me to care. Two of the three Dodger hitters struck out, swinging anxiously at every close pitch. As I went to the clubhouse I hoped that we would score more runs as had been the custom when I took the mound. We did score one and had the bases loaded when the final out was made, but almost is no cigar.

I moaned to the trainer, "Doc, what can I do? My arm's killin' me."

"Hold it straight up in the air for as long as you can. Get that blood moving out of your shoulder. You'll be all right. We'll wrap your ankle tomorrow. Looks like you get a rest for a couple of days."

"Thanks, Doc!"

August 23—Cincinnati

"Where are we going, Cot?" I said. "Willard and me. Do you think Gabe will trade us to the American League?"

"Why don't you keep us for spring training, Cot?" said Schmidt. "We could run the young pitchers for you and save your arm."

"The two of you can just stop asking me the same question over and over," said Deal. "I've told you, as far as I'm concerned you're two of the best agitators in the game today and you're making my life miserable. How do you know *I'll* be back in the spring?"

"Who would we agitate, then, Cot?" said Schmidt.

"If we're still here," I added.

"Be quiet or I'll have you both warming up."

"Don't be ridiculous, Ellis," I said. "It's too hot today. Let Newcombe work. He can afford to lose weight. *We're* almost down to our playing weight now. Right, Willard?"

"I want to go to Kansas City," Schmidt said. "Fix it up for me will you, Coach?"

"My home's in Chicago, you know, Cot," I said. "Surely you can work something out with either the White Sox or the Cubs."

"Why don't you both shut up and watch the game."

"I got a better idea," I said. "We'll play manager. Willard, you manage our side and I'll manage the Cardinals since I know the personnel. Every time a strategy move comes up we'll call it, and see if Hutch and Hemus do the same thing."

"You manage both clubs," said Schmidt. "I'm more 'coach' material than 'manager' material."

"Okay. I'm running St. Louis. You criticize me, now, Cot. You were a manager. First thing I do is give Cunningham a raise. An incentive raise so he wins the batting title. I told him before the game today that he's the best hitter in the league."

"It's not a good idea to give raises during the season," said Deal.

"Why not? When I was with the Cubs we got incentive raises. I got going so good that they traded me."

"Seems to me you must be making more money than you let on, Brosnan," said Schmidt.

"Just barely making expenses, Will," I said. "My wife's thinking of going to work this winter so we can have another baby."

"Knock it off! If I had your money I'd be a successful cattle rancher and quit this game."

"Don't do it, Willard. I'm going to buy you for my bullpen. Cunningham needs somebody with a good sense of humor, to keep him loose off the field."

"He and Kasko make a real funny pair," said Deal. "They

240

could beat Martin and Lewis when they get started."

"How come Cunningham is called Flakey, Cot? When did that start?"

"People that don't know him call him that. He's got an odd-ball sense of humor, and at the same time he's so damn serious about baseball that you'd think he's two different people. 'Flakey' means people don't understand you. You don't have to understand Cunningham to appreciate him as a hitter, though. Look at that."

Cunningham lined a single to left, but like his other four hits in the series it went to waste. We won three in a row to take over fifth place from the Cubs. The Pirates were only four games away.

August 25 — Cincinnati

AMONG the folksy traditions of the Cincinnati baseball season is Family Night at Crosley Field. Wives and children of the Redleg ballplayers are led onto the playing field to receive varying degrees of applause, depending upon the size of each domestic group. Gus Bell, a hunk of potent virility the likes of which has seldom been seen in organized baseball, had seven Bells ring around him. The applause was deafening.

My wife had her usual complaint three hours before the gala event. "What am I going to wear, Meat? I haven't got a thing."

"Wear a maternity dress so it look like we mean to belong to the club," I suggested. "Most of these guys have three kids or more, or have their wives pregnant."

"Do you know that your father wants Timmy to wear a little baseball uniform?" she said.

"A nauseating suggestion if I ever heard one. The suit's cute but it's out. Timmy can wear Bermudas and a polo shirt. One comic figure to each family on the ball field."

"You do look awful in your uniform, Meat," she said. "For some reason or other you've got the wrong shape. I guess you just weren't cut out to be a ballplayer." She laughed at my sorry mistake.

"Listen, love, baseball is feeding you pretty well even if you haven't got anything to wear."

Jay Hook was introduced to the crowd after us, and he came out of the dugout cheered by the approving fans behind home plate. Only twenty-two and married just two years, he carried a baby and led his pregnant wife carefully by the hand. They picked up fishing rods and a check from the management, then lined up next to us.

"Gee, that's a lovely dress, Mrs. Brosnan," said Mrs. Hook. "I sure hope I'll get to wear one like that again." She smiled wryly at her husband.

Hook joined us later in the bullpen as the game began.

"Good boy, Jay-bird," I said to him. "You never know when you may pick up some useless information down here. Brooks, show Hook how to fire a rocket. He's an engineering student. Maybe he can help us reach the scoreboard from here."

Lawrence peeled the foil from a pack of Wrigley's Spearmint gum ("We use the best materials in our rockets, Hook") and wrapped it carefully around the head of an unlit match. "Hand me the launching pad, Broz," said Lawrence. I gave him the broom which we used to sweep cigarette stubs and candy bar wrappers from the bullpen. Setting the "rocket" upright in the broom, and pointing it toward the field, Lawrence lit the foil-covered head. Five seconds passed as the flame gradually heated the foil. Then, streaming smoke, the match arched over the railing of the bullpen into the grass beyond the left field line. "Tracking stations please measure the shot," Lawrence said.

"Dr. Wernher von Lawrence, you've done it again," said Deal. "Now let's watch Purkey slip the green weenie past Banks."

"Slip the what past Banks?" I asked, my ears twitching.

242

"Where in the world did you pick up an expression like that, Ellis?"

"That's an old baseball term," he said. "I've been using it for years."

"Sure, but what does it mean?"

"Oh, I don't know," he said. "I guess it means give the batter something he doesn't like."

"You guys come up with the damnedest expressions," I said. "Brooks made one last week. We were talking about sex and he comes out with, 'Say you're trying to make a home in some other town.' Now I never heard of any phrase like that. It's a definition for pursuit of happiness on the road, isn't it, Brooksie?"

"Why do you always ask for definitions, Brosnan?" Lawrence said. " 'Where did that word come from? What does that word mean?' What's with you? You writin' a book or something?"

"Nope, I'm just trying to learn the language."

Deal let go with several familiar terms.

"What happened, Cot?" said Lawrence.

"Purkey just hung a slider and Neeman hit it out of the park. Willard, you better put that book down and loosen up. What in the world are you reading, anyway? You haven't said a word all night."

"*Lady Chatterley's Lover,*" said Schmidt. "It's Brosnan's book. He said it would improve my mind. Who gets it next?"

Powers reached for the book and handed Schmidt the warm-up ball. "Dutch will catch you, Willard," he said. "It's my turn on the book."

Every pitcher in the bullpen but Lawrence eventually got into the game. I told Deal that I didn't think I could go very far because my wrist still hurt from last week's tumble, but Hutchinson left me in for three scoreless innings . . . to test it, I guess. I could have sworn I wouldn't be able to throw my slider.

We lost the game 8-5, but we'd just won three in a row.

"You can't win 'em all. Losing gracefully is gallant and sportsmanlike," I said to myself philosophically as we climbed the ramp into the clubhouse. The door to Hutchinson's room slammed shut, and the sound of falling chairs and upset tables reverberated throughout the clubhouse. Hutch disjoints furniture instead of dismembering his failing athletes. Which is his only mark of restraint when he loses a ball game.

He makes it difficult to be complacent.

August 30—St. Louis

THE sights and sounds of the scoreboard in most National League parks are sources of constant and pleasurable occupation for the bullpen crew. Careful attention to the numbers and letters, the flashes and signals on the scoreboard provides conversational material to keep each bullpen member alert. Or at least awake. Who's pitching for whom? What's the score in Pittsburgh? In Milwaukee? In our game? Who relieved the starting pitcher at L.A.? What did the scorer call that play? A hit! He must be out of his mind!

Scores are posted on the board manually in some parks, electronically in others. The sound of magnetized numbers clinking into place in Milwaukee is a signal for somebody in the bullpen to move. For the scoreboard can't be seen from the bullpen bench. This is true in Philadelphia, also, where in the daytime the numbers are flashed in color so dim that they are practically invisible to the naked eye. (Fortunately most bullpens have field glasses to aid the interested observer. The first row of the second deck is usually interesting.)

In St. Louis a neon Cardinal bats neon baseballs over the scoreboard, and a huge neon eagle flaps in Busch family colors whenever a home run is hit. Crosley Field's scoreboard flashes individual batting averages for the batter at the plate. Some hitters complain of embarrassment, as do most pitchers. (It's better to have no hits than just a few; the fans may assume you have not yet batted officially during the season when your average reads .000. It's a sobering reflection for bullpen pitchers to comment, seriously, on the prowess of the pitcher coming to the plate only to have the scoreboard indicate that this "good-hitting pitcher" is batting .089 in August.)

The Wrigley Field scoreboard in Chicago is the most imposing, towering more than a hundred feet above the center field fence. It serves as a roof for some of the liveliest gamblers in the Midwest, who will lay odds that the next batted ball will fall into the first row of seats along third base and strike a blonde on her left wrist. In rain, snow, sunlight and smog, the Wrigley Field gamblers huddle near the scoreboard, a scene of togetherness in a frequently raucous and loudly individualistic bleacher crowd.

The clock atop the Cub scoreboard has been two minutes slow for the last five years, and has its counterpart in the ball-and-strike operator, who is frequently one pitch behind the umpire. Closer attention is paid by the bullpen, however, to the posting of scores in other major league games. A blank panel in the board is replaced with a numbered panel. The speed with which this switch is made usually indicates whether or not a run has been scored in that particular half-inning. Zeros are painted on the opposite side of the blank panels; numbered panels must be retrieved from stacks inside the scoreboard. Many a beer has been bet in the bullpen on how many runs will be posted to replace an empty panel. It's a split-second wager to be made only by experienced bettors.

In St. Louis on the last Sunday afternoon in August Jay Hook battled the Cardinals while all eyes in our bullpen watched the posting of the Pittsburgh score. The Pirates, instead of fearing us, were talking pennant and playing like they meant it. They won Friday and Saturday while the Cardinals beat us; and when Hook gave up four runs in the first two innings our fourth-place ambitions looked bleak. But Hook shut the Cardinals out the rest of the way and we scored six

245

to win. In Pittsburgh, the Pirates won the first game 2-1, but Philly jumped out with five to start the second game. We rooted for Philadelphia. "Just hold 'em right there till we get a chance at 'em Tuesday."

September 2—Cincinnati

It RAINED on Tuesday. We couldn't play.

It rained Wednesday. We shouldn't have played but we did. The field was sloppy.

"Do you think a slow track helps us more than them, Whiz?" I asked Whisenant. We sat in the dugout watching the ground crew tug the tarpaulin off the infield so that we could take batting practice.

"Bross, it won't make a damn bit of difference. We're gonna hit everything out of sight, anyway."

"How come you don't come down to the pen any more, Whiz? We miss you."

"Hutch wants me on the bench to keep everybody awake. He says I liven up the bench. Ho! . . . Ha! . . . And a Cha! Cha! Cha!"

"For Christ's sake, Pete," I said, stumbling into him, "a man has to take out insurance just to talk to you."

"This infield is better than that rockpile in Pittsburgh, isn't it, Bross?"

I nodded my head. The Forbes Field infield is adapted for the Pirate type of baseball. Swift runners beat out many base hits because of the abnormally high bounces that batted balls take off the hard ground. But then it is an accepted practice for ball clubs to "fix" their own ball parks.

Back in 1949 when I was at Macon, Georgia, in the Sally League, our manager, Don Osborn, always supervised the ground crew in preparing the field. Since we had three sinker-ball pitchers on our club, a soggy area around the plate was

246

bound to benefit us. Any batted ball that hit within ten feet of the plate picked up mud like a snowball and could hardly get through the infield. We won the pennant by fourteen games. Every little bit helps. Each manager tries to fix his home field to his best advantage.

"Not many ways to fix this field to help the pitchers, though, Bross," said Whisenant, laughing.

"I suggest the government drop a bomb on second base and blow those fences back to where they belong," I suggested.

Lawrence came up to us and said, "Let's get our running in, partner, and we can play a couple of rubbers. Hutch just said there won't be any hitting."

Ever since I'd learned how to play bridge I'd been looking for a partner like Lawrence. We won twenty-three straight games from July through August. A number of combinations of players challenged us. Newcombe and Willie Jones had us down four hundred points one evening before a game, but Hutch called all the pitchers out of the clubhouse for a running session—the first time all year I jumped at the opportunity. (Amazing how virginity sublimates the desire to compete against odds. A spotless record we had, and, by Goren, we'd have it when the season ended!)

Lawrence plodded alongside me to the center field fence where we met several Pirate pitchers running their own ten laps. (Where *we* plodded, *they* ran. The paper had quoted Pirate manager Murtaugh—"We still got a chance for the pennant.") Harvey Haddix, a fellow resident with Lawrence of Springfield, Ohio, and Benny Daniels, the Pirates' Negro right-hander stopped to say hello.

"Hey, Mullion-man!" Lawrence said to Daniels, and they grinned at each other.

Lawrence and I turned to run back to the left field line for our last lap. "How do you spell 'Mullion,' Brooks?" I asked him.

"I don't know. I just say it. I don't spell it."

"It's a Negro term, isn't it? I asked. "I first heard it this

247

spring over at St. Louis. Every colored player in the league seems to be using it this year. Who started it?"

"How do I know, Brosnan? Don't bug me on that, now. You're always buggin' people on words."

"But what does it mean, Brooks?" I persisted. "Even the o-fays on this club are using it now." "*O-fay*" is a Negro word that means white man, and is one word from the fascinating Negro language that I'm familiar with.

"Where'd you pick up *that* expression, Brosnan?" asked Lawrence.

"O-fay? I read a lot. Don't bug me on words, man."

"Well, I couldn't spell 'Mullion' but it means . . . like, not pretty. Not a queen. You know. Ugly, you might say," he said.

"Okay. I dig. How come everybody's a Mullion-man this year?"

"There aren't many good-lookin' ones goin' nowadays, I guess. How do I know? Let's go play us some bridge."

Hutchinson didn't bother with a pep talk. He knew we knew this was it. Either we won both of these games from Pittsburgh or we were out of the money for sure. O'Toole started the first game for us. He retired the first man, then gave up a single to Groat, a triple to Clemente, and a tremendous home run to Stuart. As the ball sailed high over the left field fence, I thought, "There goes the first division." But I said, "There goes my record for the Long Ball of '59."

O'Toole was shaken up by Stuart's blast, and he shut out the Pirates the rest of the game. In our eighth, with two men on, Roy Face relieved for the Pirates. The crowd applauded the little guy and his 17-0 record. In our bullpen, however, the amazing record got short shrift. "Let's get this little squirt one time," said Powers.

Willie Jones hit a home run off Face's third pitch. That was enough for us to win. We had just one more trick to pull for game and rubber, so Hutch led his ace of trumps. Big Newk strode arrogantly to the mound and dared the Pirates to hit him. You can't beat the trump ace; we took both games. Pittsburgh's pennant chances disappeared and our chance to catch them looked good again.

"Newk, you really had it tonight," I said as we sat at our lockers.

"Yeah! Listen to the 'Tiger' roar!" he roared.

September 7—Cincinnati

"It worked, Cot," I said as we settled back in the bullpen for the Labor Day game with Philadelphia. "We lost two out of three to the Braves but Hook won the big one."

"We should have won all three. The Pirates lost two out of three, too," he noted. "Why was Hook's game any bigger than the others?"

"Jay-bird and I both want to drive our wives home tomorrow, see. He had to win a game so Hutch would be in a good mood when we asked his permission. *You* said we wouldn't be allowed, remember?"

"If we don't win this game today we might just work out tomorrow," he warned.

"Oh, no, I'm already packed for the trip," I protested. "Listen, give me some more advice. Should I ask Gabe for a new contract before the season ends?"

Purkey interrupted, "Don't, Broz. Let him call you in first. That's the only way to do it. Don't let 'em know you're anxious."

"Listen, Purkey, Cot and I are talking bullpen business. What are you doing down here, anyway?"

Deal said that he agreed with Purkey.

"To hell with the both of you," I grumbled. "I'm going to ask him anyway. I can't stand the suspense of waiting for a new contract all winter long."

249

"What *are* you doing down here, Roomie?" asked Schmidt. "Hutch run you off the bench?"

"I think he wants me to learn how to pitch again," said Purkey, sadly. "Ever since I had the flu and missed a week of throwing I seem to have lost all my rhythm on the mound. I'm throwing too hard, and my ball isn't moving at all. Nothing works."

For some pitchers too much rest is a catastrophe. Any disturbance of their pitching habits can hamper their effectiveness on the mound. Purkey, whose fast ball sinks at an odd angle, can't afford to be too fast. He has to throw at a certain controlled speed or his ball won't move properly. Moreover, the slider, which is Purkey's secondary pitch, has to be rigidly controlled. A strong arm may cause the slider to break too much; a weak arm, not enough. A week-long layoff causes any pitcher to think of his arm as too strong, or too weak. The arm doesn't change much physiologically, but the pitcher tends to *think* it has. (Some baseball men say that pitchers should give up thinking.)

With Purkey's rhythm erratic, and Nuxhall out with a bad knee (and probably doomed to a similar ineffectiveness for a while if he returned before the season's end), our starting rotation included the two kids and Big Newk. Our task of catching the Pirates didn't look any easier. A pitching hand that included an ace and two spots seemed hardly good enough to bid on. Two double-headers in a row faced us in Chicago. Hutchinson had to make a true psychic bid.

To top off a shaky pitching foundation Newcombe couldn't wangle any runs from our hitters. In five games he gave up no more than three runs per game and yet won only two of them. The sportswriters had insisted that the Reds were scoring five runs per game, and that the horrible pitching was responsible for our position. This twisted misrepresentation did nothing to help Newcombe's morale.

The Phillies did nothing to help it, either, on Labor Day, bombing Newk in the sixth inning. We lost the game, to the relief of the Pirates, who must have been watching our score in Milwaukee where they lost two games to the Braves. In four days we had lost a chance to pick up three and a half games.

"We should be in fourth place already," muttered Hutchinson as he paced back and forth through the clubhouse after the game. Hook and I showered and dressed quickly to sneak away before he changed his mind about letting us drive to Chicago. As I passed the blackboard next to the door I read the notice: "Meeting with Frank Scott in Pittsburgh, Sept. 19." (Scott runs the office of the Major League Ballplayers Association.)

"What are we voting for, Broz?" said Hook as we walked into the parking lot.

"You can get a ballot from McMillan, Jay," I said.

The one big issue to be decided by the ballplayers was whether or not to have two All-Star games in 1960. The players would play the games under the condition that four days in a row would be set aside in the schedule during which time the games would have to be played. Or . . . Do you vote *yes* for an extra day off, Brosnan?

Why not?

September 10—Chicago

BREAKFAST on the second day of our two-day stand in Chicago was extra-heavy. Daylight double-headers mean no meal for ten hours between breakfast and supper. I prepared one of my special egg dishes with wine and cheese, ate six tablespoons of wheat germ instead of four, poured a third cup of coffee, lit one last pipe, and sat down with the morning paper.

"Oh, no, you don't!" my wife said. "You're home for two days, spend most of the time at the ball park, and you want to waste time reading the paper. I wanted you to cut the grass, or wash windows, or something. This house is a mess."

"But we've been away for a month!" I protested.

"Yes, but it's dusty. And don't forget, the Clarks will be here sometime today. Bring some beer home with you for Phil."

Phil and Gay Clark had promised to drop in for a day on their way to Georgia from St. Paul, where Phil had finished the season.

"Good," I said. "I'm looking forward to seeing Gay again."

"Gay!" she said. "What do you mean by that suggestive tone?"

"We're both looking forward to seeing the Clarks, aren't we?" I said. "Well, you look forward to your Clark and I'll look forward to mine. It'll be good to see Philip, too. Wonder how he made out in the Dodger system? That organization is loaded with pitchers."

"You better hurry or you'll be late," she reminded me.

Leaving her with the lawn mower, I drove to Wrigley Field. The wind blew gustily at my back, as I walked into the park. I hoped it would stay that way all day. In my years of pitching relief for the Cubs I seldom got into ball games when the wind blew in, only when the breeze roared straight into the center field scoreboard. In the third inning of the first game, however, I got my chance. O'Toole, starting for us, had some trouble with his co-ordination. Even with a 9-1 lead he didn't seem to be able to find the strike zone. He threw ten straight balls, enraging his father, who sat behind our dugout. Hutchinson, also, was not amused. He bade the umpire to seek a relief pitcher for O'Toole.

An eight-run lead to a relief pitcher is like gold to a penniless prospector. When Hutch, irritated at O'Toole's wildness, had wagged his hand for someone to warm up in our bullpen, there was concerted rush for the mound. Having long legs and a greedy ambition I won the right to be first. "Long relief," according to Casey Stengel, "is a dirty job." But it has its moments.

As I stood on the mound looking for the sign, I felt for the wind. It was still at my back. *"Ils ne passeront pas,"* I said to

252

Walt Moryn, who already had a count of two balls and no strikes. "Wha'!" he said back to me. "Thou shall not pass, O Moose," I repeated, and struck him out. A pinch-hitter was next. "Why do they bring these kids up at the end of the season to confuse my mind?" I wondered. "This man isn't classified yet. How do I pitch him?" He hit a ground ball through the third baseman's legs, and the next batter lined a single to left center.

By now Lawrence was heating up hastily for us and actually waving his arm at Hutchinson to indicate that he was ready to relieve me. "Oh, no, you don't, Brooks," I said, and retired the side.

"Bear down out there now," Hutch said to me on the bench. (The Big Bear!) "You'll get yourself an easy win."

I don't know why people said it was so easy. Six innings of pitching is work in any man's game. The similarity of this game and my first win of the year back in May struck me, however, as Banks drove a five-iron shot toward Milwaukee. The wind toyed with the ball, let it drift toward the left field seats, but dropped it into Pinson's glove at the 390-foot marker. That's the way this game should be played. They've taken everything else away from us pitchers. Let us have Mother Nature on our side.

Don Studt sat in the first row just behind our bullpen during the second game. I introduced him to Willard Schmidt. "Willard, I'd like you to meet the champion free-loader of all time. Don's wife and son came to the game on my two passes. They got tired—or bored—during the first game so they went to Don's office down the street, gave him the ticket stubs, and he got in to see *this* game. Congratulations, Studt, you'd have made a great ballplayer."

Willard laughed as if he thought I was kidding, and Studt laughed because he knew I was. "You should have seen Brosnan in the first game, Don," said Schmidt. "He was so anxious to get into that game he spiked me and knocked Lawrence flat on his face."

"The way he beats the Cubs, he should," said Studt. "That's

253

six times since they traded you last year, isn't it, Jim? Why don't you pick on somebody else? How can I be a loyal Cub fan when you keep giving me passes to see you beat 'em?"

Phil Clark repeated the same question when I got home. He added that I should also beat the Cardinals six or seven times in 1960, "and do it once for me, hyah?"

We killed a half-case of beer before the night ended, cutting up managers, organizations, and progressive education. Philip needed just one more semester for his teacher's degree.

"But ah can't make any money teachin'," he said. "Just two more yeahs of baseball and ah would have been set. Hemus sure wrecked mah plans."

"His opinion has been wrong before and since," I said. "The papers quoted him the other day in L.A. saying he didn't know what kept the Dodgers up where they are. And Bavasi—you know, the Dodgers' general manager?—said, 'Maybe Hemus doesn't know what's holding our team up, but I know what's holding his down.'"

"Jim, you're somethin' else," said Gay Clark.

"Well, I didn't say it, hon, but I wish I had."

"Who are you calling 'hon,' Meat?" said my wife.

"Everybody's 'hon' tonight, honey. Smile a little. You're with a winner."

September 11—Milwaukee

HOME plate in Milwaukee is 450 feet away from the bullpen. The visitors' dugout is set back another thirty feet from third base. There, Hutch growled back and forth, tearing gum wrappers into confetti as our game with the Braves began. The manager's only connection with the bullpen in County Stadium is via telephone; he can't see what's going on, who's laughing, who's smoking, who's sleeping. If he suspects that there may be a certain lack of attention at times, he's right.

254

Bullpen conversations cover the gambit of male bull sessions. Sex, religion, politics, sex. Full circle. Occasionally, the game —or business—of baseball intrudes.

"Look at that stupid pitch!" Whisenant wagged his finger at "that"—a home run into the right field stands by Ed Mathews. "A stupid curve ball. Bailey's dumb for calling it, and Hook's dumber for throwing it." Whisenant fired his catcher's mitt into Cot Deal's stomach, saying, "And you're responsible, you dumb coach."

Deal laughed a little less heartily than the rest of us. He flipped the glove back to Whisenant, and said, "Well, Pete, now just what should he have thrown right there?"

"You gotta jam him with the fast ball," Willard Schmidt said, interrupting.

"Hit him on the hands with a slider," said Brooks Lawrence.

"Slow up on him once in a while, then jam 'im with the slider," I suggested.

"Bross, you're gonna throw that high slider once too often to Mathews," Whisenant said. "Ed told me he's been looking for it."

"Let him look," I said, bravely, considering some of the drives Mathews has hit off me in the past. "There's only one way to pitch him. You gotta get into him."

Heads nodded in agreement. Deal, as pitching coach, pushed the argument. "Well, Hook tried to jam him twice with his fast ball, and missed. He got behind and he had to come in with a strike. If he'd thrown a good curve, and gotten a strike on him, then he could go back to jamming him."

"Hook ain't got a good curve," said Whisenant. "He's got to go with his best pitch to a guy with a hot bat like Mathews. That run's liable to beat us. He'd be better off walking him . . . or something." Pete's voice trailed off as his argument weakened. *Nobody* is supposed to walk *anybody*. "Make 'em hit the ball!" Outfielders scream it, infielders shout it encouragingly, catchers plead, managers moan. It's up to pitchers to decide what pitch to make the better hit, though.

"How's he gonna pitch Adcock, Cot? Goofy's got a hot bat, too. Against us, anyway." I asked the question hopefully, expecting to get a general opinion that would coincide with my own. Adcock has hit too many shots through my legs and off my glove or shins to make me confident that I know positively the best way to pitch him.

"First thing you gotta do," said Whisenant, interrupting, "is knock him down. Then, go away and stay away. Sliders, curves, fast balls."

"Knuckle balls, spitters," Schmidt added, a grin wrinkling his face.

"Get serious, Willard," said Pete, kicking dirt on Schmidt. "Here I am trying to help you dumb pitchers out, and you try and make a joke out of it."

Adcock lined a double down the right field line, and the phone rang in our bullpen. Deal answered. "Yeah? . . . Okay . . . Willard, loosen up a little," he said as Lee Maye stepped into the batter's box and Bailey walked out to talk to Hook. "Orlando, you might as well throw a little, too," Deal added.

Whisenant grabbed his glove and ran to the other end of the bullpen. "Hurry up, now, Willard," he yelled. "Hook's gonna bail out in a minute and you'll be in there for a couple innings. We'll watch you and learn how *not* to pitch. That way we'll learn the right—" Pete dodged a curve ball that snapped off in front of the plate and caromed away. "Save that good stuff for the game, you dumb German. Throw a curve like that to Crandall and he'll never touch you."

Eyes turned to the field as the crack of a bat solidly hitting a ball reached our ears. "What was that pitch?" I asked. Frequently in Milwaukee I have to ask that question because I just can't see the plate, even with my glasses. If I ever go to coaching I'll need Zoomar lenses. Actually I hadn't seen the pitch thrown.

"Maye's a high-fast-ball hitter so that must have been a high fast ball. Right?" said Brooks, watching Vada Pinson catch the long drive at the base of the center field fence.

"Looks like you have to move the ball around on Maye," said Deal. "I'd suggest you mix in a change and give him the good hummer on his hands if you want to strike him out."

"Cot, you're a genius," we all agreed.

"If I'd only done what I knew I should do I wouldn't be here," said Deal, ruefully acknowledging the fact that all our observations were worthless if we couldn't use them in the game. It's easy to say, "Jam him," or "Mix your speeds," or "Keep the slider away and he won't touch you." But some pitchers don't even have a slider to throw! Like young Hook, who walked Logan on four curve balls. That's what he was supposed to throw Logan and he tried, but he didn't get them over the plate. So off he went to the clubhouse and Hutchinson waved in the next pitcher. Hook had retired just two men; four days earlier he had gone nine on a five-hitter against the same team. Inconsistent youth!

"Who is hitter?" asked Pena, as he grabbed his jacket and headed for the motor scooter that would take him to the mound.

"Get the damn ball over!" yelled Whisenant. "Don't worry about how to pitch him."

"Mantilla playing tonight?" Pete went on. "Or Avila? Don't matter. Couple of bean bandits just like Pena. Keep everything down to both of 'em. That Avila can really rip that high pitch."

"He's a pretty good breaking-ball hitter, they say," said Johnny Powers.

"Stay out of this, J.C.," said Schmidt. "You outfielders think just 'cause we let you warm us up out here that you can tell us how to do our job."

"Jeez, Willard, I was just telling you what they say," said Powers.

Pena got Avila on a sinker, third to first, and we were out of the inning.

"Who else they got in there today?"

"Joey Jay's a pretty good hitter," I said.

"Curve him. He's a pitcher. Pitchers can't hit a major league curve ball." Whisenant ticked off the whole Brave pitching staff . . . Spahn, Burdette, Buhl, Rush. "Curve 'em."

"How we pitching Aaron?" I asked.

"And Bruton. Ya forgot Bruton," said Powers.

"Bruton murders that low inside stuff," said Lawrence.

"I say he's a high-ball hitter the way he hits the ball to the opposite field." Whisenant flipped his glove at me as I was stuffing a wad of tobacco into my mouth. "How about that, Bross?" The tobacco nearly choked me as I dodged the glove.

"I've had better luck with him high than low," I recalled.

"Me, too," said Schmidt.

"Shut up, Willard," said Whisenant. "We're still talking baseball."

"Try to move the ball around upstairs on him," said Deal. "Same as Torre. They don't strike out much, and their power is low. Give 'em leverage on a ball down and in, and they might hurt you."

"Gorgeous deduction, Cot," we agreed.

"Now, how about Henry? How you pitching No. 44?" said Powers. His eyes gleamed, a leer lighted his face. Hitters love to see pitchers in trouble.

"We'll get to Aaron in a minute. Anybody got a score card?" I asked.

Deal reached for the card. "Let's see, they got Lopata—you jam him or curve him. Good stuff. And they got Mickey Vernon—I'd say, overpower him. He's too smart for you to be cute with him."

"Wonder if Schoendienst will still be able to hit that fast ball like he did?" Schmidt said. "You could throw him ten off-speed pitches in a row, and then come in with a good hummer. Whomp!"

"Once a good fast-ball hitter, always a good fast-ball hitter. He won't play, anyway." Deal shoved the score card under the telephone. "Let's get some runs."

258

"What about Aaron?" asked Powers.

"Knock him down, first pitch," said Pete.

"Curve him away," said Willard.

"Jam him good. He'll swing at the ball a foot inside, sometimes," said Brooks.

"Change up on him once every trip," I suggested.

"Boys, I think Pena just struck him out on a spitter," said Deal.

"Good pitch," we agreed.

The Braves looked good. All year long they had looked like each guy was waiting for the other guy to start moving. Now each guy had decided the other guy wasn't going to do it, so he better do it himself. With their material, the Braves should have had the pennant sewed up already.

"Now," said Willard, "let's get down to some serious conversation." And we came back to it again. . . . Full circle.

September 14—San Francisco

IT WASN'T till we landed in California that we learned Pittsburgh had also won Sunday. Our win over the Braves gained us nothing in our race. San Francisco papers, agog about the pennant race, hardly mentioned our fight with the Pirates for fourth place. The *New York Times* sent John Drebinger to report on the Giants for nervous New York fans who once booed the Giants at the Polo Grounds. Drebinger's appearance on our bus to the ball park in the morning did not surprise Don Newcombe, who interviewed Drebinger all the way to Seals Stadium. If the *Times* was truly seeking All The News That's Fit To Print, Big Newk would oblige. After Drebinger had a look at Rigney and the Giants twitching nervously on the field he would have some Fits that were New to Print.

The Giants still held first place, but the poll of other National League teams predicted an imminent breakdown.

"Antonelli will keep us in first place," wrote the hopeful sports editors as they threw off the mantle of objective journalism and cheered like die-hard fans. "Brosnan will start for the Reds," said Hutchinson. The odds on the game jumped to 5-2 for Frisco, according to reliable cab drivers who checked our bus as we arrived at the ball park. "What's the story?" Schmidt said to me in the clubhouse. "Is Hutch betting on the Giants?"

I gave him my best nervous sneer and went to the telephone to call various hosts who had fed me during the 1959 season. My brief appearances previously against the Giants had gone unattended by my friends. I would repay my free-loading debts with passes to see me pitch. ("We know you play for the Cardinals or Reds, but when do you ever pitch?" they had inquired.)

My passes did not swell the crowd visibly. It was a Monday afternoon, and weekends in San Francisco are traditionally tough. I received one delayed acceptance. From Dr. S. I. Hayakawa, the editor of *ETC.*, the Semantics Quarterly. (My acquaintance with Don Hayakawa has been my only brush with the erudition that the more literate members of the bull-pen ascribed to me.) He asked for a raincheck on a game, though. "I could come tomorrow. Could you pitch then?" he asked. If my luck over the years against Antonelli held out I might very well be able to do that. But I put a brave front. "No, Don," I said. "I don't think so. I'm starting today, and I'm going all the way." He said he was sorry about that. He wanted to see me pitch.

I wished *him* luck, anyway, and reported to the trainer for a pregame rub-down. Doc Anderson said my arm felt fine so far as he could tell. Johnny Powers caught my warm-up pitches and said, "Ya got good stuff today, Broz. Hang in there." This injudicious blend of contrasting sentiment was soon followed by Hutchinson's last words of advice: "Go as far as you can, now. We got plenty of help down there when you need it." Not even *if* I need it, but *when* I need it!

Antonelli had no trouble in the first inning. I asked Conlan for a new ball when I reached the mound. Jocko winked at me as he tossed a ball to me. "You got good stuff, kid," he'd said years ago.

"Now, let's see some of it," I said to myself. We hadn't gone over the hitters before the game. "You've pitched against them enough," said Hutch.

Bressoud took two pitches, then half-swung at a good slider and popped it up. A half-swing pop-up of a slider is not as encouraging as a full-swing strike. He could obviously see it break just before the ball got to the plate and his strike zone.

McCovey, the second hitter, usually took one pitch just to get a look at the stuff. I laid a flat slider in for a strike, then broke one off on his hands. He popped it up. Ah ha! Give Old Broz a pitch and he'll take two.

Mays stepped into the box and stared at me. Willie constantly asks me what I throw him that he can't hit. "Why d'you do me like that, man?" he asks, with a terribly hurt expression, as if I deliberately got him out! The first year I threw him nothing but high fast balls away from him. The second year he had to hit sliders away. This year it was the old Red-Ball Express again, but in on the hands. I have just one more pitch left; perhaps Mays will retire in 1962.

Willie popped up a jammer that broke his bat, and I had lasted one inning. (Money changed hands in the press boxes.) Antonelli had little trouble in the second, getting Bailey on a called third strike for the last out. Bailey screamed at the call, and Conlan threw him out of the game. Hutchinson charged Conlan with having a quick thumb, and Jocko threw him out, too.

While Hutch told Jocko what he could do with his quick thumb I strolled to the mound muttering to myself. With Bailey out of the game, I not only would have to throw each pitch, but would have to decide which pitch to throw. Bailey was familiar with my stuff and knew better than I did sometimes which pitches were working best. We'd breezed through

261

the first inning together. Why did you leave me, Gar?

I stared at Cepeda, the fourth Giant batter. There's only one way to pitch him, of course. I threw him a slider on the outside corner for a strike. He leaned over the plate looking for another one and caught a sinker on his bat handle. Cursing in Spanish and shaking his hands in pain, he jogged toward first as his little fly ball settled into Kasko's glove. If Cepeda ever gets smart, and thinks two pitches ahead instead of one, he'll hit .400.

Kirkland ran up to the plate, eagerly. My old homer-hitting buddy. Six home runs off me in three years. I stepped back off the mound to hate Kirkland with my eyes. (Early Wynn says a pitcher will never be a big winner until he hates hitters!) I growled a negative growl at Dotterer's sign. No, sir, if Kirkland hits a home run off me on this pitch it will be from a prone position. Down he went. My control was excellent. He fouled off the next slider, fouled off a curve, and fanned on a fast ball right under his chin.

Well, that pitch did it. When a pitcher can rid himself of the feeling that he can't get a certain hitter out, he *knows* he's got good stuff. The Giants stared at me for six innings, waiting to see Old Broz, Old Nervous Broz, start to waver, start to think on the mound. They waited in vain. Today I *knew* that I could pick a pitch, decide where to throw it, and do it with good stuff on each and every pitch. "Want this slider two inches inside to McCovey? Okay, Professor, fire away!" Try a side-arm curve on Spencer; break it off the outside corner. Well-fanned, Broz!

Mays, still looking for a slider to hit, caught me thinking he might be taking one pitch as he had done on his first two times at bat. He hit a flat slider into the parking lot behind left field. A man is entitled to make one mistake in a game.

I didn't make another. Hutch called me into the runway behind our dugout at the end of the seventh. He said, "Now, I want you to tell me if you're tired. This is the first time you've gone this far in months."

262

What could I say? Any time I pitch seven innings I get tired. It's in my record. "I had a little trouble getting loose last inning," I admitted.

"Does your finger bother you?" he asked.

I shook my head.

"I think you're tired," he said finally. "Let's let Brooks finish up for you."

(Well, now, that's good enough for me, Hutch. My bridge partner and I are undefeated so far this year. Every game we've both been in, bridge or baseball, we've won. We had a 3-1 lead. Let's let Brooks finish up. Why not?)

Lawrence had nothing but good cards left. We won.

September 17—Los Angeles

A LONG-DISTANCE phone call from Bakersfield awaited me at the Sheraton-West in L.A. A Dodger fan greeted me by my first name and pledged eternal friendship because I'd beaten the Giants. The Dodgers *had* to win the pennant, he said. I asked him how much he'd won on my game and why didn't we split. He said he never bet on baseball games, so I hung up. He was an obvious liar. Baseball fans bet on every game during the season, according to statistics. My Bakersfield buddy was a baseball fan. Therefore he obviously bet on every baseball game. That's Formal Logic, something else I learned in school that I haven't used since.

"Whiz," I said to Whisenant as our final game with the Dodgers began, "I hear you went out to Hollywood today. Screen test, of course, wasn't it? You should be a great success, Peter. With your body? Cinch. Look what they did for Marilyn Monroe."

"You don't know the half of it, Bross," he said, "Come here, sweets. I learned a new technique today."

"Get away from me! Come on! Hey! How about it? You going to stay out here this winter?"

"I might just do that, Bross," said Whisenant. "What are you gonna do?"

"If I get a contract before I leave Cincinnati, I may just hibernate all winter. I've made a good salary drive this last month. It's time to hit 'em, I think, before they review the rest of my lousy year."

"Do you really think you ought to ask for a contract now, Bross?"

"Hell, yes. Why not? How can I tell what kind of year I had till I find out how much they think it's worth? Don Osborn, one of the best managers I ever had when I was a kid, told me that the best way to determine how good a year you had is by how much money you make out of it."

"Why, Bross, I thought you played baseball because you loved the game," he said, banging me in the ribs. He danced away, shuffling down the line of players seated on the dugout bench, shouting at them, "Wake up, boys! The neons are on! Time to open up your eyes! That a boy, Willard, open up. AAGH! They're bleeding! Doc! Doc! Take a look at Willard!"

The score of the Pittsburgh game in St. Louis flashed on the board. "They won, boys. We gotta go. Time's running out. Come on, Purk!" Deal yelled as Purkey walked out of the dugout to the Coliseum mound. Several pairs of eyes focused on Deal in the midst of his threatening exhortations. For two weeks we'd been "going," and getting nowhere. The best we could do was play .500 ball. Even if we won this game, we'd trail the Pirates by two and a half games. All they would need would be one win from us over the weekend. That would be it. Next year already looked better than this year.

September 20—Pittsburgh

WE LOST both games to Pittsburgh.

The light of our first-division dreams flickered on Saturday as the Pirates won in twelve innings, 4-3. The season then ended, practically, at two o'clock the next day.

I started the Sunday game. Every other pitcher on the club went to the bullpen except Newcombe, who had pitched the day before. Most of them got into the game. To start with I struck out the first Pirate batter. Superstition has it that it is bad for a pitcher to retire the first hitter on a strikeout. That's ridiculous, of course. It's not the first out but the last out that you should worry about. I didn't have to worry about the last out. I never even saw it. Two walks and four singles sent Pirate runners circling the bases around me. I felt like the operator of a merry-go-round, everybody else getting a kick out of the ride but me. The base hits weren't hit very hard, and the walks were intentional. But four base-runners scored.

"There goes my winning streak," I thought as Hutch silently took the baseball from me and gave it to Willard Schmidt.

"There goes my E.R.A.," I said to myself in the showers. From below 3.00 it soared to 3.47 in fifteen minutes.

"There goes my salary drive," I thought as I dressed and left the ball park.

"That's enough for one year," I hoped. It had been a long season.

September 27—Pittsburgh

THE last day of every season comes, eventually.

The last time to pack the duffel bag with gloves and shoes, jock straps and jackets, souvenirs and clippings that litter each locker.

The last hours of a Team. (For a new season must mold a new team.)

The last moment to say, "Good-by" . . . to say, "Good luck!"

But it's also the time to say, "See you in the spring, buddy!" Every ballplayer thinks he can come back again, to play another year. On the last day of the season baseball is a game that professionals really do *play;* it no longer seems like work to them. It is virtually impossible for a ballplayer to convince himself that he will never play the game again. On the last day of the season baseball, truly, is in his blood.

I stuffed my glove into a duffel bag, and picked up the last shirt from my locker. The empty locker symbolizes the cold, blue sadness of the last day of the season. There is something poignant and depressing about clearing out, for good; abandoning your own place in the clubhouse. They even take the name plate down, and who's to know what player dressed in which locker?

We won both games during the final weekend, ending the season on a positive note, and almost bringing a smile to Hutchinson's face. Four nights earlier, Philadelphia had beaten us in a double-header, forever quenching the aftertaste of our fourth-place ambitions. Actually, we needed no such reminder that we didn't deserve to finish in the first division, but the Phillies kicked us anyway.

To add to the insult, the bus driver, hired to drive us to the airport for our flight to Cincinnati, lost his way. Aimlessly he drove through the midnight-quiet streets of the city, finally reaching a dead-end in the railroad yards. His tired, subdued passengers, at first annoyed, became increasingly hilarious at this final, farcical coincidence. When we had a bad day, we had ourselves a mess!

A railroad watchman asked, in a bewildered voice, "How in the world did you ever get that big thing in here?" as if the driver had accomplished an impossible feat. A voice from the back of the bus asked, "Any of you bums want to take the train?" as a freight rumbled down the tracks behind us. And a cab suddenly appeared, the driver grinning as he inquired if he could guide us back to the highway. Hutchinson hired him immediately.

As the bus bumped onto the main road headed toward the airport, Frank Robinson yelled to the driver, "What's the matter, Bussy, you ashamed to be seen with us?" The nearly possible truth of this question convulsed everyone, including the bus driver, who almost drove off the road.

We had nothing to be ashamed of. Or, rather, we would prefer to think of those days which we could be proud of. Every baseball season is just long enough for each player to do something to which he can look back with satisfaction. On the last day of the season those are the moments you want to remember, and probably those are the memories that make you a little sad.

That final look at the empty locker brings no smile to a ballplayer's face. No matter how successful his season, he must feel sad at the sight of his locker, finally swept bare of tangible remembrances of the long season. No more sweaty, dirty uniforms to hang there; no more fan letters, newspaper clippings, baseballs and other souvenirs to clutter the locker with his own personality. A ballplayer can stuff the shirts, the glove, and the souvenirs into a bag and take them home for the winter, but they lose some of their appeal when they're removed from the locker. It's their natural setting. They belong there.

On the last day there really is not much tangible evidence

of the sweat, the tears, the applauding cheers of the season passed by, that a ballplayer can take with him. A bagful of gloves, shoes and jock straps; a fistful of clippings and fan mail; a line of statistics following his name in the record book. Of these, only the record will remain, permanently a part of him. Something he can never change, or replace. Something he can use that will never wear out. (Or, if he's had a bad season, something that can be used against him.) I'd already used my line in the book: "Brosnan, James Patrick, Cincinnati, Won 8, Lost 3, E.R.A.—3.36." (There are some figures for my months with St. Louis, too, but I slough over them. My record with the Reds is what they were interested in.)

Gabe Paul had said, "We liked what you did for us this year. We expect you to do better next season. We're happy to have you with us." Then he offered me the contract that I was after and I signed it. I wanted no more baseball problems till February, 1960.

Shoving two World Series tickets into my jacket pocket next to the copy of my 1960 contract, I made the rounds of the room, saying my *au revoirs*. Hutchinson was last in my tour of the clubhouse. He looked up from the trunk into which he had packed his equipment, shoved a huge bear paw at me, and said, "Good luck. You did a good job for me. Have a good winter." And he almost smiled.

I thanked him and went home.

Glossary

(These are some of the words and phrases I heard and recorded during the 1959 season. Professional ballplayers have their own technical language and slang, just like any other business. The definitions given are those which my twelve years' experience in baseball have led me to believe are reasonably accurate.—Jim Brosnan)

Bad Hands A physical affliction common to ballplayers with poor fielding averages. Symptoms include awkward fumbling of easy ground balls. There is no known cure.

Bean Bandit A Latin-American ballplayer.

Bloop A weakly batted base hit; a short line drive, or low fly ball that falls in safely between infield and outfield; often has the sound of a soft tomato struck by a broomstick.

Bo-Bo A ballplayer who is considered by his teammates to be the particular pet or favorite of the manager, the front office, the newspapers, the broadcasters. He draws more favorable attention than other players for no immediately recognizable reason.

The Book Unwritten laws of baseball strategy; traditional, sometimes superstitious, lore of years, and ballplayers, passed by. Most managers "go by the book" in certain situations, like the hit-and-run, or bringing in a right-handed relief pitcher against a right-handed batter.

Bombed Said of pitchers whose pitches return from the plate traveling faster than they were going when they arrived.

Breaking Stuff Pitches thrown in such manner as to not describe a straight line from pitcher's hand to catcher's mitt; e.g., curve balls, sliders, screwballs, etc.

Brush-Back A pitch thrown at a spot approximately six inches in front of, and on a line with, a batter's Adam's apple. Purpose of the pitch is to let the batter know the pitcher may, occasionally, lose control, and to keep him from digging in at the plate with confidence.

Bush Used to describe a social faux pas in the baseball world. A player who does things he shouldn't do, or says things he shouldn't say, is likely to be called "bush."

Caddie A player who frequently substitutes for one other particular player, usually in the late innings of games. As a rule the "caddie" is younger, quicker, but has less experience and makes less money than the player for whom he is substituted.

Change-up A pitch thrown apparently with the same power, energy, and intensity of expression as the fast ball, but which (ideally) does not reach the plate until the batter, his timing upset by the phony motions of the pitcher, has started to swing his bat. A cunning, deceitful artifice of the pitcher that will probably be outlawed by baseball rules-makers, who are constantly seeking new advantages for the batter. (Also **change-of-pace, letup, slow stuff.**)

Creaming a Pitch See **Bombed.**

Draft An annual ceremony in which major league club owners or general managers select minor league ballplayers in a ritual as complicated as it is stylized.

Drag From "drag bunt" as opposed to push bunt. A left-handed hitter drag-bunts down the first base line; a right-handed hitter drags down the third base line.

E.R.A. A pitcher's Earned Run Average is determined by dividing the total number of innings he pitches into the total number of earned runs (those not scored as a result of errors or attributable to a preceding pitcher) charged to him during the season, and multiplying the result by nine. Theoretically, the final result represents the pitcher's effectiveness during any nine-inning game. On a pitcher's record, the E.R.A. can mean everything or nothing depending on which general manager he's talking to.

Fist Him See **Jamming.**

Flakey A character, or characteristic, of eccentric or unusual behavior, verbal or physical, on or off the ball field. Any ballplayer who is considered hard to figure out is called "flakey."

Flip Him See **Brush Back.** (A good "flip" may require that the pitcher throw the ball at a spot where the batter would be if he didn't know the pitch was obviously meant just for him, and duck.)

Get a Jump In base-running, to start toward the next base just as the pitcher begins his pitching motion toward the plate.

In fielding, to move unerringly and swiftly toward the spot where a batted ball will eventually drop. More often used negatively, to describe a poor fielder—"He get a lousy jump on a fly ball."

Give Him the Line A defensive direction given to left or right fielders, first or third basemen, so that they will play farther than usual from the first or third base foul lines.

Gopher Ball Similar to the ordinary, legal-size baseball, but dangerous for pitcher to handle. Invariably, it can be observed sailing over an outfield fence in fair territory during a game. Should be avoided. (Also **long ball.**)

Handle Hit A batted ball struck with the narrow, or wrong, end of the bat, which falls for a base-hit and causes the pitcher to curse his scowling Destiny.

Hanging Curve   A curve ball that starts to "break," or curve, at eye level instead of belt-high; it usually ends up out of the ball park rather than in the catcher's mitt. For a pitcher, a mortal sin. He who hangs too many curves, soon hangs up his glove forever.

Heavy Ball   In pitching, a fast ball thrown with an eccentric spin. It causes more than ordinary pain or "sting" to the hands of a player who bats or catches the ball.

Hit a Ton   To collect a better than average number of base hits, often for extra bases.

Homer   To umpires, an insulting word inferring partiality is being given to the home team. Sometimes used by ballplayers who wish to be thrown out of the game.

Hot Dog   A ballplayer who exaggerates his place in the mortal scheme of things. His estimate of himself is often several times larger than that of even his closest acquaintance.

Hummer   A fast ball.

Iron Mike   A machine that throws baseballs as fast but not as cleverly as a pitcher.

Jamming   To pitchers, throwing the ball so that the batter can hit the ball only with the lower, or weaker, half of his bat. (Also **fist him, jammer, pitch him on his hands.**)

Knock Down   See, under **Flip Him,** a "good flip." Condemned by the A.A.U.

Knuckle Ball   An uncontrollable pitch that (according to batters) "dances," "wobbles," or "flutters" as it approaches the plate.
   The pitcher grips the ball with the knuckles, or (more frequently) with the fingernails, of his second, third, and fourth fingers.

Lollypop   Any ball thrown with less than average speed or energy by any player on the field.

Long Ball   See **Gopher Ball.** Often used as a nickname for catchers who signal for too many bad pitches.

Long Man   Pitchers are divided into three classes—Starter, Short Relief Man, and Long Man. The last-named enters the game usually when his team is behind and the starter has not yet pitched at least six innings. Also answers to **Mop-up Man,** or "Who in hell wants to pitch?"

Meat   A term of indiscriminate affection.

Off the Hook   Used to describe a state of nervous relief which a pitcher sometimes enjoys who leaves the mound trailing in the score and who then watches his team tally enough runs to tie the score again and eliminate the possibility of his being charged for a defeat.

Optioned Out   To be demoted to another ball club, usually in a lower minor league, on the condition that the club return the player at the end of the club's playing season. Like, to be put down, man.

271

Out-Man   A batter of little talent at the plate. There are few of them left now, since pitchers have learned to hit.

Pepper Game   A warm-up exercise in which a batter stands thirty to forty feet away and tries to hit pitched balls at, past, or through two or more fielders, usually pitchers. Theoretically used to improve the reflexes of the fielders.

Pick-ups   A warm-up exercise for pitchers designed to produce physical exhaustion. A coach stands a short distance from the pitcher, and rolls a ball to his right. The pitcher chases the ball, picks it up, and tosses it back to the coach, who has just rolled a second ball in the opposite direction. The pitcher repeats the exercise until he falls on his face as he leans over for the last pick-up.

Play Deep and Cut Across   Advice to outfielders from a pitcher who doesn't feel well and expects to be shelled off the mound during the game.

Play Straight Away   To assume, as a team, defensive positions that divide the playing field into nearly equal sections. Also because "I don't know which direction he's gonna hit the ball."

Pushing the Ball   For a pitcher, an awkward, feminine motion contrary to his usual delivery. Often caused by fatigue.

Rabbit Ears   A physical phenomenon that enables a ballplayer or umpire standing in a ball park before a crowd of 50,000 noisy fans to hear his name whispered in the opponent's dugout twenty-five yards away.

Red-Ball Express   A fast ball.

Rinky-Dinks   On any ball club those players (excluding pitchers) who play irregularly and infrequently.

Sailer   A fast ball that moves, or curves slightly, from a straight line between the pitcher's hand and his target. The movement stays in a horizontal plane, in contrast to breaking balls (curves, sliders, etc.), which drop, or break down, as they near the plate. Not a dependable or controllable pitch.

Save   A pitching credit recorded when one pitcher relieves another with his team leading in the score, and who finishes the game, helping the relieved pitcher get credit for the win.

Shade in the Hole   For a shortstop, to play nearer than usual to the third base line, thus closing the left-side "hole," or gap; similarly, the second baseman moves nearer to the first base line to close the right-side hole between him and the first baseman.

Shelled   See **Bombed**. (Also **clobbered**.)

Shot   Any ball hit with exceptional force, usually on a line. It often stuns a momentarily paralyzed defensive player; sometimes is hit over or through an outfield fence.

Sinker Ball   A pitch that looks like a fast ball as it comes to the plate from the **mound,** yet which curves, as it reaches the plate, like a slider, only in the opposite **direction.** (Damn good pitch.)

Slide Ball   Same as **slider.**

Slider   A pitch that is not quite so fast as a good fast ball, nor curves quite so **much** as a good curve ball, but which is easier to throw and control than either of **them.** Often called a "nickel curve" by old-time ballplayers who didn't have to hit **against** it. Worth $10,000 to any major league pitcher today; many would give their **last** penny to own a good one.

Squib   See **Bloop.** (Usually hit on the ground.)

Swinger   A batter who will try to hit any pitch that doesn't hit him.

Taking   To a batter, being forced to watch a pitch cross the plate that he **obviously** would have hit out of the ball park if the manager had only permitted him to **swing.**

Throwing Aspirin Tablets   Pitching the ball so swiftly that it looks smaller than **it** actually is. The best way for a pitcher to cure his manager's headache.

Tommy-hawked   In batting, having swung at a high pitch in a downward, chopping stroke. Frequently used in reference to line drives, home runs, and other such **disasters.**

Walking the Ball Park   For pitchers, issuing so many bases-on-balls that **sportswriters** grumble, fans scream, and managers cry. The quickest way to be taken out of **the** game.

The Players

The following ballplayers whose names are mentioned in the journal appeared in at least one major league uniform during the 1959 season. Some players were traded, sold, released, or optioned to the minor leagues during the year 1959. In most cases these changes are noted. Nicknames are those used in the journal.

Aaron, Henry (Hank, No. 44), outfielder, Milwaukee

Acker, Tom (Rooms), pitcher, Cincinnati —traded to Kansas City, winter

Adams, Bobby, infielder, Chicago Cubs— released, midseason

Adcock, Joe (Goofy), infielder, Milwaukee

Alou, Felipe, outfielder, San Francisco

Altman, George, outfielder, Chicago Cubs

Anderson, Bob (Andy), pitcher, Chicago Cubs

Anderson, George, infielder, Philadelphia

Anderson, Harry, outfielder, Philadelphia

Antonelli, Johnny, pitcher, San Francisco

Ashburn, Richie, outfielder, Philadelphia

Averill, Earl, catcher, Chicago Cubs

Avila, Bobby, infielder, Milwaukee

Bailey, Ed (Gar), catcher, Cincinnati

Banks, Ernie, infielder, Chicago Cubs

Bell, Gus (Ding-Dong), outfielder, Cincinnati

Blasingame, Don (Blazer, Blaze), infielder, St. Louis—traded to San Francisco, winter

Blaylock, Bob, pitcher, St. Louis

Blaylock, Gary, pitcher, St. Louis—traded to New York, midseason

Bouchee, Ed, infielder, Philadelphia

Bowman, Bob, outfielder, Philadelphia

Boyer, Ken, infielder, St. Louis

Brandt, Jackie (Flakey), outfielder, San Francisco—traded to Baltimore, winter

Bressoud, Ed, infielder, San Francisco

Broglio, Ernie, pitcher, St. Louis

Brosnan, Jim (Boom-Boom, Bross, Broz, Four-Eyes, Prof, Professor), pitcher, St. Louis—traded to Cincinnati, midseason

Bruton, Bill, outfielder, Milwaukee

Burdette, Lew, pitcher, Milwaukee

Burgess, Forrest (Smokey), catcher, Pittsburgh

Cepeda, Orlando, infielder, San Francisco

Cheney, Tom, pitcher, St. Louis—optioned to Omaha, midseason

Chittum, Nelson, pitcher, St. Louis—sold to Minneapolis, spring

Cimoli, Gino, outfielder, St. Louis—traded to Pittsburgh, winter

Clark, Philip, pitcher, St. Louis—optioned to Omaha, spring—sold to St. Paul, midseason

Clemente, Roberto, outfielder, Pittsburgh

Covington, Wes, outfielder, Milwaukee

Crandall, Del, catcher, Milwaukee

Crowe, George, infielder, St. Louis

Cunningham, Joe (Joey), infielder, St. Louis

Dark, Alvin, infielder, Chicago Cubs

Davenport, Jim, infielder, San Francisco

Demeter, Don, outfielder, Los Angeles

Dotterer, Henry (Dutch), catcher, Cincinnati

Drysdale, Don, pitcher, Los Angeles

Durham, Joe, outfielder, St. Louis—sold to Vancouver, spring

Elston, Don (Elsie), pitcher, Chicago Cubs

Ennis, Del, outfielder, Cincinnati—traded to Chicago White Sox, spring
Essegian, Chuck, outfielder, St. Louis—optioned to Rochester, midseason—sold to Spokane, midseason—purchased by Los Angeles, September

Face, Elroy, pitcher, Pittsburgh
Fairly, Ron, outfielder, Los Angeles
Flood, Curt, outfielder, St. Louis
Ford, Whitey, pitcher, New York
Fox, Nelson, infielder, Chicago White Sox
Fowler, Art, pitcher, Los Angeles—sold to Spokane, midseason
Freese, Gene, infielder, Philadelphia—traded to Chicago White Sox, winter
Friend, Bob, pitcher, Pittsburgh
Furillo, Carl, outfielder, Los Angeles

Gilliam, Jim, infielder, Los Angeles
Goryl, John, infielder, Chicago Cubs—sold to Minneapolis, midseason
Grammas, Alex (Greek, Cool), infielder, St. Louis
Green, Gene, catcher, St. Louis
Grissom, Marvin (Uncle Marv), pitcher, St. Louis—released, midseason
Groat, Dick, shortstop, Pittsburgh

Haddix, Harvey, pitcher, Pittsburgh
Hamner, Gran, infielder, Philadelphia—traded to Cleveland, midseason
Hearn, Jim, pitcher, Philadelphia—released, midseason
Hegan, Jim, catcher, Philadelphia—traded to San Francisco, midseason
Henrich, Bob, infielder, Cincinnati
Henry, Bill, pitcher, Chicago Cubs
Hoak, Don, infielder, Pittsburgh
Hobbie, Glen, pitcher, Chicago Cubs
Hook, Jay (Jay-bird), pitcher, Cincinnati
Hyde, Dick, pitcher, Washington

Jablonski, Ray, infielder, St. Louis—traded to Kansas City, midseason
Jackson, Larry (Cocky), pitcher, St. Louis
Jackson, Randy, infielder, Chicago Cubs

Jay, Joey, pitcher, Milwaukee
Jeffcoat, Hal, pitcher, Cincinnati—traded to St. Louis, midseason
Jones, Sam (Sad Sam), pitcher, San Francisco
Jones, Willie, infielder, Philadelphia—traded to Cleveland, thence to Cincinnati, midseason

Kasko, Eddie, infielder, Cincinnati
Kellner, Alex, pitcher, St. Louis—sold to Rochester, winter
Kirkland, Willie, outfielder, San Francisco
Kline, Ron, pitcher, Pittsburgh—traded to St. Louis, winter

Landis, Jim, outfielder, Chicago White Sox
Landrith, Hobie, catcher, San Francisco
Lawrence, Brooks, pitcher, Cincinnati
Lockman, Carroll (Whitey), infielder, Cincinnati
Logan, Johnny, infielder, Milwaukee
Long, Dale, infielder, Chicago Cubs
Lopata, Stan, catcher, Milwaukee
Lown, Omar (Turk), pitcher, Chicago White Sox
Lynch, Jerry, outfielder, Cincinnati

Maglie, Sal, pitcher, St. Louis—released, spring
Mathews, Ed, infielder, Milwaukee
Maye, Lee, outfielder, Milwaukee
Mays, Willie, outfielder, San Francisco
Mazeroski, Bill (Maz), infielder, Pittsburgh
McCovey, Willie, infielder, San Francisco
McDaniel, Lindy, pitcher, St. Louis
McDevitt, Danny, pitcher, Los Angeles
McMahon, Don, pitcher, Milwaukee
McMillan, Roy, infielder, Cincinnati
Miller, Stu, pitcher, San Francisco
Mizell, Wilmer (Vinegar Bend), pitcher, St. Louis
Moon, Wally, outfielder, Los Angeles
Moryn, Walt (Moose), outfielder, Chicago Cubs
Muffett, Bill, pitcher, San Francisco—optioned to Phoenix, spring

Musial, Stanley (Stash, The Man), infielder, St. Louis

Narleski, Ray, pitcher, Detroit
Neal, Charlie, infielder, Los Angeles
Neeman, Cal, catcher, Chicago Cubs
Newcombe, Don (Tiger), pitcher, Cincinnati
Noren, Irv, outfielder, St. Louis—traded to Chicago Cubs, midseason
Nuxhall, Joe, pitcher, Cincinnati
Nunn, Howie, pitcher, St. Louis—optioned to Rochester, midseason

Oliver, Gene, outfielder, St. Louis
O'Toole, Jim (Rocky), pitcher, Cincinnati

Pafko, Andy, outfielder, Milwaukee
Pena, Orlando, pitcher, Cincinnati
Philley, Dave, outfielder, Philadelphia
Phillips, Taylor (T-Bone), pitcher, Chicago Cubs—traded to Philadelphia, midseason
Pinson, Vada, outfielder, Cincinnati
Post, Wally, outfielder, Cincinnati
Podres, John, pitcher, Los Angeles
Powers, John, outfielder, Cincinnati—traded to Baltimore, winter
Purkey, Bob, pitcher, Cincinnati

Ricketts, Dick, pitcher, St. Louis—optioned to Rochester, spring—recalled to St. Louis, midseason
Roberts, Robin, pitcher, Philadelphia
Robinson, Frank, infielder, Cincinnati
Rodgers, André, infielder, San Francisco
Roseboro, John (Rosie), catcher, Los Angeles

Sanford, Jack, pitcher, San Francisco
Sawatski, Carl, catcher, Philadelphia—traded to St. Louis, winter
Schmidt, Bob, catcher, San Francisco
Schmidt, Willard (Will), pitcher, Cincinnati
Schoendienst, Red, infielder, Milwaukee
Singleton, Elmer, pitcher, Chicago Cubs—optioned to Fort Worth, midseason

Skinner, Bob, outfielder, Pittsburgh
Smith, B. G., outfielder, St. Louis—optioned to Rochester, midseason
Smith, Bill, pitcher, St. Louis—optioned to Omaha, spring—recalled by St. Louis, June—optioned to Rochester, midseason—traded to Philadelphia, winter—optioned to Buffalo, winter
Smith, Hal, catcher, St. Louis
Snider, Duke, outfielder, Los Angeles
Spahn, Warren (Spahnie), pitcher, Milwaukee
Speake, Bob, outfielder, San Francisco—optioned to Phoenix, midseason
Spencer, Daryl, infielder, San Francisco—traded to St. Louis, winter
Stuart, Dick, infielder, Pittsburgh

Tate, Lee, infielder, St. Louis—optioned to Rochester, midseason
Taylor, Sam, catcher, Chicago Cubs
Taylor, Tony, infielder, Chicago Cubs
Temple, John, infielder, Cincinnati—traded to Cleveland, winter
Thomas, Frank, infielder, Cincinnati—traded to Chicago Cubs, winter
Thomson, Bobby, outfielder, Chicago Cubs—traded to Boston, winter
Torre, Frank, infielder, Milwaukee
Turley, Bob, pitcher, New York
Trowbridge, Bob, pitcher, Milwaukee—traded to Kansas City, winter

Vernon, Mickey, infielder, Milwaukee
Virdon, Bill, outfielder, Pittsburgh

Wagner, Leon, outfielder, San Francisco—traded to St. Louis, winter
Walls, Lee, outfielder, Chicago Cubs—traded to Cincinnati, winter
Whisenant, Pete (Whiz), outfielder, Cincinnati
White, Bill, outfielder, St. Louis
Wynn, Early, pitcher, Chicago White Sox

Zimmer, Don, infielder, Los Angeles